The Elements of Inquiry

A Guide for Consumers and Producers of Research

Peter J. Burke, Ph.D.

Director, Education Doctorate Program
Edgewood College
Madison, Wisconsin

 Pyrczak Publishing
P.O. Box 250430 ❖ Glendale, CA 91225

"Pyrczak Publishing" is an imprint of Fred Pyrczak, Publisher, A California Corporation.

Project Director: Monica Lopez.

Cover design by Robert Kibler and Larry Nichols.

Editorial assistance provided by Cheryl Alcorn, Randall R. Bruce, Jenifer Dill, Karen M. Disner, Brenda Koplin, Jack Petit, Erica Simmons, Mel Yiasemide, and Sharon Young.

Printed in the United States of America by Malloy, Inc.

ISBN 1-884585-85-X

Contents

Notes

Detailed Contents

Detailed Contents

Introduction

This book provides the basic principles to be considered when consuming and producing original research. While these principles are stated as "rules," the real idea is to have a manageable inventory of standards, benchmarks, or touchstones—basically, a list of process steps or stages—that describe what researchers or consumers should consider or include when reading or conducting research in order to be authentic.

Distinctive Features of This Book

- The concept of research is set in a larger context of inquiry, and a discussion of the philosophical basis and historical growth of research as inquiry is provided.

- The rules for research provide a reference for reading research reports to individuals not familiar with the basic techniques. These rules allow readers to analyze, synthesize, interpret, and use research reports based on the widely accepted tenets of professional inquiry.

- The research rules in the text provide a checklist for individuals carrying out authentic research.

- The exercises at the end of each chapter provide an opportunity to consider and apply the constructs discussed in the chapter. Flexibility in the responses allows for application and extension across the wide range of topics that exist in research.

Why Is It Important To Know the Basic Rules of Research?

- Inquiry and research are the basic tools used to increase the knowledge base in any discipline. Consumers and producers of research must follow the accepted path for creating and interpreting research in order to make the results applicable.

- Data-based decision-making is essential for assessment and evaluation that leads to change and improvement in many professions. Using valid and reliable data to reach conclusions that lead to program enhancements requires an understanding of the process and techniques of research.

- An understanding of the foundations of research paradigms and their appropriate use is essential for the interpretation of research projects.

Suggestions for Using This Text

- Clearly, one basic use of this book is as a textbook for a short course on research and research methods. Selections from the annotated bibliography can be used to emphasize one or more research types with more depth of coverage.

- Another basic use of this book is as a reference tool when reading research reports. For instance, a reader may ask, "Is that an accepted method of drawing a sample?" The answer can be found by checking the section on sampling in the text.

- A third use is as a checklist for conducting research. A student can plan a project by using the rules as steps in the process, making an educated judgment as to whether, and how, the rules apply.

- Finally, this book should become a desk reference for those who are not full-time researchers, but who are called upon occasionally to conduct a data-based project or who need to review the research literature to aid in a professional decision. By checking the book's index and finding the succinct discussion of the item that needs exposition, the reader can refresh her or his memory of that particular research topic.

Acknowledgments

First and foremost to be recognized are the students of research who have interacted with the content of this book in its several forms prior to formal publication. Student reactions to the use of the raw materials helped immeasurably in determining the final presentation of the rules, and the work done by graduate students provided real-life examples of the use of the rules. The people and the supportive environment at Edgewood College helped to make the idea become a reality. Dr. Thomas Wermuth, former director of research for the Edgewood College Doctoral Program, provided valuable comments in the early stages of preparation for the text and its framework. Thanks, Tom! Finally, a very special debt of gratitude is owed to the late Professor Glen G. Eye of the University of Wisconsin, Madison, who gave me a hand-written note at the end of my graduate work over 30 years ago, with the title, "Handbook for Consumers of Research Reports." That was the impetus for this book, and it took only 30 years to get it done. Thank you, Professor Eye, for your huge part in my preparation for a life of educational administration, and for the encouragement to not only practice administration but also to think about it and write about it as complementary activities. I am also grateful to Drs. George W. Burruss, Matthew Giblin, and Nicholas Corsaro of Southern Illinois University, Carbondale, and Dr. Deborah M. Oh of California State University, Los Angeles, for their contributions to the final draft of this text.

Dedication

This work is dedicated to four generations of family, on whom my professional life and the resources generated from that life have always been focused. To my parents, Wayne and Rose, for bringing me into the world and providing the encouragement and support to live a good life; to my wife, Lynn, who helps me to live that life; to my children and their spouses: Amy, Andy and Melissa, and Maggie and Stephen, who give me encouragement that the next generation is strong; and to my grandchildren: Josh, Noah, Jack, Michael, Owen, and Carolyn, who provide the link to the future and who give so much joy. This work is dedicated to you all, and to those still to come in our family.

Peter J. Burke
Edgewood College
Madison, Wisconsin

Notes

Preface

Inquiry is a formal investigation of a situation or circumstance to determine the facts or condition of a phenomenon. Inquiry as investigation most often involves a formal process of research and writing. Research and writing are two components of professional communication that are essential not only between individuals, but also for growth and development in agencies, programs, or personnel in order for improvement to occur. Inquiry, and the research and writing that accompany it, are essential to the growth of a knowledge base in any topical area. Research and writing are very much intertwined. To conduct inquiry using research is to test theories or hypotheses, or to analyze and appraise situations, circumstances, or events. In order for the results of research to be communicated, the basic features of professional writing must be mastered. In addition to the rules of writing, there are, of course, basic structures to the research process that must be mastered as well.

A great deal has been written about inquiry and research, and the aspects of professional communication necessary to convey a message. For writing, one book is referenced and used more often than any other on the long list of rhetorical support books. That book is *The Elements of Style*, 4th Edition, by William Strunk, Jr. and E. B. White (Strunk & White, 2000). This text is still in print and is still widely recommended as a support document for writing clearly and concisely.

The rules of writing in this text, first published in 1959, date back to a 1919 edition that the student E. B. White used in Professor Strunk's English composition class at Cornell University. What Professor Strunk authored and called "that little book" has become a classic for writing at all levels, in all fields. The author of this text can still see his high school English teacher holding up an early edition of the book 40 years ago and exclaiming "Rule 13! Omit needless words!" Rule 13 was one of several basic rules continued throughout the many revisions of this valuable tool for writing. This rule became Rule 17 in later versions, but here it is, from the original text:

> "13. Omit needless words—Vigorous writing is concise. A sentence should contain no unnecessary words, a paragraph no unnecessary sentences, for the same reason that a drawing should have no unnecessary lines and a machine no unnecessary parts. This requires not that the writer make all his sentences short, or that he avoid all detail and treat his subjects only in outline, but that every word tell."[1]

---

[1] Strunk, W. Jr. (1918). *The elements of style.* Ithaca, NY: W.P. Humphrey. Retrieved August 2, 2005, http://www.bartleby.com/141/.

The point of including this reference to Strunk and White (2000) is to remind the reader that good writing is timeless. Those rules recommended in 1919 are still valid today. The use of language, like the foundation of a building, must be solid and well constructed at the very basic level in order for successful expansion to occur. This is true for inquiry as well.

Inquiry means the examination or investigation of some topic, and research is most often the tool used to conduct the inquiry. Research, like composition, also follows basic rules. Much has been written about conducting research as well. The tomes devoted to the study, analysis, and implementation of research are, for the most part, lengthy texts that delve deeply into, and attempt to explain thoroughly, the minutest aspects of the research process. Interestingly, much has been written about conducting the research, but little about consuming it. What this text offers is a concise look at the process of inquiry, including some basic rules that can be used by the producers and consumers of educational research, so that the stability and veracity of the research can be assured.

This text is designed to help build a solid foundation for consumers and creators of research. Like *The Elements of Style*, *The Elements of Inquiry* is a very basic book that will serve multiple uses. First, it will be helpful to consumers of research reports as a touchstone to measure the validity and accuracy of the published inquiry. Consumers will be able to use the structure provided in this text to judge the value of written research reports when they are conducting inquiry at their workplace.

Second, this book will serve as an outline for readers interested in inquiry, or those who may become producers of research. The text will aid in the initial organization of an inquiry or research project. One of the most difficult elements in undertaking a research project is getting started. This text provides the rudimentary structure for a neophyte researcher to organize her or his thoughts around a process of inquiry. Topics covered include questions to ask, data to collect, how the data should be organized and analyzed, what conclusions are warranted, and how to select salient features for reporting. Work teams focusing on a specific project may find this text valuable as an organizational tool when conducting action research projects.

As with rules for writing, the rules for inquiry provided in this book are not intended to be a linear step-by-step process. Just as there are ebbs and flows in the writing process, the research process may have circular influences, depending on method, which should not be lost in the rubric of strict rules. However, a generally accepted construct for inquiry is reflected in these rules, which all consumers and producers of research should keep in mind.

The most valuable use of *The Elements of Inquiry* may be that of companion to the larger treatises regarding research—the books that are often used in research courses. This shorthand version on the structure of inquiry should prove valuable as a side text to help students map a path through a research course.

Finally, it also may be used as a supplement to discipline-specific courses that include authentic (genuine and original) inquiry as an instructional tool. The student who needs to read the research, write a research paper, or carry out a basic or applied research project in any discipline, or who is a member of an action research cooperative group, will find this text valuable as a reference for those inquiry tasks and more.

Those who read professional literature to keep abreast of the changes and improvements in their profession need a basic understanding of what they are reading when it comes to research articles or inquiry reports, especially when a replication or program change is planned based on the published research. This book will fill that need. Sometimes, even peer-reviewed and published reports may not meet the standards applicable to the research method used. The consumer of research can use this book to validate the procedures and techniques used to ensure that the results reported are reliable prior to adaptation, replication, or other use.

Those tasked with carrying out authentic research will find the book helpful at the very beginning stages of design and development. As mentioned above, the most difficult part of any inquiry endeavor—as with a lot of things in life—is often just getting started on the project. The rules in this book will outline a structure that will provide an impetus to support that beginning for most new researchers, especially those working alone or at a distance from a supportive environment like a college campus.

The author of this book is a faculty member in a department of education, so many of the examples and exercises come from inquiry and research in education, particularly educational leadership. It is important to remember, however, that the basic research concepts provided apply to all fields of study. Examples of the process of inquiry described in this book can be found in the education profession. The field of education has been replete with the use of most of the various heuristics in inquiry. In fact, for education professionals, the federal legislation in the No Child Left Behind Act of 2001 includes a specific focus on research. While this legislation has a narrow view of what constitutes usable research, it has pushed educators to become more efficient consumers and producers of scientifically based research. This book was written to help professional educators and others do just that.

As a result of the No Child Left Behind Act, educators were required to provide evidence that federally funded programs can be documented with scientifically based research. This meant that program planners needed to read and interpret the research literature in education. Another consequence was that educators were pushed to create and carry out the research on topics or issues in which no current research existed, or in which previous research had been inconclusive. This book will support the continuation of both tasks.

Also considered as the book was planned and written were those students who are left to their own devices to fulfill a requirement for a research paper, a research project, or even a research dissertation. Many colleges and universities have instituted a research culture at the undergraduate level as well as at the graduate level. This text can guide those students through the process of academic inquiry. While not exactly a checklist of things to do, this book provides rules to consider when designing and carrying out a research project. The references provided to additional existing literature in research, along with the annotated bibliography, will aid those students in moving through the steps necessary for completion of the research task.

Actually, it is precisely the latter circumstance that led directly to the writing of this book. The author, as a faculty member in, and director of, an education doctorate program, realized the need for a simple and direct text on research techniques for students designing and completing a doctoral dissertation. This is especially true when those students are professional educators who are employed full-time, not to mention full-time students. The class notes and handouts prepared for the research classes—notes that were supplemental to the more wide-ranging research textbooks—have been compiled and edited, and they form the basis of this book.

Of course, the basic rules of research presented here transcend more areas and disciplines of inquiry than just education. Care was taken to provide research students and consumers with something similar to what Strunk and White have provided for rhetoricians for decades: an easy-to-use reference text that gets at the nub of the inquiry process and provides the basic rules to consider for reading and conducting research. There are four distinct parts to this book, and each could stand alone in its use.

First, in Chapter 1, there is a very basic description of the different, commonly accepted types of research and their applications. These descriptions set the stage for the consumer and practitioner to build on the foundations of research types without delving too deeply into one or more of the techniques. Basic assumptions and principles of each type are discussed, and an attempt is made to reduce the research lexicon to more usable lay terms.

Second, there is commonsense advice for consumers of professional inquiry projects. When the research literature is reviewed regarding any topic in any profession, the basic structure provided in Chapter 2 should be helpful. The common pitfalls that occur in research, like bias or miscalculation, are exposed for the reader so that bad research is not replicated or used for program development because of the good faith of the reader. Recommendations for points at which the consumer can stop consuming are provided.

Third, and most important, there are the rudimentary rules of research in Part II, Chapters 3 through 12. Really more a list of points for consideration than a set of absolute regulations, these rules apply across techniques and topics, and provide a foundation for all types of inquiry. The rules should at least be considered, if not followed, by anyone planning to carry out authentic research. Like the 22 rules of style in Strunk and White (2000), the 10 rules of research in Part II are intended to provide an elemental structure to professional inquiry. As mentioned above, the rules are not intended to be a step-by-step process. Rather, they are touchstones to help guide the reader through a research paradigm. Then, Part III brings these basic rules together into a sequence for the reader to plan and carry out a research project. In order for the reader to get started, the steps in the research process are provided in a logical and sequential order with specific, real-life examples of their use.

There are questions at the end of each chapter. These are provided for the independent reader to reflect on the content provided, or for the class or group using the text to substantiate what they may have learned in the chapter. Group discussions of these points may help readers to better comprehend the concepts.

The fourth and final component in this text is the annotated bibliography. The annotated bibliography of larger research texts found in Chapter 14 is provided as a bridge from the early stages of reading and conducting research to the more complex stages. Suggestions for expanding one's reading of research, at the end of each chapter in Part II, are linked to the annotated bibliography entries in Chapter 14. As the rules for research are presented in Part III, many of the seminal and current texts in research are cited. The annotated bibliography at the end of this book gives the reader the opportunity to select those references that fit the category of research under consideration, or in use, and to take the next step in understanding the research or designing the research project.

As a whole, this book provides the foundational elements of what academic inquiry and research are all about, from the research paper to the doctoral dissertation. The author's hope is that teachers and students across the many levels of education and the many disciplines of study find this text helpful. The contents certainly have helped many former students of this campus.

Notes

Part I

The Beginning

Notes

Chapter 1

Research As Inquiry

What is inquiry? Why is research a human endeavor? Humans are a naturally curious species imbued with an unquenchable thirst for new knowledge and a natural inquisitiveness that stems from a basic need for substantiation and verification of events, circumstances, or behaviors. Inquiry—a seeking or request for truth, information, or knowledge—has been a human trait from the earliest recorded times. Classical inquiry began with the Socratic method of asking the right question, expanded through the period of Archimedes' contemplation of natural conditions, and grew into Pythagoras forcefully demanding intellectual honesty in explaining phenomena like irrational numbers. Inquiry as a philosophical tradition suffered through medieval times when religion and superstition ruled the day. Then, the Renaissance ushered in the beginning of the scientific method, and inquiry developed into the concept of *research* as we know it today.

Inquiry is a formal investigation to determine the facts of a case. Research as inquiry is a productive and scholarly activity commonly accepted to be either investigation or experimentation that is used to confirm theories or ideas, solve problems, answer questions, test hypotheses, uncover and explain interrelationships between or among individuals or things, build an argument to revise old theories and create new ones, or test new theories. Research is a positive and important tool for business, government, science, industry, education, and all other professions, and, actually, for everyday life.

When a homeowner inspects an attic to determine why the living room ceiling is damp, that person is doing research. When a car buyer reviews *Consumer Reports* regarding different models that might be purchased, that person is doing research. When an investor constantly reviews the stock market trends and prices, that person is doing research. When an investigator is looking into the causes of some action or lack of action on the part of an individual or group, that person is doing research. When a voter is interested in how neighbors might vote in an election and engages those neighbors in a conversation around politics, that person is doing research. The examples are endless.

Reporting on research projects often requires careful scripting and sometimes includes the preparation of summary documents that detail the research and the results of the events that represent the research process. That is, research and writing are often combined. Research and writing are combined when a journalist interviews subjects and creates a story for a periodical or newspaper. Research and writing are combined when a market analyst surveys prospective buyers of a product and completes a report on the sales potential of the product. Research and writing are combined when a student reads several sources of literature and combines the information into a term paper. Research and writing are combined when a graduate student designs and carries out a research proposal as part of a dissertation. Once again, there are numerous examples of research as the precursor to a writing project.

Those who read research reports and those who carry out the research—the consumers and producers of research—must have a solid foundation in both the investigative and communication processes. In order for research to lead to knowledge growth or program improvement, the basic elements in the research tradition—the rules of research, if you will—must be followed, just as the basic rules of professional writing must be followed.

In order for improvement to occur in any endeavor, there must be change. Continuously and repeatedly using the same mode of operation—the same teaching or grouping techniques in education, for example—will not lead to improved results. But change just for the sake of change, with the hope that positive results may occur, could lead to disaster. That is why research has become the basic ingredient for thoughtful change. Decisions should be data-driven, and the data used should be valid, reliable, and the result of authentic inquiry.

Science is a systematically organized body of knowledge that has been the object of careful study and that has been carried out according to accepted methodologies. These scientific methods are techniques for investigating phenomena and acquiring new knowledge based on empirical evidence. Most think of research as a strictly controlled scientific event. That is not the case. None of the examples provided above would be considered strict scientific research, but nonetheless, they all are research. There is more to research than the scientific method as the basic research model. However, those interested in consuming research reports or doing authentic (genuine and original) research must be familiar with the scientific method as the basic research model. They may then use that knowledge as a basis of comparison to other research methods. The next section outlines the very basic methods used in research across all fields of study, including the profession of education.

The National Research Council appointed a committee to review the issue of scientific research in education (National Research Council, 2002). The committee report began with the premise: "At its core, inquiry is the same in all fields" (p. 2). The report went on to indicate that there are six basic scientific principles that all research must consider and follow. The six basic benchmarks for research as stated by the National Research Council are:

- pose significant questions that can be investigated empirically
- link research to relevant theory

- use methods that permit direct investigation of the question
- provide a coherent and explicit chain of reasoning
- replicate and generalize across studies
- disclose research to encourage professional scrutiny and critique (pp. 3–5).

These benchmarks provide the same basic principles for all types of inquiry and for all research methods. These scientific principles that form the standards for inquiry from the National Research Council also provide the basis for the rules of research to be considered, if not applied, which are detailed in Part II.

Research Fundamentals

There exist certain fundamentals that form the basis for what is considered authentic research. Science often provides the foundation model for what individuals consider "true" research, and the accepted steps in the research process are: *hypothesize, control, experiment, analyze, appraise,* and *conclude.* The logic of science is usually based on either the inductive approach or the deductive format. Induction involves gathering bits of information, such as observations, experimental results, or other kinds of data that may be available, and then formulating a generalization that reasonably explains all the collected pieces of information. Deduction, as a form of reasoning, begins with a generalization. Predictions are made based on the generalization, and those predictions are challenged. That is, many cases are studied, or many experiments are carried out, and conclusions for future groups or future trials are made based on the results of those earlier experiments. Deduction, in essence, is the testing part of science. This scientific model for research, also known as scientifically based research, has become the coin of the realm for many research arenas.

But not all work that is considered scientific follows the same controlled, experimental design of research. Within the scientific method there are, for example, case studies where there may be no treatment or quasi-experimental designs where strict control of some variables may be lacking. Additionally, the broad research community uses several different ways to organize and categorize the legitimate efforts made to resolve issues or solve problems that are, in fact, authentic research. Research design is, in the end, the structure, plan, or strategy of investigation that is created and assembled in order to answer the research questions. It is the overall scheme or process for the research and it may follow several approaches, each one appropriate for answering different kinds of questions.

The scientific model that was developed and refined in the hard sciences—a term used to distinguish natural and physical science from social science—is a quantifiable, or numbers-based, approach. There are research fundamentals that include other types of data and other methods of study as well. The ethnographic or qualitative approaches to research, based on words or text and not numbers, are well-accepted methodologies in the social sciences. The analysis and appraisal of archival documents that seek to explain events or other structures in the past—historical research—also form a well-accepted technique.

Today, many research efforts use a combination of qualitative and quantitative methods—an analysis of both numbers and text—to produce a well-rounded research project. This combination is often referred to as a mixed-methods approach. Action research is one common example of the potential for a combination of aspects of the scientific and the social science approaches. The next sections provide basic descriptions of these methods. The quantitative methods described are the strict scientific approach, along with the quasi-experimental method. Survey research is discussed in between quantitative and qualitative techniques. Ethnography and action research are used as examples of the qualitative approach to research, along with historical and descriptive research methods. Dissertation research, as an application of several of the techniques, is treated last.

Readers are reminded that the descriptions included here only scratch the surface of research techniques in very general terms. A more complete and inclusive description of these basic methodologies may be found in one or more of the references included in the annotated bibliography in Chapter 14.

The Model from Science

As referenced in the preface, education professionals were directed by federal law—the No Child Left Behind (NCLB) Act of 2001—to use scientifically based research to guide decisions about programs and interventions that might be used to improve learning. The NCLB Act was the reauthorization of the omnibus education support bill from Congress, the Elementary and Secondary Education Act (ESEA), and it required specific consideration of the scientifically based research approach, to the exclusion of other research designs. The U.S. Department of Education posited key characteristics of what it determined reliable research. The Department of Education literature focused solely on the application of what is termed the "Scientific Method," what Demetrion (2004) criticized as the gold standard in the hierarchy of research methods for the federal government. Evidently, the authors of the NCLB legislation were convinced that practitioners needed tools to identify and use evidence-based interventions from experimental or quasi-experimental designs in order to improve American education. For them, reliable research was to be based on a scientific model (U.S. Department of Education, 2003).

The scientific method of research is, of course, a solid technique to use when situations permit and conditions warrant its use. The first step in using the scientific method is to have some basis for conducting the research—a reason why. The "reason why" is usually generated from existing knowledge, or from a known theoretical base, with which the researcher has strong expertise. The theory that forms the foundation of the research is usually the result of earlier scientific experiments and research. In research, *theory* means the body of rules, ideas, principles, or concepts that apply to or define a particular subject.

The research topic or subject matter therefore comes from an area of interest to the researcher. The research variables come from observations that are either directly or indirectly related to the specific topic or subject matter of the proposed research. That is, in the scientific method of research, first an idea is formulated about the subject matter. For a medical researcher, this might be thoughts on how a specific drug affects a certain physical condition. For educators, this might be ideas about a new teaching technique, a different way of grouping students, a change in time allocations for instruction, or other changes in the standard operating procedures of a school.

The next step is to identify and confirm a research statement, or hypothesis, which is an attempt to explain some aspect of the observations. The hypothesis is basically a practical description of how the researcher thinks the idea formulated from the topic might work. The hypothesis is a prediction of potential outcomes of an experiment, series of experiments, or research trials. The hypothesis has two essential characteristics: It is a statement of the relationship between two variables, the independent and dependent variables, and it carries clear implications for testing.

A *hypothesis* is often referred to as a cause-and-effect statement about a specific set of circumstances. It represents a belief that a researcher holds—the researcher's conjecture about the relationship—before conducting a satisfactory number of experiments or trials. The repeated experiments or trials are used to test that belief using deductive reasoning. An important consideration in scientific research, one that is often overlooked, is that the researcher must somehow control all variables external to those being studied. Not all researchable topics can be studied in the controlled conditions of a laboratory, where outside influences that may have an impact on the results can be minimized.

Outside influences, however, must be controlled in a scientific experiment. Then the formal scientific method, at least according to the federal education requirements, follows the traditional control/experimental research design. Two groups are formed for the study. One is a treatment group, or intervention group, that is subject to the planned change. In classic research, this is the experimental group. The second is a control group that continues with the standard way of completing the tasks or is not subject to the intervention or treatment. The scientific test is a comparison of the two groups following the treatment. In a classical design, a test is used to try to disprove the hypothesis, and a level of confidence—or the probability that the conclusion may be an error—is used to describe the accuracy of the test.

In medicine, for example, a scientific experiment might be a series of trials for a new drug. The hypothesis may be that this new drug will be an effective pain reliever. In order to test the hypothesis, two groups are formed that exhibit the same physical symptoms—say, migraine headaches. The new drug is tested by dividing the group of migraine sufferers in half, giving the experimental drug to one group and either giving nothing or giving a placebo (a prescription that contains no medicine) to the other (control) group. The relief from pain is measured, and a conclusion is drawn regarding the effectiveness of the drug.

In education, the focus of a research project may be a new textbook and testing procedure. A third-grade class may be subjected to the new curriculum and assessment, while another third-grade class is allowed to continue with the existing curriculum. The hypothesis may be that better test scores on a standardized test will result from the use of the new curriculum. The students' content knowledge is measured after the application of the new curriculum, a comparison is made, and a conclusion is drawn regarding the new curriculum. Again, repeated trials are called for to ensure that the single result was not due to spurious events.

The new medicine and the new curriculum in the examples above are the *research treatments*. They are the things or conditions that allow for the research results (feeling better or learning more) to vary. The ability to assess and measure the change that occurs is essential, so the variables (how a person feels or how much a student learns) must be defined in a way that allows for measurement. Thus, those conditions that are allowed to vary must be given working definitions by the researcher, and those definitions should lead to a measurable outcome. That is, the researcher must be clear as to what is being tested and what changes are expected to occur based on the treatment. The researcher, of course, is hoping that the change observed (the variance) is predictable and that it results in a direction that will support the hypothesis.

In summary, the steps for hypothesis testing in the scientific method of research are as follows:

- become an expert on the basic *theoretical* aspects of a subject or topic
- identify or recognize a *problem*, or ask a basic *question* based on the theory
- determine the *variables* that are interacting with the problem/question/issue
- state the *relationship* between or among variables that is to be tested (the *hypothesis*)
- give operational *definitions* to the variables that allow for measurement
- *operationalize* the theoretical concepts—find a way to empirically measure the variables

- *test* the hypothesis—observe, experiment, apply treatment—repeatedly
- draw *conclusions*—accept or reject the hypothesis through deductive reasoning or generalize about the issue or problem based on the observations through inductive reasoning.

In the end, one important aspect to remember is that true scientific research does not *absolutely* prove anything. It is a technique that allows the new treatment to be tested and not rejected as an invalid approach within the limits set in the study. The scientific method requires a hypothesis to be eliminated if trials or experiments repeatedly contradict predictions. The failed hypothesis may be due to poor sampling procedures or to invalid or unreliable measurements. These are two reasons why replication is crucial before a conclusion is reached. No matter how great a hypothesis sounds, it is only as good as its ability to consistently predict results for the treatment, or experimental, group.

Extensive textbooks on the scientific method of research abound. Readers may want to review selections in Chapter 5 that deal in depth with this model (see especially Kerlinger, 1992 and Creswell, 1998). Because in many social science situations there is little opportunity for laboratory-style research to be conducted, this scientific method has been adjusted when conditions prohibit the pure scientific approach. One such adjustment is the quasi-experimental design.

Quasi-Experimental Designs

The quasi-experimental design is used when laboratory conditions that are usually used to control variables extraneous to the research cannot be identified or managed. That is, situations or circumstances other than the experimental treatment exist, and they cannot be organized, explained, or otherwise eliminated. One example of a quasi-experimental design is a one-group pretest-posttest, which is a before-and-after treatment comparison of one group. In a pretest-posttest design, the researcher has a hypothesis about what the effect of some treatment will be on a single group—say a behavior-modification technique with a group of unruly students, and the researcher measures the behavior, such as the number of students who need discipline, before and after the modification. Sometimes, the measurements or observations are noted more than once, creating a second quasi-experimental design. When repeated, this methodology is referred to as a time-series (or interrupted time-series) design.

Quasi-experimentation may be part of *ex post facto* research, in which the researcher does not have direct control over extraneous independent variables, either because they have already occurred or because they cannot be manipulated. Other basic tenets of strict scientific research may be missing as well. These could include a lack of random selection or assignment of subjects, that may be necessary for certain statistical tests to be valid, or the ability to replicate the conditions of the study. A precondition for quasi-experimental research, as with the scientific method, is that there are carefully defined research variables that are measurable. It is from the use of these measurements that conclusions may be drawn regarding the research.

Other examples of quasi-experimental research include such things as conducting treatments on a regular schedule, known as equivalent time-series design; separating groups based on a precondition and then applying different treatments to the different groups, known as regression-discontinuity design or the nonequivalent control-group design; and a design wherein controls are implemented when the design is determined inadequate during the research, known as the recurrent institutional-cycle design. In addition to these basic quasi-experimental designs, there are combinations of each, and different problems arise in each as well. These problems, often referred to as threats to validity (i.e., whether the conclusions are reasonable or justifiable), are the subject of specific research texts that are annotated in Chapter 5 (see especially Campbell & Stanley, 1963 and Mathison, 2005).

The scientific and quasi-experimental methods are often the means by which researchers are able to make conclusive statements about their studies at a prescribed level of confidence and with a minimum of bias. The level of confidence is selected by the researcher and is subject to statistical testing. Influences such as the confidence level selected, the size of the research groups, and the type of measurement used all contribute to the strength of the conclusions drawn.

The interpretation of quantitative data is extremely subject to bias. For example, the researcher may have a personal stake in the results. In fact, a huge concern in current scientific research is the source of external funding for research. Scientists are very concerned that funding sources might bias reported results. In order to minimize the influence of personal stakes and biased opinions, the use of a standard method of testing a hypothesis is expected by all members of the scientific community.

The final step of the scientific method is to rigorously and, in many cases, repeatedly test the prediction. Remember, a researcher cannot prove the hypothesis. Research results can only fail to disprove it. Unlike pure mathematics, in which there are absolute right or wrong answers, statistics allow for the consideration of errors in their conclusions. Statistical tests that provide a level of confidence around the potential for rejecting a hypothesis have been invented. Therefore, for the scientific method to work, the hypothesis must be quantifiable and testable. It must allow predictions to be made and experimental research to be conducted that confirms the predictions. The test used must adhere to the standard methods of measurement accepted by the scientific community. Too often, an inadequate or inappropriate test is applied to research data where the data type does not fit the measurement used. Different types of numerical data are discussed later in this chapter in the Quantitative Data section.

A second common error in the use of the scientific method, in addition to researcher bias, is a lack of testing. A hypothesis confirmed by common observations or common sense, but not by empirical observations, does not have scientific validity. The federal model in the No Child Left Behind approach to defining rigorous evidence is to rely on the constructs of replication and peer review. *Replication* is when several similar or exactly copied studies come to the same conclusion or find the same result. Additionally, research journals and specialty journals often publish what is termed a meta-analysis on a research subject. These meta-analyses are a single source for reviewing multiple iterations of similar hypothesis tests. One concern to keep in mind here, however, is that the circumstances that led to the same results may have differed widely.

A third issue in scientific research is the need to step back from the repeated trials and ask the question about professional significance. As a research project increases in size—as more subjects are included in the study—there is a greater opportunity for statistical significance to occur when standard measurement tools are used. A statistically significant difference simply means there is statistical evidence that there is a difference; it does not mean the difference is necessarily substantial, important, or significant in the context of the research. Sometimes, a statistically significant finding has little or no meaning in the context of the discipline being studied—such as having educational significance. Readers and researchers need to keep in mind the theoretical foundation of the project, and whether minute statistical findings have real meaning for the profession.

Nonexperimental Research

Not all research involves an experiment performed as part of the design. There are nonexperimental research projects that are just as valid and meaningful as strictly scientific or quasi-experimental designs. Nonexperimental research and the methods that define this type form another fundamental part of the research process. Data come in many forms and are found in various ways. The formal analysis and appraisal of research determines whether these data that are not the result of experiments carried out by the researcher are still valid measures of the concept, phenomena, or construct under study.

Much of social science research is of a nonexperimental nature. Terms such as qualitative research and ethnography are used to describe the work in anthropology, sociology, and other social sciences. Both numerical and verbal data are retrieved from different sources and studied, and conclusions are drawn to help understand a phenomenon, solve a problem, answer a question, explain a process, or otherwise elucidate physical or emotional circumstances. Just like the scientific method, however, the nonexperimental research project needs careful planning and professional implementation in order to communicate valid and reliable results.

The final research fundamental to be discussed here is the process of validating research projects through the peer-review process. No matter what research design is used in a research project, the results of the project, along with the methods implemented, require the scrutiny of an unbiased but informed public. That is the purpose of peer review.

Peer Review

Peer review is the analysis and appraisal of the published results of a research project by a jury of experts. It involves submitting the results of a project to professional scholars with expertise in the area being studied so that they may review the research for possible flaws. Professional journals are often referred to as peer-reviewed journals. This means that results of research projects composed in the classical fashion are sent to a jury of experts for blind review. Jurors reply to the publication's editors to inform them as to whether an article is acceptable for publication.

A problem with peer review, however, is that it is only as good as the individuals selected to perform the review. They, too, may suffer from a bias regarding the treatment under consideration and may not be able to provide an objective review. A reader needs to question the potential for bias in a reviewer's analysis of any research. As mentioned above, bias in a peer review may be the result of the selection of reviewers who exhibit a predetermined view that is consistent with the funding source for the research.

In fact, in recent years, the opportunity for peer review of research, both quantitative and qualitative, has been put in jeopardy. With the increasing use of the Internet as a tool for dissemination, and the immediate demand for results of research to support a position or an issue or to respond to a policy direction, this very important step in the process has been ignored. Unbiased and blind peer reviews are essential to the continued validity and reliability of professional research.

Types of Information and Sources of Data

The information gathered and used to answer the research question, test the research hypothesis, or solve the problem being studied is often referred to as *data*. Sometimes, in the qualitative arena, the concept of data is subsumed within the inquiry where the research participants may become, or at least provide, the information needed to move the issue forward. Research data come from a variety of sources and encompass a variety of types and formats. One easy distinction that helps to qualify data types is to distinguish between information that is in the form of numbers and information that is in the form of words or text. While the usual separation used between numbers and words as data is the distinction between quantitative (numbers) and qualitative (words) research, often there is an overlap of types of information or sources of data that may blur the lines of this basic distinction.

Outlined below are some of the most common information sources and data types for basic research projects. The basic types of numbers used in quantitative research are outlined, and the generally accepted descriptions used in qualitative research are provided. Research that makes use of these different data types is discussed in more detail in Chapter 2, in which quantitative research is compared to qualitative research and the use of mixed methods (both quantitative and qualitative) is described. The references listed in Chapter 5 will help the reader to gain a more in-depth understanding of data in any of the selected categories.

Quantitative Data

All scientific research depends on data that are numerical, or quantitative, in nature. Recall that the basic difference between the two techniques is that strictly quantitative research uses numbers and most qualitative research uses text of some kind (although qualitative research may be numerical as well as textual). With most numerical data, however, there are differences in the type of data gathered and how they are used in research.

Strict quantitative analysis of data focuses on *measurement*. Measurement begins with the assignment of numerals or numbers to objects or events in the research according to standardized rules and procedures. Remember that the variables being studied must be defined and measurable. The researcher selects the type of measurement to be used, chooses the appropriate rules for assigning the numerals or values, and carries out the research according to the generally accepted structures for the types of numbers available in the research. Analysis of numerical data is most often referred to as *statistical* analysis. Two interrelated terms used throughout quantitative measurement are *parameters* and *statistics*. Each term will be discussed briefly here.

A *parameter* is a characteristic or summary value considered a true measurement from an entire population being studied. For example, the average age of the world's population at a given point in time is a parameter. The variation in height in the adult population in the United States is a parameter. But since the average or spread of a measurement for an entire population is difficult, if not impossible, to measure, research often estimates these parameters. In addition, there are numerical collections that may not have a characteristic that can be summarized. These are referred to as *nonparametric* data. Frequency counts are the most common example of nonparametric data. Chapter 2 expands on the use of parameters in empirical studies.

A *statistic* is a calculated estimate of the actual value for the whole population, usually derived from a research sample. Statistics are estimates of population parameters, numbers generated to test research hypotheses, and numbers that are all derived from the data available in the research project; they are calculated from the data and used to verify decisions about the basic questions or to test the research hypotheses. Statistical testing is simply the application/substitution of the numbers acquired through the research in predetermined formulas that test for significance. Therefore, statistical testing is no more than the use of the numerical data collected in an orderly and prescribed way to make decisions about the basic research questions.

Computing an average value is an example of a statistic that is a measure of the population parameter. In the case of an average, the population parameter is called the mean value or population mean. So, since a researcher cannot actually measure the average age of the world's population, a sample of individuals from several countries could be selected and the average age from that sample calculated. The average that comes from the sample is the *statistic*, a number that approximates the actual population *parameter* (average age).

A researcher needs to know whether the group being studied has summary parameters that can be estimated with statistics. There are statistical techniques created for the analysis of sample data from both types of data. When research projects are designed, decisions about using either parametric or nonparametric statistical analysis are made. These decisions are based on the kinds of numbers available from the data collected.

For all of the experimental (scientific) and quasi-experimental research methods outlined above, there are statistical formulas that may be used to test the significance of the measurements derived from the data. These statistical tests go hand-in-hand with the confidence that the researcher puts in the results. The different data types lead to the different types of statistical tests that may be used to test significance. In fact, current computer programs ask researchers to identify the type of data in order to select the appropriate tests to be used (see, for example, SPSS, 2003). While being statistically significant, the test may not provide a substantive significance. That is, the results of these tests may provide a statistical significance, not necessarily an educational or professional significance. The analysis of research provided in Chapter 2 will help the reader to determine how significant the results may be for specific circumstances or situations. Not everything that is found to be statistically significant may be operationally valuable to the consumer. Statistics are just a manipulation of the research data to attempt to answer the research questions. Final judgments on the numbers generated are the responsibility of the reader.

In order to use statistics, a researcher must be aware of the kinds of numbers available to be put to the test. The next two sections provide a basic outline of how the numbers collected in a quantitative research project may differ, and how that difference leads to certain types of analysis. This is followed by a brief summary of non-numerical data and its use in qualitative research.

Categorical Data. One type of data that may be collected in research projects is sometimes labeled *categorical* data. Categorical data are divided into two basic types. There are data descriptors that have no real order in numeric values but are numerals used to label the categories. These are *nominal* data. Nominal means that the numbers represent a name and not a value. These "numbers as names" cannot be ordered in a meaningful way and they cannot be mathematically combined together with any meaning. One common example is a project that might label males as "1" and females as "2." The researcher could just as easily label females as "1" and males as "2" without changing any interpretation or analysis of the data. Another example is to give numerical labels to colors—for example, all blue cars are "1," green cars are "2," black cars are "3," and so on. The numbers have no value and are simply labels for the colors of the cars.

There are no parameters in nominal data and statistical manipulation is not possible. In the above example, there is no meaning in saying that the average gender for a group that has an equal number of men and women is 1.5. Nominal figures are simply names of individuals or groups in the research, mostly created for ease of computer manipulation of data.

The second type of categorical data does have a value or order. These are *ordinal* data that express a meaningful order to the category, but in which the distances or values between the numbers may not be equal or equivalent. In the mathematical sense, $a < b$ has meaning for ordinal data, but $a - b$ may not. Ordinal numbers that are assigned to objects or groups in a research project can be classified or ranked in a significant way. Numbers assigned to socioeconomic status, for instance, have an order (e.g., 1 = low, 2 = middle, 3 = high). Another example of ordinal data is class rank. A student's rank in class has an order, but while there is a clear order to the rank of students, the distance measured by GPA between, say, students who rank first and second may not be the same as the distance between students who are third and fourth. So the rank in class is an ordinal number.

Just because there is an order to these numbers does not mean, however, that the distances between the components of the category are necessarily equal. Grades given in school that are represented by numbers have an order (F = 0, D = 1, C = 2, B = 3, and A = 4); however, it is very difficult to argue that the distance between an F (0 points) and a D (1 point) is "equal to" the distance between a B (3 points) and an A (4 points). For example, the difference between, say, 88 (B = 3 grade points) and 90 (A = 4 grade points) is not the same as the distance between 70 (C = 2 grade points) and 80 (B = 3 grade points). In fact, an entire dissertation focused on the disparity in the grade of "F" alone when compared to other grades (Gerke, 2007).

For ordinal numbers, there are no parameters used to describe the data, but there are measurement techniques available to analyze it. These are known as nonparametric techniques because the data set does not have any numerical summary characteristics; that is, there are no parameters.

Categorical data, therefore, are either names given to the subgroups in the data set (nominal data) or actual values that do not necessarily reflect equal distances between identified points (ordinal data). The distance between the numeric values in a data set is an important distinction for the next type of quantitative data.

Scale Data. The next two types of data that are part of research projects are included in a category often referred to as *scale* data. Scale data have ordinal characteristics but are more sophisticated. *Interval* data, the first type of scale data, are those that do have a meaningful distance between the data points, so that differences between arbitrary pairs of measurements can be meaningfully compared. Operations such as addition and subtraction are therefore meaningful, but since the zero point on the scale is arbitrary, operations such as multiplication and division cannot be carried out directly with the numbers generated by the study.

Temperature in degrees Fahrenheit is an example of an interval data set. The concept of intelligence quotient (IQ) provides another example of interval data. IQ is described as a quotient because it originally represented the ratio between a person's mental age and actual chronological age—but IQs are not ratio data since there is no real zero point. The year date in a calendar is another example. Important to remember is that the difference between ordinal and interval data is that the distances between the numbers on the scale are equal for interval data. The equal-distance concept is not true for ordinal data. In the mathematical sense, the concepts of both $a < b$ and $b - a$ have meaning for interval data, but there is no real zero (no one has zero intelligence, and there is no zero date) and multiplicative operations do not apply (2008 is not twice the year 1004).

The second type of scale data is *ratio* data. Ratio data are the highest level of measurement for research. Ratio data are those numbers that have a set order (ordinal), have a meaningful distance defined between data points (interval), and provide the opportunity for dividing data into smaller increments in a meaningful way. An additional, important characteristic for ratio data is that there is an absolute-zero point. This characteristic allows for arithmetic, and therefore statistical, operations to be performed appropriately on the data set. In mathematical terms, the concept a / b (division) has meaning for ratio data.

Ratio data are the numbers in mathematics that most educated individuals have experienced in learning about mathematics. But it is important to recognize when ratio data occur in research. This is to substantiate that the use of appropriate statistical techniques is justified. The subdivisions or smaller increments of ratio data are often seen in decimals, fractions, or percentages. An example of ratio data could be the property tax mill rate (the rate of taxation applied to each $1,000 of property valuation) and methods of calculating the tax on property. Physical qualities such as mass, length, or energy are measured on ratio scales. Ten pounds is twice as much as five pounds, five yards is half the distance of 10 yards, and each scale has a zero point.

Qualitative Data

Textual data are often the basis for qualitative inquiry. As mentioned previously, qualitative research may combine data types, and use different research methods, to reach conclusions regarding the phenomenon or issue being studied. Each of the different methods of inquiry in qualitative research uses preestablished techniques for collecting empirical data. The techniques include surveys, interviews, observational techniques such as participant observation and fieldwork, archival analysis, and historical record review. Written data sources can include published and unpublished documents, company files, memos, letters, reports, e-mail messages, faxes, newspaper articles, and transcriptions of meetings or interviews. These data are sometimes referred to simply as information, or as empirical materials, to differentiate the non-numerical, textual data from quantitative data.

In the collection of qualitative data, it is a common practice to distinguish between primary and secondary sources of materials or information. Generally speaking, primary sources are those that are unpublished and that the researcher has gathered directly from the individuals, participants, or organizations. Secondary sources are materials that have been previously published, including books, referred articles, or other organizational documents. Both sources provide legitimate information for analysis in a research project.

In a case study, for example, the researcher may use field notes, interviews, or documentary materials collected on-site as primary sources. The researcher may or may not be at the site as a participant-observer who gathers original information, but may rely on others for the primary documentation. Secondary sources may be published documents that help to describe the case in a larger context, published research of a similar nature, or other manuscripts. The distinguishing feature of most ethnography as a qualitative method, however, is that the researcher spends a significant amount of time in the field. In many cases, the researcher is a participant-observer.

The fieldwork notes and the experience of living as both a participant and observer become an important addition to any other information or materials that may be used as research data. Good discussions of qualitative techniques for data collection can be found in several of the references listed in the annotated bibliography in Chapter 14, under the section on Qualitative Research.

Once materials or information that will become the grist for the research mill are collected, there are specific strategies and tools available for the researcher to use in the analysis phase. Often, categories of information are established, and the researcher selects criteria or rules for category membership from the data that are relevant and important. The information or events under scrutiny may be ordered chronologically, based on frequency of occurrence, or on the importance given to a specified criterion. The researcher should be able to articulate abstract relationships between existing categories of information and compare specific abstract and concrete features of two items from the information.

The organization of qualitative data is used to compare different sources of information for the same topic in terms of basic similarities and differences. The data are used to identify the abstract relationships that form the basis for analogies. This often includes the comparison of multiple items on multiple abstract characteristics. The researcher identifies abstract patterns of similarities and differences between information on the same topic but from different sources, and may identify important relationships between seemingly unrelated items. The researcher seeks out traits that can be used to order and classify items. Again, both textual and numerical data are important to the qualitative researcher.

Two Research Traditions

Just as there are several forms of data, there are several ways to extract those data and to use them in a research endeavor. A very basic separation of research methodologies has to do with the kind of information used to help answer the research question. If the data are numerical, the research is most often termed "quantitative." That is, there are specific quantities of data that may be reduced to numbers for comparison. The second basic methodology is termed "qualitative." Here, the information collected to answer the research question is in the form of words, or textual data. Much of the literature about research today references these two traditions—quantitative and qualitative research—and often refers to the combination of the two traditions in a mixed-methods approach to using research for problem solving. Chapter 2 provides a more in-depth discussion of these research methods.

The scientific method of controlled experimentation that was treated earlier and will be expanded upon in Chapter 3 is a quantitative approach to research. The research methods outlined in the following pages are some of the more common techniques used when carrying out a research project in addition to the experimental design method. While each method of research is a technique unto itself, there are increasingly subtle variations of the various techniques and, more important, designs that combine two or more of the basic techniques. Once again, the reader should review the texts annotated in Chapter 14 for more in-depth analyses of the basic methods and their several variations.

Quantitative Research

The scientific, experimental design for research uses measurements and numerical analysis—statistics—to study isolated events in order to make judgments about how things interrelate or what changes occur due to some manipulation. Numbers and measurements are used in research other than the strict, controlled experiments of science. There are research designs that use a comparison of numbers—data—from different sources. These are usually called correlational studies. There are also numerical studies done with the quantitative approach that try to predict outcomes or events by analyzing numbers from several different sources. These are the *causal-comparative* designs of research.

Most, if not all, research that deals with numbers and measurement is labeled quantitative research. Much of the research done in education and the social sciences utilizes numbers and incorporates textual data in the discussion that lead to conclusions. These are the mixed methods of the social scientist, a research technique that blends the best of the basic research traditions—quantitative and qualitative—and allows the researcher to substantiate findings with the authority of both.

In education and the social sciences, *survey research* is a quantitative method that is often used by researchers. Although some surveys use open-ended questions that allow for textual responses, most use a numerical scale or count specific responses to draw conclusions about the group being studied. An example of the careful use of numbers in research can be found in the use of surveys. There are two basic types of surveys. The first are the polls or status surveys that aim to measure the status quo of a population concerning one or more specified topics or research variables. Polls most often focus on the actual status or facts of a situation. For whom did you vote? Did you purchase an American-made car? The second survey type includes sample surveys aimed to measure the incidence, distribution, or interrelationships of sociological or psychological variables. These surveys focus on the beliefs, motivations, or behaviors of individuals. The data gathered include facts, opinions, or attitudes.

Surveys are conducted in several ways. The personal interview is direct contact with the individuals in the research sample, using a prepared interview questionnaire or interview schedule. Often, factual information like gender, education, income, or age is collected, along with attitudes or opinions. Personal interviews offer the opportunity to ascertain the reasons behind the behavior or opinion. Surveys are also conducted over the phone, via e-mail, and through the Internet.

A specialized survey technique is the panel approach, often referred to as the *Delphi technique*. In this approach, a panel of experts on a subject is asked to respond to an interview or survey, and is then reinterviewed or surveyed again following the sharing of the results of the initial data collected. The purpose of the second round of data collection is to determine whether opinions or attitudes change after feedback is provided.

When survey results form the research data for any project, it is important to understand the assumptions behind any calculations made from the data. Research that uses surveys to determine attitudes, values, or reactions to situations often includes a numerical rating scale from which respondents select a value that most closely approximates their feeling, attitude, or value. These response items are often called *Likert scales* or *Likert-type scales*, and are named after Rensis Likert, the originator of this survey technique (Likert, 1932). The original Likert scale had five different points to measure responses, with the middle value being a neutral or zero score. Likert-type scales change this basic design by adding more responses or by eliminating the option for a neutral position on the scale.

A refinement of the Likert scale was created by Osgood, Suci, and Tannenbaum (1957). They expanded the scale to seven values, arguing that seven typical responses are given with roughly equal frequency when subjects participate in a survey or questionnaire. The *semantic differential*, in which seven blank spaces are placed between polar traits and respondents are asked to check the blank that most closely describes their feeling or attitude, is an example of this refinement. Figure 1.1 below provides examples of the different Likert-type scales used in current research.

Figure 1.1. Examples of response scales.

Likert scale:

1	2	3	4	5
Strongly Disagree	Disagree	Neutral	Agree	Strongly Agree

Likert-type scale (after Osgood, Suci, & Tannenbaum, 1957):

1	2	3	4	5	6	7
Strongly Disagree	Disagree	Mildly Disagree	Neutral	Mildly Agree	Agree	Strongly Agree

Figure 1.1. (*continued*)

Likert-type scale (no zero term):

1	2	3	4	5	6
Strongly Disagree	Disagree	Mildly Disagree	Mildly Agree	Agree	Strongly Agree

Semantic differential (Sax, 1968):

Disagree _____: _____: _____: _____: _____: _____: _____ Agree

Statistics that are used to test hypotheses, or to draw conclusions about the data, are directly dependent upon the type of numerical data available from the research. Statistics are, after all, mathematical manipulations of the research data using prescribed formulas. Nominal data are not subject to any of the basic statistical or quantitative techniques. If the data have order, but not necessarily equal intervals, there are specific measurement formulas that a researcher may use to test the strength of the relationship uncovered. These are often referred to as *nonparametric* statistics.

Recall that a parameter is a true value of a population. It is a value that can be calculated from a sample and therefore depends on having the right kinds of numbers (interval at least). Nonparametric measures are used when the information is in the form of ordinal data—frequency counts, for instance. Examples of data that are subject to the nonparametric approach include calculations such as tallying the number of responses selected in a certain category of response or counting the number of individuals in a certain research category.

Data derived from survey research conducted as a component of a quantitative study are often assumed to be interval data. While the real distance between words like "highly satisfied" and "satisfied" and words like "unsatisfied" and "neutral" may not be equal, that assumption is made so that parametric statistics (measurements from specific formulae that describe aspects of the research population that can be computed from the research data—the average number, for instance) can be used for the analysis of the data. More will be said regarding assumptions about research populations and samples, the type of data derived from research, and the matching of statistical procedures to the data in Chapter 9 under Rule 7.

Qualitative Research

Just as quantitative data are numerical, most qualitative data are text-based. When a researcher knows that the data to be collected and analyzed cannot be effectively reduced to numbers, a qualitative approach must be planned. Interviews, focus groups, open-ended questions on surveys, document reviews, case studies, or other observations are examples of text-based data collection in qualitative research. The easy way to remember the distinction between qualitative and quantitative is that the information collected in qualitative research is, for the most part, in the form of *words* rather than *numbers*.

Qualitative research, like all of the other methods, begins with a carefully described concept or construct that is to be analyzed. There may be specific and carefully stated hypotheses just as in the scientific approach, or there may be basic research questions that the researcher will attempt to answer. The questions most often come from issues or problems that the researcher wants to resolve. The research amounts to careful appraisal of the situation resulting in a written analysis of the researcher's observations.

The ethnography of the anthropologist or sociologist formed the beginning of the qualitative approach to research. The ethnographer was an observer who recorded everyday observations in the situation being studied. The ethnographer could also be a participant-observer in that she or he might be a member of the group under surveillance. The observations were recorded in narrative form, and that narrative became the research data for analysis.

Ethnography provides the research tools needed for a qualitative study, much like the scientific method provides the rules for the quantitative studies under laboratory conditions. Sometimes referred to as *field research*, the ethnographic process most often involves direct observation and data collection in natural settings. While most data from field research are qualitative, some observations may be quantifiable as well.

Just like the experimental and quasi-experimental variations of the scientific approach, the qualitative method has an evolving set of unique variations that aid the researcher in designing the research protocol most likely to deliver the information needed for intelligent decision-making. Variations of educational ethnography may exist for studies that include the community, the school level, individual schools, school positions, curriculum, instructional methods, or educational progress.

In addition to ethnography, the basic categories of qualitative research include historical research (historiography) and descriptive research, such as case studies including grounded theory (deriving a theory from looking at specific cases), biography, and phenomenology (descriptive psychology that illustrates how thoughts and mental acts are directed at real objects).

Two often-used and basic types of qualitative research are historical research and descriptive research. These methods will be discussed in brief here, along with a review of what has been termed *action research*. Action research is used here as an example of the potential for the combination of quantitative and qualitative research designs. There are numerous text-books annotated in Chapter 5 that expand on all of these qualitative techniques.

Historical research answers the question "What was...?" The data that are used most often are earlier writings about the subject under study. The researcher collects opinions, attitudes, interpretations, and other materials written about a subject and combines the sources to draw conclusions about the events in the time period being studied. Historical research is concerned with determining, evaluating, and understanding past events, often for the purpose of understanding the present or predicting the future. The study of a single individual, either through experiences told to the researcher or through the analysis of archival documents—a biography—is one use of the historical research method.

The structure of most historical research projects begins with projecting a theory about past conditions. This may be an existing theory about conditions or results of actions, or it may be a new theory that the research has created. Then a hypothesis is stated, or research questions are posed, based on the theory. Once the questions are identified, the available resources that become the research data must then be isolated. These resources could include documents, individuals, or other information and evidence that can be used to develop an argument. Next, the resources identified must be analyzed. The researcher brings together the disparate documents and evidence, then organizes them to point out similarities or disparities between or among sources. In the final step, the researcher draws valid conclusions about the data as they relate to the research questions.

Two data sources for historical research are, first, direct or primary sources and, second, indirect or secondary sources. Direct-source data are the authentic writings or interviews with actual participants in the events under scrutiny. The researcher identifies the connection between the events and the sources as a primary source of information on the subject. Indirect or secondary data sources include other opinions written about the subject or third-party descriptions of events. The researcher looks for other historical research about the event or talks to individuals who may have interacted with the actual subjects. Historical research is an archival type of inquiry that may include analysis of numerical data from the past and, therefore, may also use quantitative methods of analysis.

Descriptive research answers the question, "What is...?" It is the real-time equivalent of historical research that is used to determine the nature and degree of existing conditions. Most often referred to as the *case study* approach, a descriptive research project aims to determine the nature and degree of existing conditions in an individual, a group, an agency, or some other variable or construct. If a shared meaning of an experience is derived from several individuals in the context of a particular situation, the research is sometimes referred to as *phenomenology.* The research describes how one or more individuals react to predetermined phenomena.

If the researcher generates a theory to explain some action or process and conducts an analysis of the action or process in context, it is referred to as *grounded theory.* The researcher reviews the data collected and generates or develops a theory from those data. A continuous interaction between data collection and data analysis is conducted to help describe the theory in the selected context.

The two basic components of descriptive research in the qualitative mode are comparative research and developmental research. Descriptive research is usually used when the researcher is present while changes are occurring, and the researcher may even be a participant in the events.

Descriptive research is marked by the need for careful selection of data sources, indepth study of the circumstance under inspection, thoughtful analysis of the information collected, and meaningful descriptions of the situation as it exists. Comparative research as a descriptive technique may look at the similarities or differences between or among groups of individuals or techniques used to derive a prescribed end, like different teaching styles. It is an analytical approach that includes the steps of watch, learn, record, analyze, and draw conclusions about what has been observed.

Developmental research in the descriptive mode focuses on one group or one issue and observes the change over time. The researcher watches the subjects or program develop and records the changes that occur at prescribed intervals of study. Often, the researcher is a member of the group and participates while capturing data for the research project. This is referred to as the *participant-observer* role in research.

The case-study approach is a descriptive technique that may be either comparative or developmental. Case studies are a research methodology in which the researcher watches defined aspects of one case—an individual, a classroom, a school, a school district, or a state, for example—and records the changes that occur. This record is applied to the basic research questions for analysis, and conclusions are drawn based on the analysis of the data. The case study is, in addition, an obvious choice for the blending of the quantitative and qualitative approaches to a research project. Often, there are numerical data collected along with anecdotal notes that may be blended into the analysis. Action research is another way of describing this blended type of research.

Two other research techniques that fall loosely under the descriptive category are the *correlational* and *causal-comparative* methodologies. Correlational research answers the question, "How are they alike?" It is a nonexperimental design in which the researcher conducts no manipulation or interventions. The data collected on two or more variables are compared to determine any relationships that may exist. If the data are quantitative, then statistical tests may be applied. There are tests used for measuring similarities between the data sets and testing for differences as well.

Causal-comparative research answers the question, "Why is it?" It is research that attempts to describe cause-and-effect relationships between or among observations noted from the research. It involves using one variable to explain another, often in a predictive way. Once again, the data may be quantitative or qualitative, and, if numerical, may be subjected to standard statistical tests that will determine the strength of the prediction.

The research methods described above are often combined so that the researcher may adjust and review data to legitimately meet the needs of the project. Three such uses are described below.

Common Uses of Research

The research methodologies just outlined are often combined in a project that requires different types of data or that leads to different types of interpretations. Three common expressions of this combination of method or use of research are action research, research conducted for formal theses or dissertations, and research carried out for program evaluation and improvement. While none of these is a particular method, program assessment, the direction of an action research project, or the writing of a thesis or dissertation may be mapped by a specific method, or, more frequently, by a cogent design of mixed methods. Many dissertations, in fact, are now based on an action research model, although many of the descriptions of action research refer to it as a group or collaborative process, not an individual event.

Action research may be at the base of the third use of research, which is the evaluation and improvement of programs. Research for program assessment is planned and carried out in various ways in order to arrive at the desired end. Research for the purpose of assessment helps the researcher and project colleagues to make informed, data-based decisions about changes necessary for improvement. Whether through the use of existing research or with newly conducted studies, decisions made based on research have the best chance of succeeding.

Action Research

Action research deals with issues that exist in a workplace that need attention. It is research focused on the effort to improve the quality of an individual's performance or the performance of an agency or organization. Action research has been called practice as inquiry, and it is broadly accepted that there is no singular and unique format for action research. Collectively, projects called action research are those that are designed and carried out by practitioners who identify the problem, collect and analyze data, and use the collected information to make data-driven decisions to improve their own practice or to improve working conditions. Individuals can conduct action research, but it is a term most often applied to work done by teams of colleagues. This team approach is also known as collaborative inquiry.

Kurt Lewin is generally considered the father of action research. A social and experimental psychologist, he used group processes for addressing issues and problems within organizations. Lewin coined the term *action research* in 1946. He characterized it as a comparative research using a process of steps that included planning, action, and fact finding. Action research is used in real situations rather than in controlled experimental studies since its primary focus is the solving of real problems or issues in the workplace. As mentioned above, it is in action research that different methods of discovery may be blended.

Blended, or mixed-model, research means that quantitative and qualitative designs, methods, techniques, or other paradigm characteristics may be mixed in one overall research project. There may be a combination of survey responses and interview results. The survey data may be subjected to a quantitative statistical analysis, and the interview data may be analyzed through accepted ethnographic techniques. Then, the results are reviewed from both perspectives to determine alignment and to permit conclusions to be drawn.

The basic steps in an action research project begin with identifying a problem or issue that needs resolution or selecting an action or behavior that needs testing. Then, planned change is introduced into the system; that is, *action* is taken, and the researcher carefully monitors the results of that change. Adjustments in the plans may be made—that is, further *action* may be taken—based on an analysis of the progress being made while the research is carried out. Summary judgments regarding the success of the project and the potential for further development or implementation are made after the project is completed. Action research has been recommended to teachers in the classroom setting as a valuable tool in experimenting with ideas that may lead to better student learning.

Thesis and Dissertation Research

Thesis and dissertation research is the learning-by-doing approach. Students are led through a research project by an academic advisor, or a committee of advisors, and the several stages in the research process are monitored carefully. There is no single research method applied to theses or dissertations. When a student identifies an issue area, the theoretical model that provides the foundation for the research most often dictates the research methodology to be used.

Clearly, students conducting research in the hard sciences will use the scientific method or some carefully planned variation of that model. Students collecting quantifiable data will look for advice on how to use statistics to interpret the data. Those who choose questions that lead to narrative data will choose the qualitative approach to analysis.

Most dissertations use a five-chapter format that includes the basic research stages. The first chapter serves as a roadmap to the entire project, and it is usually the introduction to the problem or issue. Chapter 1 in a dissertation provides the reader with a clear sense of what the study hopes to accomplish, the context of the study (where it takes place), and the connection of the study to previous research or theory. Chapter 1 should include:

- a *contextual orientation* that is a very brief description of the setting of the issue or problem being studied
- a *theoretical model* that is a description of the interrelationships of the variables or groups being studied; it may include a graphic representation of this relationship
- a *problem statement* in commonsense or reader-friendly language that is connected to the theory behind the study
- the *research questions* (hypotheses) designed to frame the study that are linked to the theory and to the research problem or issue
- *definitions* of terms used throughout the dissertation that may have a meaning unique to the research being conducted
- the *significance* of the study, which may anticipate some potential findings
- any *limitations* that may have an impact on the use of the literature or on the methodology.

The second chapter in most traditional dissertations is the review of the literature. In many cases, this may be the longest chapter of the five. Part of the responsibility of the researcher is to find, review, cite, and give appropriate credit to previous researchers who published their work. It is the place for the dissertator to deduce the question that will be studied in the research project from earlier work. The literature review should build to the problem or issue that was studied in the research. To write this chapter, a researcher must:

- find and *read* the most salient works in the field of study
- *summarize* the connection to the broader theory and the authors' findings, conclusions, or recommendations
- create a *coherent outline* of the several authors connected by the research theme or variables
- use *advanced organizers* to help with the organization of the authors by topic or subtopic

- be sure to *treat all sides* of issues if there are opposing views in the literature related to the topic being studied
- include a review of *methodological literature* as well to let the reader know that the method used was the best one for the study
- identify how the research *expands* or *confirms* previous work.

Chapter 3 in a dissertation contains the methodology of the study. While often brief and to the point, the methodology chapter details the design of the research and the plan that the researcher intended to follow in carrying out the project. It is mostly about the data—the sources, the collection strategies, the management, and the analysis. The basic format for the methodology chapter is as follows:

- a review of the formal statement of the research problem or issue, followed by a discussion of the basic questions or hypotheses being studied
- clear definitions of terms used in the research, especially the terms that label the variables used
- an orientation to the type of research used, often embedded in a discussion of the research paradigm
- identification of the data sources, especially the population and sample (participants or subjects) that are the object of the study
- a description of the strategy used for the collection and management of the data, that is, the protocol for gathering the information needed to answer the research questions
- a description of the procedure used for the analysis of the data
- any conditions or limitations that may affect the interpretation of the information collected.

Chapter 4 in a dissertation is the display of the data in summary form. Tables, charts, figures, or other devices are used to gather the information collected and explain it to the reader. Usually, data are organized to respond to separate basic questions or hypotheses, which provide an organizational tool for the chapter. Unanticipated or incidental results should also be considered and reported. Data displays should be complete and self-explanatory so that reference to the text is minimal. The usual procedure for data displays in this chapter is to introduce the table, present the table, then discuss the salient features of the data in the table.

The final chapter, Chapter 5, in a dissertation is the discussion of the information presented in summary form in Chapter 4, along with conclusions the researcher may be able to logically draw from the data. These conclusions or implications should consider each of the research questions in an orderly way. There may be a need to discuss the unanticipated results that might not be directly related to the basic questions but are, nonetheless, an important result of the research. Finally, the researcher may want to make suggestions for further research to carry on what has been started or to delve into an area only touched on by the dissertation research.

Research for Program Evaluation and Improvement

Mixed methods of research and a variety of information or data sources are used when a researcher is looking at whether or not a program has been successful. Often, funding decisions are made based on the results of program evaluation, so the collection and analysis of the data upon which decisions are made should be organized according to the strict research techniques. The same is true for analysis and appraisal of existing programs for the purpose of change and improvement. Recently, the concepts of action research as described above have been used in the assessment of program strengths and weaknesses, and the results of those projects are the basis for change decisions.

When conducting research for program change or improvement, a researcher often uses the concept of *triangulation* to assure that the results are accurate. In the social sciences, triangulation is often used to indicate that more than one method was used in a study, with a view to double-checking results or getting the same result from different viewpoints. This is sometimes referred to as cross-examination. The idea is that one can be more confident in a result if different methods of analysis, or different sets of data, lead to the same result.

When all is said and done, all research comes down to asking the right questions, identifying the proper information or data to respond to those questions, collecting those data, analyzing those data, and drawing conclusions or making recommendations based on the analysis. The brief descriptions of the foundation of research and the different methodologies contained in Chapter 1 were to provide general knowledge for all those interested in reading or conducting research. Readers are encouraged to visit some of the references in the annotated bibliography if more depth in any one topic is desired. Chapter 2 is for the consumer of research reports. It provides a roadmap to reading research studies and reports, along with a set of questions that a reader should ask her or himself after digesting the research document. Chapter 3 contains a summary of the basic rules of research that cover all of the listed methodologies.

Summary

There are a variety of techniques to get a researcher to the end of a research project, but all techniques should be comprised of the same basic components. Those components include:

- understand and be conversant with a *theory* that invites research—define and understand the theoretical basis for the project
- read and digest the *literature* that forms the theory—find out what other researchers have done that provides the opportunity for new research
- ask *basic research questions*—state a problem, isolate an issue, or write specific hypotheses to be analyzed
- recognize the *research variables*—identify the elements in the project that may or will change, or that will cause change to occur (make things *vary*)
- *operationalize* the theoretical concepts—find a way to empirically measure the variables
- identify *data sources* in terms of the research variables—find the location of the information that will allow the researcher to draw conclusions about the project
- create a *research design*—structure the project to collect and analyze information that will help to solve the problem, answer the questions, or lead to conclusions about the hypotheses
- *collect the data*—implement the research plan to gather information that may be used to answer the research questions
- ensure the *reliability* and *validity* of the measures
- *analyze the data*—apply standard research tests or appraisal methods to the information collected
- *draw conclusions* about the data—identify what the data document about the results of the project
- *report the research findings*—describe the project in writing using an accepted framework for research reports.

Exercise for Chapter 1

1. What are some cases where inductive reasoning would be better than deductive reasoning?

2. What is a research question that you would like to answer? What are the variables? How would you collect the data to answer the question?

3. In what ways could a participant-observer conducting research be biased?

4. What are some examples of population parameters and the statistics that describe or approximate them?

5. Give some examples of research that may be biased due to the source of funding for the research.

6. Why is replication important to scientific research?

7. Determine whether exit polls for national elections are experimental or nonexperimental research and identify sample statistics that may be computed on exit-poll data.

8. Give some examples of nominal variables that are not ordinal, and ordinal variables that are not interval.

9. Why is it important to read the literature in the conceptual area before you design a specific research question?

10. Outline the steps you would take to design and carry out a research project based on the question, "Does consensus bargaining work?"

REFERENCES FOR CHAPTER 1

Campbell, D. T., & Stanley, J. C. (1963). *Experimental and quasi-experimental designs for research*. Boston: Houghton Mifflin Company.

Creswell, J.W. (2002). *Research design: Qualitative, quantitative, and mixed methods approaches* (2nd ed.). Thousand Oaks, CA: Sage Publications.

Demetrion, G. (2004). *Postpositivist scientific philosophy: Mediating convergences*. Retrieved from: http://www.the-rathouse.com/Postpositivism.htm

Gerke, R. (2007). *The proper assigning of an F grade: The lack of understanding best practice in grading*. Unpublished doctoral dissertation, Edgewood College, Madison, Wisconsin.

Kerlinger, F. N. (1992). *Foundations of behavioral research* (4th ed.). New York: Holt, Rinehart, and Winston.

Lewin, K. (1946). Action research and minority problems. *Journal of Sociological Issues, 2*(4), 34–46.

Likert, R. (1932). *A* technique for measuring attitudes. *Archives of Psychology*, 140.

Mathison, S. (Ed.). (2005). *Encyclopedia of evaluation*. Thousand Oaks, CA: Sage Publications.

National Research Council. (2002). *Scientific research in education*. Committee on Scientific Principles for Education Research. Shavelson, R. J., and Towne, L., Editors. Center for Education. Division of Behavioral and Social Sciences and Education. Washington, DC: National Academy Press.

No Child Left Behind. (2002). Reauthorization of the Elementary and Secondary Education Act. Washington DC: U.S. Congressional Record.

Osgood, C. E., Suci, G. J., & Tannenbaum, P. H. (1957). *The measurement of meaning*. Urbana, IL: The University of Illinois Press.

Sax, G. (1968). *Empirical foundations of educational research*. Englewood Cliffs, NJ: Prentice-Hall, Inc.

United States Department of Education. (2003, December). *Identifying and implementing educational practices supported by rigorous evidence: A user-friendly guide*. Washington, DC: U.S. Department of Education.

Chapter 2

Consuming Research

Consumers of research reports are the first audience for this book. The second audience is those who are in the beginning stages of planning and designing a research project. This chapter is for the student or consumer who needs to find and interpret valid research in order to implement research-based projects or structures in a work environment or make data-driven decisions. It is also for those research consumers who need to stay up-to-date with the latest changes in their work environment by reading and understanding what has been studied, validated, and published as research results in the field for the purpose of making positive advances in their professional lives. In order to become a knowledgeable consumer of research, one must first possess a solid background knowledge of research methodology and, second, a basic repertoire of interpretive skills.

With the advent of the federal legislation in No Child Left Behind, authors have begun to help consumers of education research be judicious in their selection and use of quantitative data in scientifically based research reports (see especially Bracey, 2006). As educators consume research, they need to understand how data are used and abused; how data may be manipulated in politically motivated research; whether conclusions from the research are valid; and how the use of student test scores may or may not be appropriate as data in research. Bracey, for example, provides 32 principles of data interpretation that are intended to help readers of educational research sort the good from the bad in quantitative research. These principles are separated into four major theme areas:

- understanding data and how they are used—and misused
- uncovering how variables are used in the construction of scientifically based research—and manipulated in politically motivated research
- drawing conclusions about a study and deciding whether the data presented are meaningful
- assessing the data that come from standardized testing.

Consumers also need to develop a basic understanding of research reports from other research paradigms in addition to the scientific method. This would include qualitative approaches and those that use mixed quantitative and qualitative methods. Research reports in periodicals and other literature, once the appropriate sources for these reports are found, need to be understood and digested. One-stop shopping does not work. Readers of research must have the tenacity to gather an abundance of information or data from several locations, using various library resources in locating research references to build a solid foundation of supportive literature.

Once this information is consumed, readers need to understand the function of research in designing, developing, monitoring, evaluating, and conducting professional programs. It is here that the value of research is most often displayed. Actions that have been the subject of study and publication may provide the basis for informed, data-driven decisions regarding program growth and improvement. Program planners need to be aware of the "garbage in, garbage out" potential for using published research. The results from a project are only as good as the design and implementation of the project allow them to be. Program improvement relies heavily on valid and reliable research.

The Value of Research

Research as a human endeavor is a valuable way to increase knowledge and improve personal and professional situations. The successful practitioner in education or social science settings must be able to conduct, consume, and critically analyze research in many areas and in a variety of forms. Research concepts and methods explored here should be applied to current issues and important problems in specific settings.

It is essential that consumers critique research articles through the lens of applicability. The rubber meets the road when the theory is applied to practice. Situations that need exploration or issues that need to be resolved should be viewed from a broad range of research perspectives. No one method fits all circumstances, and no one model fits all phenomena. Research techniques in the broad range should be applied to policies, practices, and problems in the workplace in order for a solid understanding of the value of research to be realized.

This chapter is intended to help readers of research begin to recognize and understand the value of research and its broad-reaching utility. It begins with the basic philosophical designs and constructs that serve as a foundation for research endeavors. Often, the philosophical is overlooked and the practical is emphasized. It is important that readers recognize not only their own philosophy as it applies to their life and life's work, but also the philosophy of the writer being read. Researchers do not often delineate the philosophical basis used in their research when they produce their publications. But a careful reading of those reports can often put the research into one of the basic philosophical traditions: Is it scientific? Is it pragmatic? Does the humanism show? Then the reader must determine whether or not the philosophy fits the situation or circumstance in which the research may be applied.

It is crucial that consumers find the right sources of research, both to help her or himself understand a concept and to make judgments about program improvement; then to judge the value of the research results and apply the research findings to her or his own situation; and, finally, to have confidence that any changes recommended or implemented would be data-driven and research-based, and result in true program improvement. Using data-based sources, reading research abstracts to glean necessary and important information, understanding the design or structure of the research, judging reliability and validity of the research process, and determining research significance are the components that consumers need to be aware of, and they are the major subjects of this chapter.

Research Theories and Philosophies

What is research? The word *research* derives from French, and its literal meaning is *to investigate thoroughly*. Research is often described as an active, studious, and systematic process of inquiry or examination aimed at discovering, interpreting, and revising facts. It is an investigation that results in a greater understanding of phenomena in the world, such as events, behaviors, or theory. The intent of conducting or consuming research in many cases is to make informed or wise decisions for practical applications of the research results. While it is usually associated with science and the scientific method, the term *research* is also used to describe the studious collection of information about a particular subject. To understand research as a human endeavor, a reader must have an understanding of the philosophical bases of inquiry and the research types that fit each of those bases.

Philosophy is a basic mental exercise that creates and organizes theories aimed at some kind of understanding, knowledge, or wisdom. Philosophy is thinking—thinking that focuses on foundational concepts of human cognitive activity, such as reality, value, meaning, existence, causality, or truth. All cultures have their own unique schools or theories of philosophy, and these theories have grown from widely different propositions and approaches. The basic examples of the different philosophical foundations include the rational or logical approach, empiricism, leaps of faith or hope, and inheritance of philosophical customs. Philosophical foundations in research begin with the component that is devoted to the study of knowledge itself—epistemology.

Epistemology is the branch of philosophy that is devoted to the study of the nature, origin, basic foundations, validity, and scope of knowledge. Historically, epistemology has been one of the most investigated and debated of all philosophical subjects. The debate has focused on analyzing the nature and variety of knowledge and how it relates to similar notions, such as truth and belief. Much of this discussion concerns justification. Specifically, epistemology analyzes the grounds on which one can claim to know a particular fact.

Not surprisingly, the way that knowledge claims are justified depends on the general approach to philosophy one selects. Thus, philosophers have developed a range of epistemological theories to accompany their general philosophical positions. These epistemological theories that are well known to the general public include rationalism, realism, idealism, pragmatism, and relativism. Each of these theories is built upon a set of propositions or premises that must be accepted as true in order for the knowledge in that theory to be built. Following are broad definitions of each:

- *Rationalism* is the school of thought in philosophy that appeals to reason as a source of knowledge. In more technical terms, it is a deductive method in which the criterion of the truth is not sensory but intellectual. It is a feeling that reason has precedence over other ways of acquiring knowledge.

- *Realism* in philosophy is the study of existence or being that is considered independent of conceptual schemes, linguistic patterns, or beliefs. Realists tend to believe that current thinking is only an approximation of reality and that every new observation brings one closer to understanding reality.

- *Idealism* is the doctrine that thought (a person's ideas) makes up any complete reality. Therefore, a world of material objects containing no thought either could not exist as it is experienced, or it would not be fully real. Idealism asserts that minds are aware of or perceive only their own ideas, and not external objects. That is, things in themselves cannot be known because they are only a mental image.

- *Pragmatism* is a philosophic school that considers practical consequences, or real effects, to be vital components of both truth and meaning. It is more concerned with practical results than with theories and principles.

- *Relativism* is the idea that some element or aspect of experience is not permanently fixed, but rather dependent on (related to) some other element or aspect. It is a conviction that humans can understand and evaluate beliefs and behaviors only in terms of context because there are no absolute truths.

- *Empiricism* is another of the many epistemological theories that exist in the broad range of philosophical thought. For research, empiricism is the philosophical doctrine of observation and experience. In recent iterations, it has taken on the more specific meaning that all human knowledge ultimately comes from the senses and from experience. Empiricism is generally regarded as the heart of modern scientific method. It requires that theories be created based on testing and observation of the world, rather than on intuition or faith. Empirical research based on inductive reasoning rather than on pure deductive logic is the path to truth in this category of philosophy.

The logical chain here is that there must be a philosophical base to the research design. The basis for research is derived from the epistemological branch of philosophy, the one that studies the nature of knowledge. Within the epistemological branch of philosophy, most of the work deemed research is completed under the rubric of the empirical theory, emphasizing testing or observation and analysis. The term empiricism is used to describe a number of distinct philosophical attitudes, practices, and propositions. Empiricism refers to an emphasis on those aspects of scientific knowledge that are closely related to experience, especially as formed through deliberate experimental arrangements. Empirical research may then further be divided within the empirical theory into several camps that support their own techniques or methods. The major camps in this regard include positivism, postpositivism, phenomenology, and constructivism. Each of these may be subject to subdivision as well. Constructivism philosophy, for example, has been separated into the areas of social, cultural, radical, or critical constructivism.

Nearly every modern discussion of the theory and philosophy of research, at least in education, begins with the work of John Dewey. Philosophies that influence research have grown since the time of Dewey, and basic theories have been subdivided into more precise and focused subcategories. The discussion that follows is an attempt to scratch the surface of the basic schools of thought regarding research and to provide a foundation for research consumers as to the philosophical bases for what may be read in research reports and articles. The next several sections provide a basic outline of the empirical philosophies that helped to form the different theories of research, followed by a discussion of the different basic types of research. Once again, the reader is reminded that this is a brief overview of the philosophies and theories. Further reading is encouraged for a broader understanding of one or more of the theories, and the texts selected for the annotated bibliography in Chapter 14 will help in this process.

Positivism

At one time, empirical scientific research ruled the day, and the strict scientific method as outlined in Chapter 1 was the only method of research. All research flowed from a process that was rational and scientific. The researcher was a neutral observer and recorder of the process and results. This was referred to as the positivist way of thinking, meaning that the conditions and results of the research had to be absolute in the accuracy of the findings (e.g., the question, "Are you sure that's right?" and the response, "I've done the research and I'm positive!").

The goal of research from the positivist philosophy is to generate knowledge from research that can be used to describe experiences and phenomena, or to create new theories out of the research results. Positivism holds that the purpose of science is simply to stick to what can be observed and measured. Knowledge of anything beyond that, a positivist would hold, is impossible. In the positivist view of the world, science was seen as the way to get at truth, to understand the world well enough so that it might be predicted and controlled. The adherence to the scientific method by the federal government for programs in education represents the positivist viewpoint.

Postpositivism

John Dewey, among others, helped to promote a new approach to research that questioned the cumulative growth of scientific knowledge. Critics of the positivist philosophy felt that knowledge could not be value-free, or neutral, which was the basis of the positivist approach. This train of thought was labeled the *postpositivist movement*. Still part of the empirical theory, postpositivism is, as the prefix indicates, a theoretical position that followed, and more or less grew out of, the positivist approach. Some would argue that postpositivism was created as a drastic rejection of the positivistic, scientific approach. But in reality, postpositivists recognized the impossibility of ensuring laboratory conditions for research in the real world, especially for research regarding human endeavors. So it is more an extension of the controlled and objective scientific way of conducting research than an argument against science as research.

In the social sciences, postpositivism is used to refer to those who do not believe it is possible for researchers to view life from an objective standpoint. They recognize the importance of context, including language and culture, when dealing with research decisions. Postpositivism is a belief that theory both shapes and follows reality. For the postpositivist, the truth of science pertains to the study and description of phenomena as they are found in the real world.

Phenomenology

At the extreme of thought, there are those researchers who consider only what is presented to them in conscious experience in their quest for the truth. Phenomena are studied in their context, and sometimes the researcher is part of that context. This theory is called *phenomenology*. It is a branch of empirical philosophy that takes the intuitive experience of phenomena and tries to extract the essence of that experience. Sense experiences—what the researcher heard, saw, or felt—become an important part of the data for phenomenology, and these experiences are reported along with the results of interviews or questionnaires used to make observations or gather attitudes. Phenomenologists tend to hold that inquiry should focus on what might be called *encountering* as it is directed at objects, and on *objects as they are encountered* (Center for Advanced Research in Phenomenology, 2006). While some would argue that all qualitative research is phenomenological in nature (Imel, Kerka, & Wonacott, 2002), the commonly accepted research behavior for phenomenology is to understand and to explain an experience without reference to the question of whether that which has been experienced is objectively real or true.

Constructivism

Constructivism is a research theory at the opposite end of phenomenology. It originated in sociology under the term social constructionism and has been given the name constructivism when referring to it as a philosophy or research type. Constructivists view all knowledge as "constructed" because it does not reflect any external realities, but rather is contingent on convention, human perception, and social experience. It is believed by constructivists that representations of physical and biological reality, including race, sexuality, and gender, are socially designed and developed. The common thread for all forms of constructivism is that they focus on the constructed reality rather than merely on the nature of being or existence, as the phenomenologists do.

Figure 2.1 traces the conceptualization of thought from the broad realm of philosophy through that portion of philosophy devoted to the study of knowledge through observation or experience, with one of four possible viewpoints: positivism, postpositivism, phenomenology, or constructivism.

Figure 2.1. Organized inquiry: From philosophy to research in education.

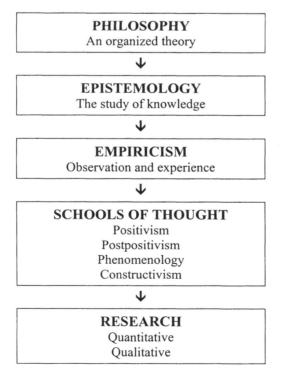

Organized Inquiry: From Philosophy to Research in Education

As mentioned at the beginning of this chapter, most published research does not enter into deep philosophical discussion regarding whether the research has a positivistic or constructionist point of view, but readers should be comfortable with their own sense of the world and their own beliefs as to how research can contribute to their work and lives. Another basis for reviewing research is to know about the different types of research, how they are organized, and how they are carried out in an appropriate way. The next section covers some of those structural elements of research.

Types of Research

While research reports may not speak to the philosophical undertones of the work, they often include a reference to the type of research or research genre that has been used. There are separate categories or distinct divisions in what the research may be called or how it is organized and moved forward. Readers need a basic understanding of how a particular piece of research fits into the broader context of all research in order to begin understanding and accepting the conclusions derived. The terms most often used to describe different types of research discussed here include *empirical research*, *qualitative research*, and *quantitative research*.

Empirical Research

The framework of thought so far in this chapter is that there is a specific branch of philosophy that provides the foundation of thought for research—epistemology. Then there are various schools of thought that may be represented in the structure of the research project, with phenomenological structures being used quite often in the social sciences. Much of the research conducted—phenomenological as well as other approaches—is empirical research, based on observation and experience. Therefore, most research published in the social sciences is *empirical* research.

Empirical research is any activity that uses direct or indirect observation as its test of reality. Empirical research may be theory-based and may use deductive reasoning to reach conclusions, or it may not be based on theory and therefore may follow the route of inductive reasoning. The empirical researcher attempts to describe accurately the interaction between an observation or a measuring device and the entity or phenomenon being observed. The researcher is expected to calibrate the device or measurement tool by applying it to known standard objects and documenting the results before applying it to unknown objects.

For theoretical empirical studies, the accumulation of evidence for or against any particular theory involves planned research designs for the collection of empirical data. Several research methods for such empirical designs have been suggested, one of the most popular of which comes from Campbell and Stanley (1963). They distinguish between preexperimental, experimental, and quasi-experimental designs. For a long time, these designs played a central role in the use of randomized experiments as the major technique in educational research.

Two basic categories of empirical research that may be referenced in research reports are fundamental research and applied research. Within these two categories, much of the research in the social sciences has been divided into two types, one based on numerical data, or quantitative research, and the other based on textual data, or qualitative research. Both quantitative and qualitative research may be either fundamental or applied.

Fundamental or basic research (sometimes referred to as pure research) has as its primary objective the advancement of knowledge and the theoretical understanding of the relations among or between selected phenomena. It is exploratory or explanatory in nature and often driven by the researcher's curiosity, interest, or intuition. Fundamental research may not have any practical end in mind, but it often has unanticipated results that may lead to practical applications. Basic research helps theory to grow and provides the foundation for further research.

Applied research, unlike basic research, is not conducted to produce knowledge for knowledge's sake. The aim of applied research is to solve specific, practical questions. It can be exploratory, but applied research is usually descriptive or evaluative in nature, attempting to make clear the salient features of the phenomenon being studied. Applied research often takes its direction from the results of basic research. Common areas of applied research include electronics, informatics, computer science, process engineering, and drug design. One current direction for applied research is the mixed-methods approach of action research, as outlined in Chapter 1. In consuming research reports, the reader may experience references to the concepts of empirical research, whether fundamental or applied; in order to make sense of the research, the reader should have a grasp of what the author means if those references are used in the study under scrutiny.

Qualitative Research

The term qualitative research has different meanings in different fields, the social science usage being the best known. While there may not be a consensus among researchers as to what the qualitative approach is, general characteristics and techniques can be categorized as qualitative research. These are described next.

Often used in the context of phenomenology, qualitative research covers a broad spectrum of research that focuses on how individuals and groups view and understand the world and how they construct meaning out of their experiences; it is essentially narrative oriented. Other researchers consider it simply to be research whose goal is not to estimate statistical parameters but to generate hypotheses to be tested quantitatively. There are uses of qualitative analysis that do involve numbers. In statistics, for example, qualitative analysis consists of procedures that use only dichotomous data—that is, data that can take only the values 0 (zero) and 1 (one). These techniques are suitable where events or entities can only be counted or classified rather than measured. The techniques themselves, of course, are numerically based.

Qualitative research methods are sometimes used together with quantitative research methods to provide a deeper understanding of the causes of social phenomena or to help generate questions for further research. Unlike quantitative methods, qualitative research methods place little importance on developing statistically valid samples or on searching for conclusive proof of hypotheses. Instead, qualitative research focuses on the understanding of research phenomena within their naturally occurring context or contexts. One aim of the qualitative researcher is to determine specific meanings that the phenomena may have for the participants.

Generally, qualitative research studies rely on three basic data-gathering techniques: participant or nonparticipant observation, interview, and document or artifact analysis. Each of these techniques represents a continuum that may gravitate from spontaneous to more ordered and controlled. Specific studies or particular techniques may rely more heavily on one data-gathering technique or another.

Ethnography or ethnographic studies, as one example of qualitative work, refers to the qualitative description of human social phenomena, most often based on fieldwork. Ethnography is a holistic research method founded on the idea that the interconnected elements of a social system cannot necessarily be accurately understood independent of each other. Several academic traditions, in particular the constructivist and relativist paradigms, claim ethnography as a valid research method.

Qualitative research is often thought of as the nonnumerical examination and interpretation of observations for the purpose of discovering underlying meanings and patterns of relationships. Qualitative research is generally considered exploratory and inductive in nature. It is used to provide a general sense of what is happening and to form theories that can be tested through further quantitative research. One criticism of the approach to qualitative research is that the definitions offered of it do not distinguish it adequately from quantitative research. One reason for this problem is that many research projects use what is called a "mixed-methods" technique in which qualitative and quantitative methods are combined. An example would be a project incorporating a numerical survey (quantitative) that is followed by interviews (qualitative). A consumer of research will see research that is either qualitative or quantitative, but very often it is a blended approach using both numbers and textual data to reach conclusions.

Quantitative Research

Quantitative research is most often aligned with the positivist philosophy and the scientific method of empirical research. Quantitative studies, however, may also observe phenomena in a natural context and address issues of meaning much like qualitative studies do. Quantitative research is based on the numerical representation of observations for the purpose of describing and explaining the phenomena. In quantitative research, the aim is to determine the relationship between one thing, referred to as an independent variable, and another, known in research terms as a dependent or outcome variable.

Quantitative research designs are either descriptive, where subjects are usually measured once, or experimental or quasi-experimental, where subjects are measured before and after some kind of experiment or treatment. Some researchers include a fourth type of design, known as a correlational or *ex post facto* (after the fact) study, as a quantitative approach to research. A descriptive study establishes only associations between variables. An experiment or correlational study may establish causality, depending on the statistical analysis carried out.

Quantitative research is all about quantifying, analyzing, and measuring relationships between variables. Quantitative research is therefore empirical research that is used both in natural sciences—like physics, biology, or geology—and in social sciences—like psychology, sociology, or education. Quantitatively based opinion surveys, for example, are widely used in the media. In opinion surveys, respondents are asked a set of structured questions, and their responses may be assigned numeric values, as discussed in Chapter 1, and then tabulated.

Basically, experimental and quasi-experimental studies are designed to examine cause and effect. These studies are usually conducted to examine the differences in dependent variables that might be attributed to independent variables or treatments. Descriptive and correlational studies examine variables in their natural environments and do not include treatments imposed by the researcher.

There is no universal standard for defining and categorizing different research designs. Often, researchers may combine design characteristics in a mixed-methods approach, they may create a subcategory of a proven design, or they may change names of designs in their discussions of them. This lack of strict categorization may cause problems when reading research because, as mentioned above, many published studies do not identify the philosophy behind the research or the design used.

Selecting Research Literature

The rapid expansion of the Internet as a resource for information has monumentally changed the landscape for finding research literature. The search engines available for any kind of research place ample data literally at one's fingertips. Of course, professionals still can, and do, subscribe to the scholarly journals and other publications in their field in a hard-copy format. In fact, the jury review of papers submitted to professional publications is one very important reason to continue receiving printed publications, although more and more professional associations are combining online publications with paper copy. The professional journals that have articles peer reviewed are referred to as refereed journals, either in hard copy or online.

Sometimes, Internet information that is not from trusted sources of research suffers from what has been known for a long time as premature publication, meaning, in most cases, that the essential peer review outlined in Chapter 1 has not been completed. Another caution is that technology is available to edit results in order to imply a desired conclusion that is, in the end, unwarranted.

Of course, libraries continue to be an excellent source for finding publications on any topic. City, county, school, and college or university libraries have always been, and continue to be, a nuclear resource for research. Most libraries are also linked to electronic search engines through which research reports from a wide range of sources may be obtained. Most libraries are not only a source for the original documents necessary for a research project, but also a storehouse for the tools needed for the acquisition of reference materials. Software, computer programs, data-retrieval sources, and other mechanisms necessary for the conducting of online research are often housed in local libraries.

Determining which resources to read has become more of a challenge than actually finding those resources. The first step in the finding process is to know the literature of the field of study. Who publishes the research in the field? In some professions, the answer is easier than in others. Fields like medicine, law, architecture, or engineering have well-known and established peer-reviewed journals that have stood the test of time with regard to providing the most up-to-date and relevant research in the profession. Many of these journals have added an online edition so that professionals can have electronic access to the articles.

These fields, and others, have specialty publications in addition to coverage of the broad aspects of the profession in the major journals. Those who practice in a specialty sub-field in the profession—surgeons in medicine, safety experts in engineering, or corporate specialists in law, for example—know the publications that focus on their field. These, too, may be available online as well as in print. Organizational bulletins or conference proceedings are other sources of information, although they may not be referenced to the extent that published articles are.

Occasionally, a consumer needs to go beyond the well-known publications or common library database searches to investigate a topic that may not have the broad appeal needed for general distribution. That is where an independent Internet search may be helpful.

Searching the Web

Sometimes, a well-organized, general search through one or more of the broadly accepted search engines is all that a consumer needs (e.g., http://www.google.com/ or http://www.yahoo.com/). Google has a scholar tab search function that facilitates a search of scholarly literature across many disciplines and sources, including theses, books, abstracts, and articles from academic journals or .edu sites (see http://scholar.google.com/). Another rich resource is a Web site known as Wikipedia (http://en.wikipedia.org/wiki/Main_Page), a free online encyclopedia that allows for constant update. This site is an open-entry database that allows researchers to add to the knowledge base, thus keeping it alive and growing. Databases of this type are subject to criticism regarding accuracy so the reader should always remember to verify the source and the information by checking other sources.

Often, it is necessary to dig a little deeper into the resources available. Research embedded in government sites, for example, may take a little more work to uncover. The consumer is advised to use the topical-search option that most sites provide to do this digging. Keywords need to be carefully selected so that the search results are in the category being used by the information seeker. Most libraries have also become automated so that the same technology that a person would use on a home or office computer to find research reports is used to search on-site stacks or other electronic databases available through the public or school library.

Report titles, recognizing the names of the report authors or the principal investigators as leaders in the field, and the source of the publication are the best beginning items for selecting reports to read. Looking through the Web of Knowledge (http://wok.mimas.ac.uk/) or some other type of citations index appropriate to the discipline being studied might result in a list of peer-reviewed journals on the topic. Questions the reader should ask include: Does the title contain the keywords that help in identifying the topic under consideration? Are the authors well known in the field of study? Are the journals well established and refereed? Lunsford (2006) provides a source map for assessing the value and accuracy of Web resources. Her steps for evaluating Web sources are:

- determine the credibility of the sponsoring organization
- determine the credibility of the author
- determine the currency of the Web source
- determine the accuracy of the information.

Web surfing for the purpose of finding research in the field can be both fascinating and frustrating. The fascination comes when one realizes the vast assortment and incredible number of sources that exist for some topics. The frustration is in sorting through the chaff to find the kernel of grain that will help the reader to find the knowledge sought. Web searches can be additionally frustrating in that sources disappear from the Web on a regular basis, and some sources have few or no attributions that would give the reader confidence in the reliability and validity of the study.

While libraries and professional associations, as gatekeepers of knowledge in a profession, are counted on to sift through the literature and keep or publish only that found to be of significance, the resources on the Web are not subject to the same filters. Because anyone can establish a Web site and publish anything she or he wants, it is very difficult to separate the accurate from the misleading. That is where the questions listed above are important in any search.

The Abstract

Once appropriate research reports are identified and selected for review, the first thing to check is the abstract, if one is written. Most published research begins with a paragraph that, in a very brief way, describes the purpose of the study, the variables being studied, the type of research used, and the major findings in the study. This is the abstract of the study, and it is most often at the very beginning of the publication, right after the title and author's name. Depending on the resource used for selection, the abstract may be the only piece of information the consumer has. Many Internet sources use titles and abstracts only as a first level in providing information about research.

The intent of the abstract is to provide a very brief summary of the research topic, the methods used in the research (including data sources and structure), and the basic conclusions drawn from the data. It provides the consumer an opportunity for an efficient review of the article contents, and it should contain many of the keywords that describe the research variables and components.

Quantitative studies contain abstracts that identify the subject being studied, the pertinent aspects of the subject, the methods used, the statistical findings, any major conclusions drawn, and any implications made. A qualitative study abstract may not contain the statistical component, but it will still describe the relevant characteristics of the object under consideration, the nature of the issue being studied, and the basic research findings or questions posed for further research purposes.

Most professional publications require a specific method of writing, following a generally accepted writing style or format. One such format often used in research is that followed by the American Psychological Association. The APA manual is an excellent source for further investigation of the purpose for and writing of abstracts for research publications.

If well written, the abstract of an article or report will tell the reader immediately whether or not the complete text is worth reading.

Reading the Report

Most research articles are separated into five main components. As mentioned above, the abstract is usually provided at the beginning of the article and summarizes each of the parts. Research articles usually begin with a review of pertinent literature, followed by the statement of the problem, the design of the research, the presentation of the findings, and finally, a discussion of the significance of the results. While this outline is not followed in every research publication, the component parts represented are very often included in some way.

The Literature Review

By selecting the right titles and reading the abstracts of the studies, a consumer of research may identify research reports that will be helpful to the issue being studied. The next step is to read the entire report or article. Reading research, like reading different genres of literature, has its own peculiarities. Research reports are not creative literature. They cannot be read like a novel. Speed-reading or skimming is not an option with research articles. Once a research report is identified for further study and the abstract has been digested, the reader needs to carefully read the entire product.

Well-written reports start with background literature that lays a foundation for the study. New research is based on existing theory, and the theoretical aspects of the issue being studied need to be made clear at the beginning of the report. Other research that has been completed in the topic should be identified and summarized. Consumers should pay careful attention to the literature selected and referenced by the research author. Questions to keep in mind while reading the report include: Is the theoretical basis of the research well founded? Are the authors selected by the researcher well known in the field? Is there variety in the research literature selected for inclusion? Are all sides of the argument included in the researcher's introduction? Does the author lean heavily on her or his own previous work to the exclusion of others'? These are some questions the reader should ask as the literature review is consumed. The reader is well advised to grant more legitimacy to top-tier journals in the field, which are often the trade publications of the major professional associations.

Areas of caution when consuming the research literature component of a research report start with recognizing the theoretical basis for the research. If the theoretical structures are easily identified, recognizable as accepted in the profession, and controlled in their construction rather than loosely tied together, the report is on the right track. If the researcher provides evidence that preconceived notions about the topic are avoided, the research is on the right track. If the variables under consideration lend themselves to appropriate testing, and the literature provides examples of previous research using the study variables, the research is on the right track.

The introduction to the research should give the reader confidence that there will be a systematic look at relationships or a careful explanation of observed relationships if the report is not an empirical testing of theory or a controlled experiment. Remember that one of the basic principles for research provided by the National Research Council is to link research to relevant theory. Additionally, a careful review of existing literature on a subject may point out gaps in a theory or in the literature describing or explaining that theory. The literature section of a report should do both for a reader—link the research to theory and point to possible gaps. See Rule 1 in Chapter 3 for more on the literature review in research reports.

The Problem Statement

The second component of most published research is a carefully designed statement of what the research is about: the problem statement. The first principle from the National Research Council's six benchmarks for inquiry is to pose significant questions that can be investigated empirically. This principle or benchmark also needs careful examination by the reader. The basic question(s), the research hypothesis, or the conceptual issue under consideration should have been outlined in the abstract. In fact, that problem statement should have been one of the more important criteria for electing to read the report. The text of the report should go into greater detail about the question(s), hypothesis, issue, or problem under consideration by the researcher.

The first part of the problem analysis for the consumer is to ensure that the issue is logically linked to the literature cited. Then the reader should look at the problem statement and ask whether the problem described is going to be helpful to the reader's understanding of the issue. The research participants, the conceptual issues, or the organizational structures of the group or agency being studied may or may not fit the reader's actual situation. The variables used in the research may not be relevant to the reader. If not, then the research may not be helpful, and the reader may decide to discontinue the review of that particular piece of research literature.

If the problem statement seems to fit the reader's needs, then the next question to ask is whether the problem being studied in the research is applicable or replicable in the consumer's own circumstance. The reader needs to be convinced that the results of the study will be valuable information for her or his own situation. This begins by accepting that the theory behind the problem is closely related to the reality of the situation the reader faces.

Another important consideration for the consumer of research at this juncture is to determine whether the problem posed is realistic. Once again, the report may be discarded if the problem seems too trivial, or too optimistic, to help with a real-world situation. Should the reading of the problem statement give the consumer confidence that these threshold questions can be answered appropriately, the next part of the report is most often a description of the methods used in the research. The reader must determine whether the techniques used match the issue outlined and are appropriate for the question under consideration. Rule 2 in Chapter 4 provides a further exploration of the issue of research topics and problem statements.

The Research Design

A research design begins with the foundations of the scientific method of knowing. The design is the structure, plan, and strategy of investigation put together to answer the research questions. Research design and research method are often used synonymously. Most research can be divided into two camps. There is the static view of science as knowledge accumulation in which new facts are derived from old. Then there is the dynamic, or heuristic, approach that is a discovery method, or a theory-building and -testing approach. Research design is a guard against preconceived notions leading to erroneous conclusions. A third principle from the National Research Council is to use methods that permit direct investigation of the question.

Empirical, or quantitative, studies most often aim to do one of two different things. They either attempt to compare constructs or they try to contrast them. A research construct is the result of systematic thought about a subject in which a complex theory or subjective notion has been created and systematically put together. A study of contrast is a study that looks for significant differences between research variables. A conjectural statement about the relationship between variables (i.e., the problem statement) is tested. One crucial aspect of a scientific research design is the control of what is called *variance*.

Consumers of research reports should be able to distinguish between the three basic sources of variance in research. First, readers should think of variance as change, and that *experimental variance* is any change due to the treatment used in the research. Researchers want this type of change to be the greatest. That is, experimental variance (the change due to the applied research conditions) should be maximized. The second important type of variance in research is the change due to outside influence. Researchers must work hard to control this *extraneous variance*, and often laboratory conditions are necessary to do this. The third type of variance readers should recognize is called *error variance*. Error variance, change due to chance, must be minimized.

As outlined in Chapter 1, the scientific approach to research design is one of control and repeated measures. Probably the most pure research is the laboratory experiment of the scientific method, in which the variance of all extraneous variables is kept to a minimum. The research is isolated in a physical situation apart from the routine of ordinary living, and one or more independent (or experimental) variables are manipulated (treatment given) under carefully controlled conditions. Outside the scientific approach, most research is conducted as a field experiment in which the situation is more realistic, but the control of extraneous variables is difficult.

In order to test hypotheses, and to measure the different types of change, statistical tests are planned into the research design. Remember that statistics are numbers that are generated by the research to test the hypotheses or to answer the basic questions. They are data generated from the research project. These data are manipulated through the use of generally accepted formulae, and are used to verify decisions about the problem statement.

There are statistical tests that researchers use to measure those differences or test those statements. In the basic scientific method, for instance, two groups are contrasted to determine whether the treatment applied or attempted had a significant impact upon the experimental group. The statistical formula used most often explains the change that may be due to chance (the error variance).

Readers of research reports do not have to be experts in the several statistical techniques used to measure the significance of the research findings. It is enough to know when a test proposed or used is appropriate and whether the conclusions drawn based on the techniques used are warranted.

The keywords for the reader to look for in the abstract and in the research design section include: *compare, contrast, differences, significant difference, correlation, commonalities, similarities, statistical significance,* or terms that describe the statistical test to be used. Readers should be concerned that the methodology used realistically matches the problem being studied. That is, does the type of analysis planned or used actually fit the situation and the data?

A comparative study looks for similarities rather than differences in the data. Two or more groups may be studied, and the similarity of response compared, in order for judgments to be made about the research topic. There are also statistical procedures to use when measuring similarities.

Chapter 1 outlined the different data types derived from or used in a quantitative study. One thing a reader can do when reading a study is to check that the data type is adequate for the research methods being used. Is the right statistical test being applied? If the research is a correlation study, for instance, the researcher should not be testing the differences between mean values (averages) from a survey. Are the data appropriate for the analysis technique selected? Or, for example, are ordinal data being forced into parametric statistical tests?

Some of the basic statistical tests used in quantitative studies, their data needs, and their meaning are listed below (remember that the types of data were defined in Chapter 1):

Nonparametric summary statistics that cannot be used to generalize about the population include:

- frequency counts (nominal data)—the number of instances or objects in a data category

- percents (nominal data)—used to summarize a sample by using a comparative ratio of 100 (e.g., 45% male and 55% female)

- chi-square (nominal data)—used to test whether the data are in a different pattern than expected (are the observed patterns different from a normal pattern?)

- rank-order correlation (ordinal data)—a ranking of frequencies in categories to compare the relationship between two variables without making assumptions about the frequency distribution.

Parametric calculations from the research sample that are used to describe the population include: *statistical*

- measures of central tendency (mean, median, mode)—ordinal data—are used to make summary statements about how scores or values cluster or collect around one score or value. The *mean* or mean value is the arithmetic *average* of a set of scores, the *median* is the *midpoint* of a distribution, and the *mode* is the *most frequently occurring* score in a data set

- measures of dispersion (range, quartiles, variance, standard deviation)—interval data—are used to measure the spread of data across the entire sample. The *range* is the difference between the lowest to the highest score in a data set; the *quartile* is dividing the data set into four equal parts; the *variance* is the mean square dispersion about the arithmetic average, or mean value (i.e., each score is subtracted from the mean, the result is squared, and the results for each score are added together and averaged); the *standard deviation* is the root mean square of the sample (i.e., how different the sample average might be from the real population mean), which is the square root of the variance. These same tests are appropriate for ratio data as well

- *t*-test—interval data—are used to test differences of average scores from a selected scale score value, or compares two samples' averages; compares a sample group to itself to weed out discrepancies

- Analysis of Variance (ANOVA)—interval data—compares the dispersion (variance) between three or more groups in the sample to the dispersion within the groups; groups can be compared across items
- correlation—interval data—is used to measure the similarity of the data derived from different variables
- factor analysis—interval data—is used to separate data into like or similar categories
- regression analysis—ratio data—is used to make predictions about the relationships between variables.

Qualitative studies also have a methodology that should be described in the research article. Whether it is a review of existing documents or the compilation of new data through interviews, surveys, or other means, the data type and the source of the data must match the questions posed by the research. Do you interview police officers to answer a question about firefighters' perceptions? Do you review financial data to measure the adequacy of storm shelters? The method of research must be directly related to the questions asked.

Qualitative field studies are an appropriate method with which to study complex circumstances, but they must be realistic, significant, and theory-oriented. The variables being studied must be isolated in the design, and the interactions being observed need to be made clear. The problems identified for resolution should be practical, and the methods used to study the problems should be carefully outlined.

The careful consumer of research may find a mismatch of methods and problems, which should cause one to discard that particular piece of research. If the methodology does seem appropriate, the next step in reading research is to digest the findings that the author selects to report. In reviewing the findings, the reader should pay careful attention to how the data are displayed, and to whether the numbers used or the texts selected are significant to the reader's own circumstance. Whatever the technique, the reader should keep in mind yet another principle of the National Research Council: the report should provide a coherent and explicit chain of reasoning. For further discussion of research design or methodology, the reader should review Rules 3, 4, and 5 in Chapters 5, 6, and 7.

Research Findings

Quantitative data in research reports are usually displayed in the form of tables or figures. The numbers generated by the research study are combined and displayed to aid in the description of the information collected and to lead to summary responses to the basic questions posed in the research. Displays usually include raw data, frequency counts, measures of central tendency, measures of dispersion, and the results of statistical tests used to determine the significance of the research data. Readers should be sure that the promise made in the methodology section is fulfilled in the findings section.

Other components of the findings that a reader should review include the scope of the data displayed. Are there enough participants to legitimately draw conclusions about the topic? Are the groups being compared roughly the same size, or do they represent roughly the equivalent proportion of the home group? Are there too many participants? Statistical tests, for the most part, rely on the number of data points in the study, and the more participants, the more likely that statistical significance can be generated.

The consumer should also look at the characteristics of the data. If data from a limited geographic area, for instance, are used exclusively in the project, the results may not transport to the reader's home location. What is true in Maine may not be true in New Mexico. If the participants represent organizations or agencies quite different from the consumer's, that, too, may be an issue for using the results. The attitudes of a heavily female sample may not hold true for males.

These characteristics should be easily read from the tables, figures, or charts the author of the research report provides in the text. If, for example, the author offers only percentages of respondents and not the actual number of participants or respondents in a category, it may be difficult to determine the real value of the data. This could be an obvious reason for the reader to dismiss the results. Another reason for dismissing the results of a report is if it combines categories of respondents or participants in an illogical way that confuses the ability to draw conclusions. Tables and charts in the document should be reviewed for these or other abnormalities.

Readers of research need to conduct an insightful analysis of the data displays while keeping in mind the setting and structure to be informed or shaped by the research. If the two are too disparate, the research may not be helpful to the consumer's purpose. If the data seem to fit the circumstance, the next construct for the reader to analyze is the use of the statistical tests selected to prove the point or describe the data. Authors of quantitative research usually include these tests in the analysis or treatment section of the report. They may be integrated into the findings section as well. In either case, the reader should ask some basic questions about the measurement used in the analysis of the data.

Some of the most common statistical techniques were listed previously. There are many variations on the basic types listed, but in each case, the tests are simply manipulations of the data derived in the research project. If the research has poor data, no statistical test in the world will help to give the research more validity and reliability—two concepts that should be part of all published research. The research concepts of validity and reliability are explained further in Chapter 8 under Rule 6, but a brief discussion of these two essential characteristics is provided here.

Validity

Validity, simply put, means that the research method and the techniques used to collect data actually measure what they purport to measure. It means that the conclusions drawn or descriptions given by the researcher for the subject or topic under consideration are accurate. Two types of validity are usually discussed in research reports. The first is *internal validity*. For experimental or quasi-experimental designs, this means that the treatment did, in fact, cause the result. For qualitative designs, internal validity means that the control, analysis, and procedures used in the study are appropriate to make the results interpretable—that the research is credible. Member-checking is a tool used by qualitative researchers to conduct an internal validity check. Because the purpose of qualitative research is to offer insights from the research group's perspective, the members of the research sample form the basic group that will judge the credibility of the research project.

The second type of validity usually used in research is *external validity*. External validity means that, in the quantitative sense, the results can be generalized to a larger group outside the research group. Statistical tests are used to substantiate the external validity and to provide a confidence level for any generalizations made from the research data. External validity allows the qualitative researcher to generalize across factors in the population being studied—evidence that the research is transferable. Here, the research design and the theoretical assumptions upon which the design is built allow the researcher to make statements about other settings based on the research conducted. External validity for qualitative research relies heavily on the commonsense approach to the research as findings are argued to be transferable.

Readers of research reports will see several varieties of validity referenced in studies. Some of the more common ones include:

- face validity—the measurement or analysis proposed is in agreement with commonly held beliefs about the subject or topic (i.e., "on the face of it," it seems logical)
- content validity—the questions asked are the right questions for the research, and they accurately represent the subject or topic being studied (i.e., they deal with the "content" being studied)
- criterion validity—there is an external criterion that is the standard for the topic or subject, and the measurements being calculated or questions being asked in the research compare well with that criterion (also known as predictive validity, because

the known standard predicts the research results). A device has criterion validity if it provides an alternative measure of the same concept as another well-accepted device (e.g., high school GPA and SAT scores have criterion or predictive validity because they both measure potential success in college)

- construct validity—the measurement device relates well to the appropriate theoretical concepts that define the study, and not to concepts for which it was not intended. A measurement device has construct validity if it provides support for the intended interpretation of the variables. Construct validity refers to the totality of evidence about whether a particular use of a device adequately represents what is intended by a theoretical account of the thing being measured (e.g., a measure of IQ may not be the best device to determine the construct of socio-economic status; there may be more, or better, measurements to determine the construct)

- substantive validity—also known as educational or professional validity—answers the question of whether or not the size of the research group (the sample) is adequate to the purpose of the study (i.e., is the group substantial enough to warrant conclusions).

Reliability

Reliability in research is the dependability or accuracy of the results. It includes the stability, consistency, and predictability of the analysis. If the project were to be replicated, reliability would indicate that the same or very similar results would be found. In quantitative research, most tests of reliability are applied to the instrument being used to collect data. Survey forms or questionnaires are subjected to a reliability analysis (most often a statistical test) so that their accuracy may be substantiated.

The basic quantitative technique for determining reliability uses accepted statistical analyses. The object is to keep the variance in the measured results that is due to chance (error variance) at a minimum. Statistical tests used to determine the stability of a measuring device need, at a minimum, interval data. Tests that are used often and may be referenced in research reports include:

- test-retest reliability—a correlation coefficient is calculated based on two iterations of the same test or instrument. Correlation coefficients most often vary from 0 to 1, and the closer the value is to 1, the more reliable the measurement device

- split-half reliability—when successive iterations of the same measurement are not possible, the device may be split into two matching items that measure the same or similar constructs, and a reliability coefficient is generated from using the two halves of the device

- coefficient alpha—also known as Cronbach's coefficient alpha—all of the possible split-half comparisons are made, and the coefficient is an average of all split-half calculations
- rank-order correlations—results measured at different times or from different groups are ranked, then used to analyze data and compare for consistency, often in tandem with nonparametric data.

Reliability in the qualitative tradition has the same meaning as in the quantitative methodology. Reliability assures that the results from the research are accurate and that they represent the topic or subject under consideration. That is, the research is dependable. Qualitative researchers must accurately describe the setting of the research and pay close attention to changes that occur during the research process. It is by cataloging and explaining these changes that the qualitative researcher provides for the reliability of the study.

Consumers of research work must be knowledgeable of the concepts of validity and reliability. If a report does not speak to either concept, or if the treatment of one or the other or both seems superficial, the reader may want to think twice before implementing a program or replicating a study incorporating the report's results. There needs to be confidence that the research is accurate (valid) and dependable (reliable) if it is to be usable. If the research seems to be valid and reliable, the next question the consumer needs to ask is: "Is it significant?"

Research Significance

The true significance of a research project depends on the care taken in the structuring and implementation of the project. As was mentioned in Chapter 1, classical scientific research includes hypothesis testing, which is a determination of confidence in rejecting the stated hypothesis. Hypothesis testing in scientific research does not directly prove anything. So readers must look at the references provided by the researcher that summarize similar studies, or at the replications that may exist in the research report, before conclusions can be drawn for the reader's own situation.

Significance in quantitative research goes back to the discussion of confidence, and to the statistical tests used to verify confidence. Readers will see researchers use levels of significance to substantiate the importance of the research results. Most commonly, the researcher chooses "1 out of 100" or "5 out of 100" as the probability level for the significance of the study. The level of significance is selected to minimize the possibility that the results are due to chance. Researchers will choose the 1% chance level and report significant results represented by $p < .01$ or they may choose the 5% chance level and report a significance of $p < .05$, where p is defined as the probability. If significance exists at one of these levels, the reader may have confidence that the treatment in the research most likely caused the results reported by the researcher.

Special caution needs to be taken with a researcher's claim in the published work that the research had a resulting effect on the group, organization, or agency being studied (i.e., when the researcher attributes causation of variables or events by or through other variables in the research). Too often, correlation studies lead the author to attribute one variable as being the cause of another when in fact the measure is just one of similar trends in the data. While there are statistics that do provide for the explanation of variance between phenomena being studied (regression analysis, for example), it is still risky to indicate that one thing actually caused another to happen in a research project.

Putting the Research to Work

Consumers of research reports consume them for a purpose: They want to put research to good use in their personal or professional lives. In order to put research findings to use, the reader must make some basic judgments about applicability. Questions to consider include:

- Were the participants similar to the individuals at the home site?
- Do the findings make sense for the field as a whole?
- Does the measurement support the findings?
- Can the findings be extended successfully to other situations?
- Does the research fit the current location (the "not in my backyard" syndrome)?
- Are there research implications that may cloud the use of the findings?
- Does the research extend the accepted theory beyond common sense?

In the final analysis, the consumer must answer the question, "What is it worth?" If the impediments discussed in this chapter are encountered in the reading and review of research reports and literature, then the consumer must decide whether to embark on a project to remediate the errors, or to simply discard the text as unusable.

Exercise for Chapter 2

1. What are the best sources of research literature for your current job?

2. Using research terms, how would you describe your own professional philosophy?

3. What is empirical research, and why is it important?

4. How did postpositivism grow out of the positivist philosophy?

5. Differentiate between fundamental and applied research.

6. How is quantitative research different from qualitative research? How are they the same?

7. What is meant by *variance* in research?

8. Give some examples of different measures of dispersion (e.g., the range of salaries on a teacher-contract salary index is $26,000 to $80,000).

9. How is validity different from reliability for measuring devices in research?

REFERENCES FOR CHAPTER 2

American Psychological Association (2001). *Publication manual of the American Psychological Association* (5th ed.). Washington, DC: American Psychological Association.

Bracey, G. W. (2006). *Reading educational research: How to avoid getting statistically snookered.* Portsmouth, NH: Heinemann.

Campbell, D. T., & Stanley, J. C. (1963). *Experimental and quasi-experimental designs for research.* Boston: Houghton Mifflin Company.

Center for Advanced Research in Phenomenology. (2006). *What is phenomenology?* Retrieved from http://www.phenomenologycenter.org/phenom.htm

Dewey, J. (1929). *The sources of a science of education.* New York: Liveright.

Dewey, J. (1938). *Logic: The theory of inquiry.* New York: Henry Holt and Company.

Imel, S., Kerka, S., & Wonacott, M. E. (2002). *Qualitative research in adult, career, and career-technical education.* Columbus, OH: ERIC Clearinghouse on Adult, Career, and Vocational Education.

Lunsford, A.A. (2006). *Easy writer* (3rd ed.). Boston: Bedford/St. Martin's.

Shavelson, R. J., & Towne, L. (Eds.). (2002). *Scientific research in education.* Washington, DC: National Academy Press.

Part II

The Rules

Notes

Chapter 3

The Theoretical Basis of Research

Rule 1: Read and Summarize the Literature Pertinent to the Subject

As mentioned in Chapter 1, there are principles of inquiry that transcend the topic, subject, or the methodology used in the research endeavor. These principles, or rules, need to be understood if research is to be done or if research results are to be used for program improvement. While not all inquiry is carried out in the same fashion, or with the same techniques, the foundation standards or principles apply in all circumstances.

This chapter and the next nine chapters provide 10 basic rules for research that must be considered whenever research is conducted in a formal sense. These rules are independent of the subject of the research or the method used. Each rule is described in a general sense, and references to the annotated bibliography in Chapter 14 are there to help the reader identify additional resources to expand her or his knowledge regarding the topic of the rule. Taken individually, these rules provide an opportunity to understand a particular part of the process. Taken as a whole, the rules provide a mosaic of the pieces necessary to understand the process of inquiry that leads to the growth of knowledge.

Nothing in life happens in a vacuum. For every action, there is a reaction, and for every invention, there is a precedent. Research-based inquiry, as a human endeavor, is a theory-building approach to knowledge used to explain, understand, predict, or control individuals, events, or other phenomena. Research adds a discovery or dynamic approach to knowing that can assure that the resultant knowledge is true and accurate. In order for the growth of knowledge to occur, there must be an agreed-upon foundation of prior knowledge upon which to build the new. Any researcher must understand and be able to use the prior knowledge base of the research topic. It is the researcher's selection and reporting of pieces of that prior knowledge that become the research-literature part of the research report. Obviously, a topical area for research has been identified, but the actual focus of the research may not be clear until after the literature on that topic has been consumed.

When knowledge from the past is reviewed for a research project, it means reading, or having read, as much of the published literature in the field of study as possible. The more extensive and exhaustive the review of the literature, the more accurate the researcher can be in designing her or his own project. How does the researcher know if the planned project has been done before unless that researcher reads all of the past works in the field?

Review of past knowledge must be based on an accepted theory—a set of assumptions, axioms, propositions, or definitions that form a coherent and unified description of a circumstance, situation, or phenomenon. Theory building begins with *concepts*. A concept is most often seen as some sort of abstraction that is formed as a generalization drawn from the observation of particular instances. Theories are sets of interrelated constructs, and constructs are theoretical concepts that are carefully defined for the research purpose.

So the observation of singular events may be built into a concept, which in turn may be described in theoretical terms—as constructs—and, when the researcher logically puts these constructs together, a theory is born. For instance, one may observe that there are individuals who seem to hold the interest and attention of others and who are able to have others act on their behalf. In order to describe this phenomenon, the concept of leadership is born. One may observe that some individuals seem to be able to finish tasks more quickly and with better results than others. From this phenomenon, the concept of efficiency is born.

If a researcher wants to study these concepts, that is, if a research project is to be designed, then the researcher *constructs* a way of looking at these concepts. The concept of leadership may be looked at in the categories of autocratic, democratic, or laissez-faire. The concept of efficiency may be operationalized as the construct of intelligence and measured through IQ. Constructs are putting concepts into measurable research terms. Constructs are also known as *variables* in the research tradition, especially when the construct is put in a context that makes it describable or measurable.

These terms—concepts, constructs, variables, and theories—are the foundation of the literature review. The researcher must conduct an exhaustive review of the literature that deals with the concept she or he is planning to study, capture the pertinent features of that literature, arrange that selected literature into a coherent order to make the case for the research that will follow, and describe the theory upon which the research will be based.

The literature selected should come from a variety of sources, should include whatever differing opinions of the theory that may exist, and should make the case for the research that is planned. It does not need to be a complete and extensive historical review of the topic. Each piece of published research should have a bibliography. By referring to that bibliography and selecting pertinent references to search out in the original, the author can add immeasurably to the literature review.

The writer should recognize that the future readers of the report have expertise in the area of study, so only those reference works that are pertinent to the specific issue or topic need to be included. Logical reference links need to be made from the past work to any recent additions to the theory, and, finally, to the proposed research.

Another part of the literature that needs treatment in the introduction to a research report is the literature on research method. While the method of the study will be treated in detail in another section of the report, the writer should put in place a confidence that the method to be used has its foundation in the literature as well. The literature in the field of study should provide the cornerstone for the research, and the methodological literature should provide the blueprint of the structure to be anchored by this cornerstone.

The best advice for authors of research reports is to begin with an outline. List the authors who will be referenced or quoted, and use advanced organizers to assure that the citations selected are on target. Outlining or diagramming the literature review prior to writing it will help to organize the references around the research construct and will assist the reader in making connections between the previous work and the proposed study.

Consumers and producers of research reports must follow a similar thought process as they digest previous research and prepare new projects. It is incumbent on both the consumer and the producer to read the background literature—the previous research—as a foundation for reading or designing new and future research. The first basic step is to read and understand what has happened in the field prior to the attempt to advance that field. That is, the first step, in short, is to *read*. Special attention should be given to the selection and evaluation of the literature selected. Keyword searches that use the basic accepted words or terms in the theoretical area being considered, that describe the variables or tools being sought or studied, and that define the phenomena under scrutiny form the beginning of materials to read.

Resources

Consumers of research in education have many tools at their disposal for finding the resources that lead to literature in research. The two most widely used search engines for all areas of study are Google (http://www.google.com/) and Yahoo (http://www.yahoo.com/). Two additional sites that may be added to the previous two for overall Web searches are Lycos (http://www.lycos.com/) and MSN.com (http://www.live.com/). A fifth Internet site that provides a researcher information both about topics and tools of discovery is an online encyclopedia called Wikipedia (http://en.wikipedia.org/wiki/Main_Page).

One traditional resource for research in education is an online database provided by the U.S. Department of Education through the Education Resources Information Center (ERIC). The Institute of Education Sciences (IES) of the U.S. Department of Education sponsors ERIC, and it is considered the world's premier database of journal and nonjournal education literature. The ERIC online system provides the public with a centralized ERIC Web site (http://www.eric.ed.gov/) for searching the ERIC bibliographic database of more than 1.1 million citations since 1966. More than 107,000 full-text, nonjournal documents previously available through fee-based services only are now available at no charge. ERIC is moving forward with its modernization program and has begun adding additional materials and sources to the database.

An example of the use of the ERIC system would be to enter the Web site uniform resource locator (URL) into an Internet browser and type in the search box something like "research literature." The result of this search (at this writing) provides references to 35,613 separate citations. Once a searcher is in this main section of more than 35,000 entries, the system allows her or him to narrow the field by adding additional descriptors or by limiting the sources to journals or other types of publications. The main page has an option to "search within results." In this example, the search was limited to "qualitative research." This narrowing produced 791 citations; one of the first was a reference to the book *Practitioner Research and Professional Development in Education* (Campbell, McNamara, & Gilroy, 2004). A link to the book's publisher is provided on the screen. Other citations resulting from this search are full-text manuscripts that can be accessed directly on the screen.

As mentioned in Chapter 2, however, nothing beats a trip to the library to begin a search for literature on a subject of interest. Bibliographic citations in items selected may lead to additional literature for the reader to consume. When looking for research literature, the search should have a narrowing rather than an expanding goal so that the help desired is realized.

In the earlier example, the search for qualitative research literature from the ERIC database resulted in both topical and methodological citations. Suppose the visitor is interested in qualitative research in the area of reading instruction. Entering "reading instruction" as a phrase in the keyword field to narrow the search results in 63 citations that deal with this topic. So the search was narrowed from more than 35,000 entries in the broad area of research literature to nearly 800 citations in the more narrow area of "qualitative research," and finally, to the specific inquiry for reading-instruction articles, which yielded 63 entries.

A typical entry from the ERIC resource provides the title of the publication, the author's name, the date of publication, the journal or other collection where the article was published, whether or not it was peer reviewed, and whether or not it is available in full text on the ERIC system. Most valuable are the abstract for each entry that is provided in the synopsis and the keywords that describe the work. The keywords may be used in further searches to locate additional citations that may not be in the original group.

Each of the rules of research may be summarized and referenced with one word. This first rule can be thought of as the need to *read* before starting any other part of a research project.

Rule 1:

READ

Exercise for Chapter 3

1. Think of a research topic and outline concepts and constructs that could be used for a literature review.

2. List some Internet sources that might be used to begin a search for research information.

3. Name some sources of literature that publish research reports. How would you access these sources?

4. Think of a source of information that you know to be false (such as negative campaign tactics in elections). Why was it published (i.e., what research standards were ignored)?

5. Sometimes, conflicting literature on a topic exists. Why is it important to report all sides of an issue?

6. Select a topic and compare the results of a Google search with those of an ERIC search on the topic.

REFERENCES FOR CHAPTER 3

American Psychological Association (2001). *Publication manual of the American Psychological Association* (5th ed.). Washington, DC: American Psychological Association.

Ary, D., Jacobs, L. C., & Razavich, A. (1985). *Introduction to educational research* (3rd ed.). New York: Holt, Rinehart & Winston.

Badke, W. B. (2004). *Research strategies: Finding your way through the information fog* (2nd ed.). New York: iUniverse, Inc.

Beasley, D. (2000). *Beasley's guide to library research.* Toronto: University of Toronto Press.

Bryant, M. T. (2004). *The portable dissertation advisor.* Thousand Oaks, CA: Corwin Press.

Campbell, A., McNamara, O., & Gilroy, P. (2004). *Practitioner research and professional development in education.* London: Paul Chapman Publishing.

Council of Biology Editors EPC (1990). *Ethics and policy in scientific publication.* Bethesda, MD: The Council.

Galvan, J. L. (2006). *Writing literature reviews: A guide for students of the social and behavioral sciences* (3rd ed.). Glendale, CA: Pyrczak Publishing.

Gebhard, P. (1997). *The reference realist in library academia.* Jefferson, NC: McFarland & Company, Inc.

Mauch, J. E., & Birch, J. W. (1998). *Guide to the successful thesis and dissertation* (4th ed.). New York: Marcel Dekker, Inc.

Pyrczak, F. (2008). *Evaluating research in academic journals: A practical guide to realistic evaluation* (4th ed.). Glendale, CA: Pyrczak Publishing.

Vierra, A., Pollock, J., & Golez, F. (1998). *Reading educational research* (3rd ed.). Upper Saddle River, NJ: Merrill.

Chapter 4

The Purpose of the Study

Rule 2: Specify the Research Topic

One of the most difficult challenges in the research process is selecting and narrowing or focusing on an appropriate research topic. It is true that the general topical area must be selected in order for the literature review to take shape, but it is after consuming that literature that the specific focus of the project is generated. It is crucial that the researcher have a very specific topic about which meaningful questions may be asked and answered. Too often, the theory behind a research project is broad and overarching, not nearly focused enough for delineating tangible research efforts. The prospective researcher may have some vague notions about what to study, and these general notions must be sifted and winnowed until there are specific ideas for the research. The topic needs to be well defined and narrow so that the data collected can be linked directly to the questions and answers can be posed.

When defining a research topic, *change* is the operative term. To conduct research is to observe and measure change that occurs for reasons that may be described. Once the researcher has a solid handle on the theory and the literature surrounding the issue area, a reasonable description of what the research is all about needs to be composed. It starts with a problem area that may surface either in the literature or in the real-life situation of the researcher. One reason to read the research literature is to get to the bottom of this problem, which may have been solved by other researchers. If it has not been solved sufficiently for the researcher, then a structure to solve that problem needs to be organized. The first step in this problem solving is to conceptualize the topic.

There must be unanswered questions about the problem. For the researcher, there must be a basic question to be answered at the core of any research project—not just any question, but a question that flows from the literature, that is grounded in the theoretical constructs discussed in the literature, and to which an answer can be found through observation, interaction, or experimentation. The research topic must be analyzed according to its constituent parts, and a clear and concise question must be posed regarding these theoretical constructs. The researcher needs to arrive at a generalization that results from a perception of things read or experienced, and that generalization is the researcher's conceptualization of the problem.

Often, the theory that forms the basis of the research has well-identified and acceptable theoretical constructs that may be used in identifying the research topic and its components. Sometimes, it is up to the researcher to create these constructs from other existing concepts within the theoretical area. Whatever method is used, the researcher must make it very clear what she or he plans to do with the constructs in the research project. It is very important to note that the research constructs—the variables—need definition. This is the beginning of the transition from concept to operation. By defining the variables that are to be part of the study, the researcher has made a start in the operational aspects of the project.

Well-defined variables are also an essential component of stating the research topic in hypothesis form. The hypothesis is a more sophisticated version of the planned research than the basic question. Most often, the hypothesis is a statement of expected outcomes between one independent variable and one dependent variable, and it serves to identify a question to be answered in the research. Most good hypotheses and basic research questions can be alternate forms of one another. They both flow from a problem or issue that the researcher needs to know more about, and they both define exactly what will be done to quantify this knowledge. Because change is the operative concept in research, the questions or hypotheses must be measurable in order for the research to be made operational.

The hypothesis lays out the expected relationship between or among the variables that are based on the theory or the previous research. Hypotheses, like the basic questions, are formulated in order to guide and direct the development of a research design. One typical form for writing hypotheses is to use an "If...then..." syllogism. For instance, a research hypothesis may be, "If students are provided more direct instruction in mathematics, then their math scores will improve." The variables here are time in direct instruction and math test scores. The relationship is one of looking for a positive correlation. That is, as instructional time increases, math test scores will increase.

Another form of hypothesis writing is to use a null and alternate form. First, a null hypothesis is written. The null hypothesis is considered to be true, but subject to testing. In the scientific approach, the null hypothesis states that there is no difference between the control and experimental groups; then statistical tests are conducted to refute that assertion. The null hypothesis is set up to be refuted, or nullified, by the results of the research in order to accept or support an alternative hypothesis. For instance, a null hypothesis might state: "There will be no change in reading scores if class size is reduced." Then the *contrapositive* of the null hypothesis is stated as an alternative hypothesis: "Reducing class size will improve reading scores." Once again, there are two variables, reading test scores and class size, and the relationship to be studied is correlational as well.

Whether with the use of basic questions, problem statements, or hypotheses, the design for the research—or the research paradigm—is the model or pattern to be followed when carrying out the research project. In selecting and defining an area to be researched, the investigator should:

- be knowledgeable of the *theory* that defines the area of study
- review the relevant *literature* in the area of study
- visualize a *problem* or *issue* that is connected to the theory
- identify the *concepts* to be studied
- create or define research *constructs* (or *variables*) from the selected concepts
- *define* the constructs (variables) in operational (measurable) terms
- ask a *basic question* or state a research *hypothesis* to be tested
- project how information can be collected to answer the question or test the hypothesis (the research *paradigm*).

Linkage

Just as the research behavior behind the first rule was to *read*, the inquiry behavior behind this second rule, easily enough, is to *think*. Actually, it is not a separate behavior, but one inextricably bound with the first (to *read*), and one that should result in some note taking to capture the thought process for future review and use. All of the time spent reading should be "think time" as well. Whether the reader is looking to answer a question, solve a problem, or design a research project, the time spent reading the literature is the time to start posing the question that the literature may help to answer, which may lead to a potential research design. Once the researcher or reader has consumed what is possible or available from previous research, cognitive processes must take over to identify connections, to question spurious conclusions, or to design a model for future work. This thought process must make direct and logical linkage to the literature, or between research studies, and must provide the next level of growth for the profession or for the workplace.

Using the example begun in Chapter 3, the reader may see in the ERIC search a reference to a study of reading instruction in the first grade. One such entry was, "A Comparison of First Graders' Reading with Little Books or Literature-based Basal Anthologies," written by S. Menon and E. H. Hiebert in 2005. The ERIC citation identifies the source of the article as a journal called *Reading Research Quarterly*. The abstract provided says:

This study examined the effectiveness of a little book curriculum in facilitating the independent word-solving skills of first-grade readers. The curriculum was based on a theoretical model that identified two critical dimensions of text-based support for beginning readers: linguistic content and cognitive load.

This entire document is available online through the Web site of the journal, which is provided by ERIC. In this way, the reader may review the complete manuscript in two clicks of the mouse, focus on one or more areas of direct interest, refer to the bibliography provided in this document, perhaps follow up on one or more of the references, and draw a logical conclusion about the next step in the process.

To help the reader's or researcher's thought process within this topic, the additional citations in the first text may be sought out in the original, or the references and summaries provided in the text may move the thought process forward to a logical conclusion. Attention should be paid not only to the definitions of the issues being studied, but also to the way in which the study is conducted. This provides a roadmap for new research. Additionally, the references within the citations may provide a deeper understanding of the issue and, therefore, help the thinking component of the research-design process. The reader of the literature cited above may wonder, "How would the linguistic-content technique work in my classroom?" This question would lead to a design for a research project.

The first two rules of research, linked together, tell a researcher to first *read* about the subject, especially the existing research already completed, and then to *think* about what she or he wants to do in a research project. These two activities, taken together, form a solid foundation for the individual embarking on a research project.

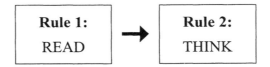

Exercise for Chapter 4

1. Using the concepts and constructs you outlined in the exercise for Chapter 3, identify specific variables and state a relationship between or among the variables.

2. Using "time on task" and "reading comprehension" as variables, state a research hypothesis in an "If...then..." syllogism. How could this be stated as a research question?

3. Write null and alternate hypotheses for the relationship between the variables "teacher salary" and "job satisfaction."

4. Why are operational definitions important for research?

5. Using teachers and administrators as research groups, state a relationship that represents a difference between the groups. State a relationship that represents a similarity.

6. Put the relationships from Question 5 into a research question.

REFERENCES FOR CHAPTER 4

Best, J. W., & Kahn, J. V. (2006). *Research in education* (10th ed.). Boston: Pearson Education, Inc.

Bryman, A. (1992). *Quantity and quality in social research*. London–New York: Routledge.

Creswell, J. W. (2002). *Research design: Qualitative, quantitative, and mixed methods approaches* (2nd ed.). Thousand Oaks, CA: Sage Publications.

Eden, C., & Spender, J. C. (Eds.). (1998). *Managerial and organizational cognition: Theory, methods, and research*. London: Sage Publications.

Eichler, M. (1991). *Nonsexist research methods: A practical guide*. New York: Routledge.

Fawcett, J., & Downs, F. S. (1999). *The relationship of theory and research* (3rd ed.). Philadelphia: F. A. Davis.

Gomm, R., Hammersley, M., & Foster, P. (Eds.). (2000). *Case study method: Key issues, key texts*. Thousand Oaks, CA: Sage Publications.

Menon, S., & Hiebert, E. H. (2005). A comparison of first graders' reading with little books or literature-based basal anthologies. *Reading Research Quarterly, 40*(1), 12–38.

Stringer, E. (2007). *Action research* (3rd ed.). Thousand Oaks, CA: Sage Publications.

Notes

Chapter 5

The Design of the Study

Rule 3: Select a Research Methodology

The basic types of research were a topic of discussion in Chapter 1. Quantitative research was differentiated from qualitative research by distinguishing the types of data used. Quantitative research needs numerical data; and qualitative research most often, and sometimes exclusively, relies on text—or words—for data. Each of these basic types has specific submethods that are selected for use based upon the different types of information collected and on the sources from which they are gathered. The type of data that will be collected determines the way the researcher designs the study. The design, or research paradigm, is the structure or framework for carrying out the work. It is the pattern the researcher uses to complete the project.

The scientific research method relies on the experimental approach to design. It is a quantitative methodology that analyzes numerical data. Theories, or new propositions regarding the theory, are built and then tested under controlled conditions. The research design is established to plan the strategy of investigation that will either answer the research questions or be used to test the research hypotheses. Control of the variables, classically referred to as control of the variance, is the cornerstone of the scientific/experimental approach.

As mentioned earlier, treatments may be applied to one or more of the groups in the research or certain conditions may be manipulated while others are held constant. Then the influence of the manipulation that results in changed conditions is measured and evaluated. So if a researcher knows that she or he is planning to change or manipulate a condition in the research project, and feels confident that other (extraneous) variables can be held constant, then the design of the project should follow the experimental or scientific approach.

If the researcher does not change or attempt to change conditions, or influence the variables in any way, the research design may be nonexperimental. As mentioned in Chapter 1, the research that is in between these two types—quasi-experimental research—is the manipulation of conditions when there is no potential for control of outside influences. So in designing the research, the researcher must:

- know the type of data that will be collected
- determine whether or not change will be introduced into the system
- recognize whether or not outside influences can be controlled.

If the data are numerical, and if there is change introduced with the guarantee that external influence can be controlled, then the research method is an experimental design and can also be considered scientific research. If change is introduced and the data are quantitative, but no control is possible for outside variables, then the quasi-experimental method is the design of choice.

If the data are not numerical, or if the researcher introduces no change, then the research design clearly falls under the nonexperimental methodology. It is important to remember, however, that numerical data, as well as textual data, are very much a part of non-experimental research. Good qualitative research is most often the product of mixed methods, in which some quantitative analyses are embedded into a textual review of the issue or basic question.

Several research designs or paradigms that are in common usage in research today are outlined below. The reader is encouraged to refer to the references listed at the end of this chapter to expand on the introduction provided here.

One-Group Designs

Symbolically, experiments often use an "E" to signify *experimental* group, a "C" to represent the *control* group, an "O" to signify an *observation* or measurement of variables under study, and an "X" to represent a *treatment* applied or the introduction of a stimulus for change. The treatment (X) is often referred to as an *independent variable*, which is an antecedent to change or a presumed cause of the expected change in the dependent variable. In the examples that follow, the subscripts represent the successive iterations of observations or treatments. Thus, O_2 is a second observation on the same phenomenon, and X_2 is a second, or different, treatment.

Research designs that use only one group for analysis do not incorporate a control and experimental group used in comparison. One-group designs for research include the following:

Pretest-posttest design. O_1 X O_2

An observation is made at the beginning of the research, a treatment or intervention is introduced, and a second observation or measurement is noted. Conclusions are drawn based on the differences in the two observations. Usually, some measure of central tendency or a comparison of dispersion is used to test the strength of the relationship. For instance, a teacher may be interested in how much students learn following an instructional unit. The teacher may give a pretest that includes the information to be taught (O_1), then teach the lesson (X), then give a posttest on the material (O_2). Comparing the results would allow conclusions to be drawn regarding the instruction.

Correlational designs. $O_1 O_2$

Two observations or more are taken on the same phenomena, and those observations are compared for similarities or differences either between groups or within the same group. The correlational design is nonexperimental because no manipulation or treatment takes place with the subject group.

Interrupted time series. $O_1 O_2 X O_3 O_4$ or $O_1 O_2 O_3 X O_4 O_5$, and so on.

Observations are made to determine trends over time before any manipulation or treatment is introduced. Then a series of observations is completed following the treatment to determine change over time. Log-linear models (outlined by Knoke and Burke [1980] for ordinal data using the logarithm of the odds for each cell) or regression analysis may be used to test the strength of the relationships.

Longitudinal designs. $O_1 O_2 O_3$, and so on.

Extending the correlational design over several observations allows for a longitudinal look at the circumstance. Sequential comparisons may be made at each stage or the sum total of the measurements may be used for the final analysis.

Multiple-Group Designs

Multiple-group designs are used when there is both a control group (C) and an experimental group (E) being observed. When the researcher wants to compare the results of an intervention or treatment to a group that has not had such change introduced, the multiple-group design is used. The different design paradigms using multiple groups include:

Experimental/control. $E X O_1$ and $C \quad O_1$

The subjects of the research must be part of the same research population. Subjects are assigned randomly to the two groups. One group is given the treatment, and the other is not. Both are subject to the same measurement following the treatment of the experimental group, and the results of those observations are compared so that a judgment can be made about the value or strength of the treatment. When each member of the control group is matched with a member of the experimental group to provide a one-to-one correspondence, the research method is referred to as a *matched subjects* design.

Pre-postexperimental/control. $E O_1 X O_2$ and $C O_1 \quad O_2$

Two observations of both the experimental and the control groups are taken, one before the treatment to the experimental group, and one following the intervention. Comparisons of the first observation are made to assure that the groups are roughly similar in the trait being studied, then the second observations are compared to determine the difference introduced by the treatment. Because this is a very common design, an example might help. A research hypothesis might be that exposure to violent video games does not increase the aggression level of high school students (null hypothesis). The alternate hypothesis would be that exposure to violent video games increases the aggression level. The experiment (research) would be to separate a group of high school students into control and experimental groups and conduct a pretest on aggression (O_1). Then the experimental group would play violent video games (X), and the aggression level of both groups would be measured again (O_2). This research design, in diagram form, is provided in Figure 5.1.

Figure 5.1. A pre-postexperimental/control research design.

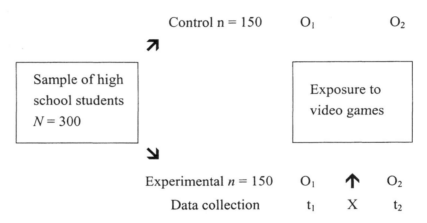

Three-group pre-post. E O_1 X O_2, C_1 O_1 O_2, and C_2 O_2

Sometimes in the preobservation of a control group, there may be the introduction of change not attributed to the experimental condition. To help measure whether or not this is occurring, a second control group is established, which is not subjected to the first observation.

Solomon four-group. E O_1 X O_2, C_1 O_1 O_2, C_2 X O_2, and C_3 O_2

One classic control/experimental design for research is referred to as the Solomon four-group design. Four samples are taken from the research population, or one sample is randomly assigned to four groups. The experimental group is measured, given the treatment, and measured again. The three control groups are set up to once again assure that the differences found following the treatment are not due to spurious events. One control group is subjected to both observations, a second control group is given the treatment but subjected only to the second measurement, and a third control group is only subjected to the second observation.

Ex post facto. $X_1 O_1$ and $X_2 O_1$

An observation or measurement is noted only after two separate treatments with differing effects are applied. *Ex post facto* research is sometimes put in the same category as quasi-experimental research because direct control is not possible, there is no manipulation by the researcher, and random assignment of research subjects is not feasible. The thinking behind random assignment is that by randomizing treatment assignment, the researcher ensures that the group attributes for the different treatments will then be roughly equivalent. Therefore, any effect observed between treatment groups can be linked to the treatment effect and is not a characteristic of the individuals in the group. Because this approach is usually applied to an intact group, the researcher does not have control of the preconditions of the sample, but she or he is able to define the manipulation and measure the consequences.

Factorial designs. $E_1 X_1 O_1$ and $E_2 X_2 O_1$

Factorial designs, which use cross-breaks of the sample, are structured when separate categories within a group are to be compared along with the overall effect of the manipulation applied. Factorial designs allow the researcher to judge the *main* effect of the treatment, while also assessing the *interactive* effect of the defined subgroups. The most used of the factorial designs is the *Latin square* research design, which is a two-by-two cross-break of the research sample. Figure 5.2 provides an example of the Latin-square approach with the sample divided by gender.

Figure 5.2. A Latin square research design.

Treatment	Female	Male
X_1	E_1	E_1
X_2	E_2	E_2

Other Nonexperimental Designs

Chapter 1 contains much information about qualitative research and the types of research designs used in this methodology. Most qualitative research is nonexperimental, and the data collected are textual rather than numerical. That does not mean, however, that a solid research design is not possible. Field studies include research that focuses on the relationships among values, attitudes, perceptions, or behaviors of individuals or groups. Field studies are an appropriate method to research complex situations, and they may result in a stronger variable effect because they are conducted in a realistic setting (the *variable* is a measurable factor, characteristic, or attribute of an individual or a system, and the *effect* is the result of a treatment or observation of that individual or system). They are often the structure used to test different methods of doing things or to determine solutions to practical problems.

Field studies have specific requirements for structuring a research project, too. Research designs that do not include experimentation as part of the structure include:

Historical. Historical or archival research is concerned with determining, selecting, analyzing, appraising, and understanding events of the past for the purpose of understanding current events or predicting events in the future. Historical research answers the question, "What was…?"

Descriptive. Descriptive research, most often conducted in a case study approach, is used to determine the nature and degree of existing conditions and to explain those circumstances from a data-driven viewpoint. Descriptive research answers the question, "What is…?"

Correlational. Correlational research takes the descriptive one step further and attempts to uncover the degree of the relationship between two or more phenomena in the research project. It looks at the basic similarities or differences of groups or structures and is often conducted to formulate predictions about the relationship. It is an attempt to answer the question, "How are they alike (or different)?"

Causal-comparative. One step beyond the correlational, the causal-comparative design is an attempt to describe cause-and-effect relationships between or among observed phenomena. The question asked is, "Why is…?"

Action Research

As in Chapter 1, a note needs to be added regarding the concept of action research. Action research is not, in and of itself, a separate research methodology. It is a combination of several accepted techniques, or the field-based implementation of one or more of the techniques described above. Professions are informed by a knowledge base, and practitioners are expected not only to make use of that knowledge, but also to contribute to the development of their knowledge base. Action research is a structure of disciplined inquiry that helps working professionals to use and create work-based knowledge for the purpose of problem solving or process improvement.

Action research has three interrelated stages of implementation:

- initiating action (an intervention)

- monitoring and adjusting action
- evaluating action.

Action research is usually described as a five-step process:

- problem formulation
- data collection
- data analysis
- reporting of results
- action planning.

Action research uses several techniques to provide data for reflection and action:

- diaries, logs, journals
- checklists
- surveys
- interview schedules
- tests
- disaggregation by subpopulations.

Most action research falls into the qualitative category of research, but may include field experiments as a technique. Most data are textual, but there may be numerical data, such as test scores or survey results, that can be quantified. To say that one is doing action research is to say that one or more of the several research methods is/are being employed to solve a work-site problem.

Considerations

The thought process regarding a research project should result in the researcher fine-tuning the concepts, topics, variables, or phenomena that are to be the research subject. This thought process leads to the third step in the process, the *design* phase. Obviously, if the reader is not interested in designing a research project, but only in finding data-based substantiation for program development or change, then the design stage is not essential.

Part of the attention paid to reading other research should be on the use of design. In the examples in the earlier chapters, there was an emphasis on methods for the research on teaching reading. The example selected from the literature was a study that compared two different techniques in the teaching of reading, one using basal readers for two first-grade classrooms, the other using little books leveled according to features of linguistic content and cognitive load for two other classrooms. This design is a typical Solomon four-group design, with two different treatments being compared between two sets of data. If put in a null-alternate hypothesis structure, the null hypothesis would be, "There is no difference between types of reading instruction," and the alternate would be, "Using little books as an instructional method in reading will produce better comprehension on the part of the students."

When considering how to design a research project, the reader should ask herself or himself the following:

- What hypotheses can be tested?
- What basic questions need to be answered?
- How can the tests be carried out?
- How can information be gathered to answer the questions?
- What research design works best?
- What has been used in the past?
- What will work in the future?

The researcher who reads the research citations used in the example above, and who has asked herself or himself a question about the success of one type of reading instruction as compared to another, now needs to design the research project. References have been read about methods of research, and results of studies in other fields of work have been consumed, so these background manuscripts may be used to design a research project to study this issue. Concepts from the earlier work could be translated to the current situation. In this example, the researcher may take the two techniques and create a survey for teacher colleagues with a numerical agree-disagree continuum of response. Then the researcher may decide to send a survey to a select sample of teachers in the field to determine whether or not an opinion exists that supports one technique over the other. The design then becomes one of survey research.

Another design technique might be the interview. The questions asked may be put in the form of interview questions for teachers, such as, "Have you used the little-books approach to teaching reading? If so, did you use it according to features of linguistic content? Did you consider cognitive load? How would you compare the little-books approach to the basal reader technique?" Then the researcher would make individual appointments with the research participants to collect the data, and the results could be captured on audiotape.

Beyond this example, the researcher has an abundance of potential research designs to use, some of which are outlined in this text. Others are available in the references provided in the annotated bibliography. *Replication* is a customary and very well-accepted approach to designing a research project. Perhaps the teacher interested in the two approaches to reading has a colleague who is teaching at the same level and would be willing to participate in a research project. The two approaches could be used in the two classrooms, modeled after the work published in the research journal. Then the teachers could compare their own results to those in the literature and make a decision about the techniques in their own environment.

Three steps or basic rules of doing the research, or of understanding what has been read, have been covered. The person conducting the inquiry must read the literature, think about what was consumed, and create a plan of action to move forward to the next step in knowing.

Therefore, the third step in the process is to *design* the project.

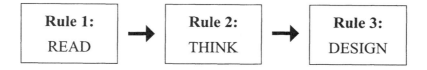

Exercise for Chapter 5

1. Construct a one-group research design using students as a data source on the topic of behavior.

2. Construct a two-group research design using teachers and students as a data source on the topic of students' behavior.

3. State a cause-and-effect relationship (causal-comparative) using teachers and students as participants, and learning and behavior as variables.

4. How would a researcher structure a case study on the services available to students in a high school?

5. How would you structure a historical study regarding special education policies?

6. What research design would allow you to make confident statements about the difference in performance in math and science between English-speaking students and English-language learners?

REFERENCES FOR CHAPTER 5

Ader, H., & Mellenbergh, G. (Eds.). (1999). *Research methodology in the social, behavioural, and life sciences.* London: Sage Publications.

Berg, B. L. (2000). *Qualitative research methods for the social sciences* (4th ed.). Boston: Allyn & Bacon.

Black, T. R. (1999). *Doing quantitative research in the social sciences: An integrated approach to research design, measurement, and statistics.* Thousand Oaks, CA: Sage Publications.

Bogdan, R. C., & Biklen, S. K. (2003). *Qualitative research in education: An introduction to theory and methods* (4th ed.). Boston: Allyn & Bacon.

Borg, W. R., Gall, J. P., & Gall, M. D. (1993). *Applying educational research: A practical guide* (3rd ed.). New York: Longman.

Campbell, D. T., & Stanley, J. C. (1963). *Experimental and quasi-experimental designs for research.* Boston: Houghton Mifflin Company.

Creswell, J. (1998). *Qualitative inquiry and research design: Choosing among five traditions.* Thousand Oaks, CA: Sage Publications.

Gall, M. D., Borg, W. R., & Gall, J. P. (2003). *Educational research: An introduction* (7th ed.). Boston: Allyn & Bacon.

Glesne, C. (2006). *Becoming qualitative researchers: An introduction* (3rd ed.). New York: Allyn & Bacon.

Isaac, S., & Michael, W. B. (1995). *Handbook in research and evaluation* (3rd ed.). San Diego: EdITS Publishers.

Keane, D. & Burke, P. J. (1980). *Log-linear models.* Beverly Hills, CA: Sage Publications.

Kerlinger, F. N. (1992). *Foundations of behavioral research* (4th ed.). New York: Holt, Rinehart, and Winston.

Lattal, K., & Perone, M. (Eds.). (1998). *Handbook of research methods in human operant behavior.* New York: Plenum Press.

Lee, T. W. (1999). *Using qualitative methods in organizational research.* Thousand Oaks, CA: Sage Publications.

Leedy, P. D., & Ormrod, J. E. (2005). *Practical research: Planning and design* (8th ed.). Upper Saddle River, NJ: Pearson-Prentice Hall.

Merriam, S. B. (2002). *Qualitative research in practice: Examples for discussion and analysis.* San Francisco: Jossey-Bass.

Patten, M. (2005). *Understanding research methods: An overview of the essentials* (5th ed.). Glendale, CA: Pyrczak Publishing.

Sagor, R. (2000). *Guiding school improvement with action research.* Alexandria, VA: Association for Supervision and Curriculum Development.

Schwab, D. (1999). *Research methods for organizational behavior.* Mahwah, NJ: Lawrence Erlbaum Associates.

Stake, R. E. (1995). *The art of case study research: Perspectives on practice.* Thousand Oaks, CA: Sage Publications

Yin, R. K. (2003). *Case study research design and methods* (3rd ed.). Thousand Oaks, CA: Sage Publications.

Chapter 6

Know the Evidence

Rule 4: Identify the Data Source

Two frequently used terms that represent research concepts common to most, if not all, research are *population* and *sample*. The information, documentation, or evidence of a research project must be generated from some source. Once the theory that is grounding the research has been established and the topic and methodology have been selected, then the researcher needs to identify the source of the information that will be used to determine the results of the research. The research method selected will be directive in the source of data to be used. Historical research relies on archival textual data or a survey population with historical knowledge. Experimental research relies on subjects from whom measurements may be drawn and compared. Every method will project a population for the study.

The research population is the universe of all subjects or objects that could be included in the study. The research sample is a portion of the population selected by the researcher for scrutiny in the research project. Also called a probability sample in experimental research, the sample is usually selected without replacement. That is, once a subject or object is drawn from the population, it is in the sample and is not returned to the universe for selection.

The theory that forms the foundation of the research study should define the population. Sometimes, the population defined for a study is quite large (all individuals over the age of 18, for instance), or it can be quite small (all individuals who have won a Nobel prize and who live in Rhode Island). When it is small, the researcher is often able to work with the entire population and sampling is not an issue. Results from using an entire population for the research do not need to be inferred because the results represent the population parameters. One example of drawing information from an entire population is a census. All members of the population are counted and specific parameters are measured. When a population is large, and drawing a sample is necessary, there are different kinds of samples defined for researchers.

Sampling

It is important that samples represent the basic characteristics of the research population. Samples must be typical in makeup to the population if the researcher wants to make generalizations about that population. If parametric statistics are to be used, it is important that the sample be a *random* sample (also known as a probability sample), where participants are randomly assigned to the different research groups. Remember that a parameter is a common characteristic or value of the entire population—like average age or average height—that can be calculated or estimated by the sample. Simply put, a random sample is one in which all elements of the population have an equal chance of being selected for the sample. Sometimes, the sample involved in an experimental research project is selected according to one of the nonprobability, nonrandom techniques described below. Then the researcher needs to recognize the difficulty of making generalizations to a larger population and to assure that random assignment of subjects be done in experimental research to avoid bias and to ensure internal consistency or validity.

Statistical formulae used to answer questions or test hypotheses in a quantitative study require that a representative sample be randomly selected, most often from what is considered a *normal* population. For a population to be considered normal, the distribution of the elements or members of the populations must be grouped according to the normal probability curve, or bell-shaped curve (see the appendix at the end of this book).

Once again, the research method will have a lot to do with predicting what kind of sample is selected. Some typical types of samples include:

Stratified sample. The researcher creates different categories or partitions of the population—different strata—and randomly selects subjects from each stratum in either a proportionate or a disproportionate way. Gender, age, height, race, or income levels are examples of strata often used to separate a research population.

Cluster sample. The researcher randomly selects predetermined groups from the population as clusters. Students in a classroom, teachers in a school, and administrators in a state all serve as clusters for sampling purposes.

Purposive sample. One of the nonprobability samples, the sample is selected with a purpose in mind, and the researcher makes a deliberate attempt to include specific subjects to provide guaranteed representatives from identified groups in the sample. One or more predetermined groups may become the subject of the research.

Accidental sample. Also known as haphazard or convenience sampling, the sample is limited to subjects at hand and available for the researcher; it is also a nonprobability sample. Much of what is termed action research uses accidental samples because the subjects are limited to the workplace where the action is taking place.

Quota sample. The researcher selects a specified number of subjects that is a quota from defined groups or strata in the population. Quota sampling is most often a nonrandom method of sampling that is widely used in opinion polling and market research. Interviewers may be given a quota of subjects in specified categories to attempt to recruit—for example, an interviewer might be directed to select 10 adult men and 10 adult women for interviews.

Interval sample. This is also known as systematic sampling; the researcher randomly chooses a starting point and uses a rotating method to select the sample—taking every other subject, or every tenth subject, for instance. Systematic sampling is to be applied only if the given population is logically homogeneous, because systematic sample units are uniformly distributed over the population.

Just as the research method predicts the kind of sample to be used, the kind of sample selected directs the researcher to the actual data subjects. In scientific research, the data subjects must be selected randomly, with each data element having the same chance of being selected as any other. Additionally, the sample must be large enough to guarantee that it is representative of the population being studied. Most qualitative research does not attempt to derive representative samples, but rather seeks to include individuals or situations within a project that will prove the most pertinent information, given the nature of the research question; this is known as a purposive sample, as discussed above.

Whatever sampling method is used, it must be compatible with the research method. In the end, the researcher should feel confident that the data cells have authentic evidence that will help to unravel the research quandary. Rule 5 in Chapter 7 deals with the research subjects or objects.

Research Decisions

Unless the research is limited to the group of individuals on hand or data that exists already, the concern over sampling is ever-present. Questions are often asked about how large is too large—or how small is too small—for a legitimate sample. There is not one good answer to the sample-size question for all the different types of research, and most research in education is limited to the students or educators who are available or willing to participate in the project.

If statistical tests are to be used, and if the researcher knows the anticipated spread of the data and the precision level selected, then an estimate of the sample size needed to complete the project and more or less guarantee some sort of meaningful statistical result can be made. Statistical formulae are, after all, algebraic relationships and, as such, may be used to determine target figures such as sample size. This is done by calculating the statistical formula as an algebraic problem where the number figure (n) is the unknown. In order to use this calculation, some basic statistics are needed. The formula uses Z-scores, which are standard or normal scores provided in a normal probability curve (see the appendix at the end of this book). The Z-score indicates how many standard deviations an individual observation is found either above or below the mean. A measure of precision, also called the alpha level or level of significance, is a probability number that determines the probability that the research results are due to chance.

The basic formula that may be used to determine a sample size is:

$$N = [(Z\text{-score}) (\text{standard deviation})/\text{precision}]^2$$

An example of the use of this formula would be to know that the Z-score for precision at the 0.05 level is 1.96, then estimate the standard deviation for the sample—say, for instance, a 0.5 standard deviation of response on a seven-point Likert-type scale. Then that estimated standard deviation (0.5) is multiplied by the Z-score (1.96), and the result is 0.98. This number is then divided by the selected precision level (.05), and the quotient, 19.6, is squared, resulting in 384.16, which is the value for N. This tells the researcher that if there are approximately 385 participants in the sample, there will be a good chance of finding statistical significance at the .05 level. Using the same standard deviation estimate (0.5), and calculating for significance at the 0.01 level, where the Z-score is 2.58, the formula would be:

$$N = [(2.58) (0.5) / 0.01]^2 = [1.29 / .01]^2 = 129^2 = 16,641$$

So, in this instance, the sample size should be more than 16,000 participants to provide a good chance that there would be statistical significance at the .01 level. In essence, for most quantitative research, the larger the sample size, the more likely there will be a result of statistical significance. Therefore, these estimated figures are at the top end of a sample size, and smaller samples with less spread in the data (smaller standard deviations) may result in better confidence in the conclusions drawn based on statistical tests.

It is important to note here that statistical significance does not mean professional or educational significance. A statistically significant finding from a calculation on a set of data values may provide no insight into the actual difference of the population under scrutiny. That is, while there may be statistical significance, there may not be practical significance within or between the actual measures being compared. For example, a t-test, which is a statistical comparison of two mean values, may be calculated on the average response to a survey item between male and female respondents. One average might be 3.2 on a 5-point scale and another 3.7 each with a small standard deviation. While the test statistic may be significant, the real result is that both men and women have an average score between 3 and 4 on the scale, which may offer no real educational or practical significance. The reference listed at the end of this chapter and in the annotated bibliography by Box, Hunter, and Hunter (2005) is an excellent source for further discussion on the difference of statistical significance and data-based decision making.

In the end, there may be other practical conditions that dictate samples and sample sizes. Factors such as budget, time, cooperation, permission, and availability all may have an influence on drawing an appropriate sample for a research project. It is also important to remember that using sample size as a factor to determine significance is not proportional to the size of the population. While there is a feeling that the larger the sample, the more potential there is for a significant finding, there is a point of diminishing return. An example is that national election polls can make a rather accurate prediction of outcome based on a small sample, and increasing the sample size has little impact on increasing the confidence of the finding.

The fourth piece of the inquiry puzzle can be described, in one word, as *assess*. A researcher needs to assess the available sources of information, then choose the right one for the project. Linked together at this juncture, the pieces include:

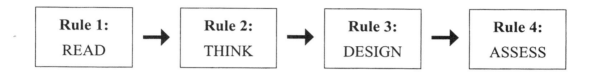

Exercise for Chapter 6

1. Define some strata for sampling school board members.

2. How would you draw a sample of students to assure that all ability levels were represented?

3. Describe how a cluster sample (choosing preexisting groups of participants) could be used in educational research.

4. What does it mean for a sample to be "random"?

5. What would be the best source of information for a research project on teacher discipline by administrators?

6. How would you categorize poll-watching at an election site as a sampling technique?

7. What can be said about results from a research project that uses an entire population as its data source?

8. What caution is necessary regarding the concept that the more data you have, the more likely you are to find statistical significance?

REFERENCES FOR CHAPTER 6

Bassey, M. (1999). *Case study research in educational settings*. Philadelphia: Open University Press.

Batavia, M. (2001). *Clinical research for health professionals: A user-friendly guide*. Boston: Butterworth-Heinemann.

Box, G. E. P., Hunter, J. S., & Hunter, W. G. (2005). *Statistics for experimenters: Design, innovation, and discovery* (2nd ed.). Hoboken, NJ: Wiley-Interscience.

Clandinin, D. J., & Connelly, F. M. (2000). *Narrative inquiry: Experience and story in qualitative research*. San Francisco: Jossey-Bass.

Greenwood, D. J., & Levin, M. (1998). *Introduction to action research: Social research for social change*. Thousand Oaks, CA: Sage Publications.

Holstein, J. A., & Gubrium, J. F. (1995). *The active interview*. Thousand Oaks, CA: Sage Publications.

Johnson, A. P. (2002). *A short guide to action research* (revised printing). Boston: Allyn & Bacon.

Maier, M. H. (1995). *The data game: Controversies in social science statistics* (2nd ed.). Armonk, NY: M. E. Sharpe.

Reason, P., & Bradbury, H. (Eds.). (2000). *Handbook of action research: Participative inquiry and practice*. Thousand Oaks, CA: Sage Publications.

Chapter 7

Know the Evidence Source

Rule 5: Identify the Data Subjects or Research Participants

Part of the research design or paradigm should be the outline of what kind of evidence will be used to satisfy the research conditions and help to make statements about the research hypotheses or answer the basic questions. Research data sources include measurements, objects, and subjects. There are both primary and secondary sources for research data. Once the researcher has determined the population and sampling technique to be used, then the actual subjects for the research need to be assessed. Potential data sources must be identified, analyzed or measured, and appraised in light of what the research plan requires.

In the controlled laboratory conditions of experimental research, the data come from observations and measurements. The data source being measured must be a random and representative sample of the research population. Then that sample must be carefully organized, meaning randomly separated into control and experimental groups. Treatments or interventions may then be implemented, and measurements can be taken. Conclusions depend on the results of the measurements as compared through classical statistical methods.

Careful identification and description of the sources of information are crucial. The population being studied should be defined in research terms and the techniques used to select from that population must be outlined. If a researcher is testing an instructional technique in secondary mathematics, for example, the data source will be high school students. The actual research data may be test scores, or responses to an attitudinal survey completed by the students, or a combination of both. In order to substantiate the effectiveness of the technique, the researcher may need to collect data from students who did not experience the new technique. The data source is the same, high school students, and the data are generated in the same way. Ancillary data may be collected from the adults directly involved (teachers) or tangentially touched (counselors, parents, or guardians) by the instruction.

Many research projects, both quantitative and qualitative, use predetermined groups within a research sample to test hypotheses or answer the basic questions. Referred to as research categories, or partitions of the data source, these categories have a specific set of rules to follow when research populations are subdivided. The rules are that categories must be:

- set up according to the research questions using one level of discourse (based on a sample drawn from a single population)

- exhaustive (all subjects or objects in the sample are used up)
- mutually exclusive (each data element is in only one category)
- independent (being in one group is not dependent on being in a second group)
- derived from one classification principle (just age, or just gender, but not both, for example).

While these categories must be independent, disjointed, exhaustive, and mutually exclusive, much research is done on the cross-partitions (cross-breaks) of two or more of the categories. The researcher must be sure that the individual categories used in the measurements meet the requirements listed above before combining categories for analysis.

In field experiments and field studies, the data come from observations and measurements in the field. Once again, a research population is identified and, in many cases, a sample is selected to represent that population. There are those occasions when the researcher may use the entire population defined for the study due to its small size, proximity, or ease of access. If the research question deals with principal effectiveness, for example, the data sources may be teachers, students, parents, or textual information in the principal's communication or budget decisions. The researcher must select the appropriate source for the data to answer the research questions posed.

A field experiment is structured much like a laboratory experiment, except that it is conducted in a more realistic setting—in the field and not in a laboratory. While extraneous influences may not be controlled in a field experiment, the results from the selected data sources may be stronger because they may rise above the outside influences. Field experiments under the banner of action research are often used to determine solutions to practical problems, and they offer an appropriate medium for studying more complex circumstances. The data sources for field experiments may be limited and may not have the characteristics of classical samples (random and representative). Many times, the sample is a volunteer group or is drawn from limited subpopulations of the entire population.

Field studies include the analysis of relationships among values, attitudes, perceptions, and behaviors of individuals and groups. They are realistic, significant, theory oriented, and heuristic. Field studies may be exploratory or hypothesis testing. Exploratory field studies are often used to probe an existing situation in the field in order to discover relationships within the population, or between population subgroups, that might generate concepts for future study. Before going into the field, the researcher needs to identify clearly the anticipated sources of information. If the question deals with an organizational structure within a school, such as the existence of a professional learning community, she or he needs to define the traits that, when observed, confirm or deny the basic question. Then the researcher must assess the potential sources of data and select the source that will provide a clear and measureable data set upon which a decision may be based or a conclusion drawn.

Hypothesis testing in field studies amounts to an in-depth analysis of the relationship between defined variables in the sample to determine how accurate conjectural statements made about the research population might be. The researcher watches the selected component of real life that is the basis of the research as it plays out in the sample selected, then either formulates new concepts regarding the population or draws conclusions regarding the interactions observed. You make an educated guess about how things fit together, or how one thing influences another, then you gather information to see if your guess is accurate.

Data sources for qualitative research come from many locations and are identified through a variety of means. A researcher needs to carefully identify the absolute best location from which to gather information (collect data), then select those sources that will provide the best documentation for the issue being studied. You can squeeze all of the turnips in the world, but you will not make orange juice from them. That is, for the results to be meaningful and helpful, the data sources must be the right ones for the research being designed.

Implications

In one of the examples discussed earlier, survey research was selected as the research tool. In this case, the researcher must then create a survey instrument to be used as a data-collection device. The items for the survey should flow from previous work in the area, or from the researcher's knowledge and experience in the area. The researcher will need to determine whether the survey is sent to the subjects or is to be used as an interview tool.

In either case, the information collected––the data gathered––must come from reliable sources and be gathered in a systematic and intelligent way. Do survey items have a numerical scale for response? Then it should be sent to the participants. Are the items open-ended responses that will need probing? Then the interview technique should be used. Form follows function when collecting data in research.

The reading example previously compared two sets of classrooms. The research participants, or subjects, in this study were first-grade students. The data collected were their scores on basic reading inventories. Word lists and graded passages from the Qualitative Reading Inventory (QRI) served as the pre- and posttest measures in this study. The researchers used chi-square analyses to show that children in the little-books group performed at significantly higher levels on the posttests than their counterparts in the basal reader group. This was a pretest-posttest design to determine, first, whether there was gain in the reading scores, and, second, whether one technique ended up with significantly better scores than the other. A pretest-posttest design like the reading example is used very often in education.

The researcher interested in designing a project based on the topic used here has several sources of information from which to choose. The original project used students as the data source. The example used teachers as a source for survey or interview data. For a project that deals with reading instruction, parents or administrators might be data sources as well.

The research design should lead directly to the type of information or data needed to move the project forward, and the next step is to go forward and gather or collect those data. Data collection takes many forms, but research rules exist for careful handling and treatment of that research information. Care is necessary in gathering what is needed and in recognizing that not all data may lead to the same end. Care is also needed in recognizing what data pieces are important to collect, and which may be left uncollected. Chapter 8 outlines several methods used to gather evidence, or collect data, in a research project.

At this point, there are five rules that one needs to consider while building an inquiry project. The new addition, in one word, is *select*. After the source of data has been carefully assessed by the researcher and the potential research participants identified, it is time to select the research sample. The first five elements in building the project at this point are:

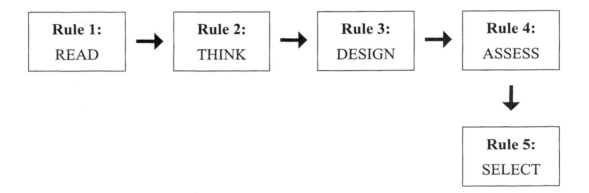

Exercise for Chapter 7

1. If you were to conduct research using all the teachers in a school, what subcategories for analysis might be created?

2. When would it be acceptable to consciously omit specific students from an action research project in a classroom?

3. If you use a control group and an experimental group in a research project, why is it important to ensure that the two groups are very similar?

4. What kinds of data may be gathered through the use of surveys?

5. How are interview data different from survey data?

6. Write five interview questions for a panel of elected officials on the topic of property taxes.

REFERENCES FOR CHAPTER 7

Babbie, E. R. (1998). *The basis of social research* (8th ed.). Belmont, CA: Wadsworth.

Gummesson, E. (2000). *Qualitative methods in management research* (2nd ed.). Thousand Oaks, CA: Sage Publications.

Marshall, C., & Rossman, G. B. (1999). *Designing qualitative research* (3rd ed.). Thousand Oaks, CA: Sage Publications.

Newman, I. (1998). *Qualitative-quantitative research methodology: Exploring the interactive continuum.* Carbondale, IL: Southern Illinois University Press.

Patton, M. Q. (2002). *Qualitative research and evaluation methods* (3rd ed.). Thousand Oaks, CA: Sage Publications.

Sales, B. (2000). *Ethics in research with human participants.* Washington, DC: American Psychological Association.

Notes

Chapter 8

Gather the Evidence

Rule 6: Collect the Data

Up to this point, the researcher has delved deeply into a theory of how structures or phenomena act, react, or interact; has read the literature regarding experimentation or other research with this theory, and has summarized the pertinent features of that literature; has structured research hypotheses, or asked basic research questions; has determined the data source (population and sample); and has identified the data subjects or objects. Now it is time to gather the evidence for the research—to collect the data that will be used in answering the basic research questions.

As evidence is gathered in experimental research, the concept of variables comes into play. A variable is a research construct that provides for a logical grouping of properties or attributes inherent in a sample or population. Anyone who has studied algebra knows that, mathematically, X is a variable, and in the end, X has a numerical value. Variables in research have the same meaning as variables in algebra. They are a research construct that can take on measured values.

Variables fall into categories of their own. There are variables that may be considered the cause of a behavior or other research result. These are referred to as the independent or antecedent variable. The independent variable can be thought of as the "if" part of a hypothetical syllogism, "If A, then B." Dependent variables are those that are the presumed effect of the independent variable action—the consequence of the research, or the "B" part of the syllogism.

Other categories of variables that form a structure for data collection include: *active* variables—those that are manipulated in the research, that is, a treatment is introduced to the variable and the effects of that treatment are studied and recorded; *attribute* variables—those that can be measured, but not manipulated (gender or age are two examples); *categorical* variables—those that define a group or subset of the sample (nominal numbers may be assigned to the categories; e.g., 1 = female and 2 = male); and *intervening* variables, also known as "latent" variables—those that are internal to the sample and, though not observed, account for resultant behavior (temper or frustration, for example).

The data collected in a research project must have meaning in order to answer the basic questions, and the variables defined for the research provide that meaning. There are a variety of techniques to collect data in research. The measurements in a laboratory are gathered with precision and accuracy through the use of tools and techniques defined for the researcher in earlier work in the field. Standards of measurement exist, and researchers are careful to use those standards so that the peer review of their work is meaningful and accurate.

Data collection in the qualitative approach takes on several forms, but each has its own framework. Variables in qualitative research include behaviors, sociological facts, opinions, and attitudes. *Behaviors* are characteristics of individuals or other research subjects that are observed or self-reported routines (e.g., reactions to stimulus). *Facts* are attributes of research subjects regarding their membership in a predetermined group (e.g., gender, race, or occupation). *Opinions* and *attitudes* are psychological variables that are often interrelated with facts to determine significant characteristics of selected groups (e.g., opinions on property tax based on occupation).

Data collection to fill in the measurements for these variables can take several forms. These include observations, interviews, questionnaires, surveys, tests, focus groups, and the use of secondary sources for data. *Observation*, simply put, is looking at what the research subjects are actually doing and recording those inspections in a uniform way. In an *interview*, the researcher actually talks to the participants to gather pertinent information regarding the research topic. *Questionnaires* are self-reported data-collection instruments used to gather and compile information in an orderly way according to the research construct. *Surveys*, which may be done person-to-person or through other means, are a form of questionnaires that may be used in a variety of circumstances. *Tests* are standardized measures of personality traits or of subjects' knowledge that have been scrutinized by the researcher for accuracy through reliability and validity checks. In all cases, the sample is a group of individuals who become the research participants and who provide data on the existence, incidence, distribution, or interrelationship of the characteristics under scrutiny.

Interviews

Interviews are a much-used data-collection method. The subjects of the interviews are those members of the research population who have the knowledge or reasoning ability to support the researcher in the quest for documentation upon which to build a case for the research findings. Personal interviews are a direct-contact method of obtaining information. A prepared interview questionnaire or schedule is used. Factual information, along with attitudes or opinions on selected topics, can be obtained. Two important components of the interview method of data collection are: First, the researcher can ascertain the underlying reasons why an individual does or believes something, and second, there is the ability to probe the interview candidate to clarify confusing or misleading responses. A third part of face-to-face interviews is that the researcher is able to read body language as responses are given. Gestures, images, impressions, or tones are all data that may represent reality as the subject sees or experiences it.

Telephone interviews, similar to personal interviews, are a good way to collect data for the research project. While the researcher is speaking person-to-person to the research subject, there is not the ability to rely on nonverbal cues or communication for help with the interpretation. The body language is missing from telephone interviews. The benefit of telephone interviews is that the researcher is able to reach research subjects who may be geographically dispersed and not easily accessible or readily available for face-to-face interaction.

Group interviews are also used in qualitative research to gather the information necessary to answer the research questions. In formal settings, such as focus-group interviews, a small group of research subjects interacts with a predetermined group moderator whose job is to keep the discussion focused on the research topic. Group members in this type of data collection are often given the opportunity to react to the collective wisdom of the group and to analyze the summary statements at the end of the process. This member-checking at the end of the interview provides the researcher with additional strength of data. Groups assembled for the purpose of data collection may be asked to respond to a paper-and-pencil survey.

Another type of group interaction that is used as a data-collection technique is the review of an issue by a carefully selected panel of experts. Called the *Delphi Technique*, this data-collection procedure was named for the Ancient Oracle of Delphi, a focal point for intellectual inquiry where scholars would congregate. In this technique, the researcher identifies and selects a sample that represents the best minds—the experts—in the field of study. The subjects are provided open-ended questions for response, and the researcher codes the responses and creates a rating scale based on the coded responses. Then, the rating scale is sent to the panel for rating and returned to the researcher. The results of this rating are shared with the panel members, and they are asked to perform a second rating based on the combined results of the earlier responses. This may be continued until consensus on the topic is reached.

Surveys

The survey technique for data collection refers to the use of questionnaires, opinionaires, or polls as instruments for gathering information for a research project. It is, except for the group enterprise mentioned above, an indirect method of collecting data; that is, the researcher is not present when the subjects for the sample read and react to the questions or situations being presented for response. These research interrogatories are sent via the mail, through automated telephone response channels, or through the Internet.

The survey technique relies on the willingness of the research-sample participants to respond to and return prepared data-collection devices. The use of Internet services has made surveying more efficient, but it relies on the sample participant being able to respond using a computer. An issue with mail surveys is ensuring that the targeted sample has received the survey, then having the confidence that the subjects will interpret the items uniformly. Another issue with survey research is generating an adequate response, or being able to make the case that the nonrespondents are not significantly different from those who do respond. Follow-up of some kind is often necessary in order to increase the response rate.

Some basic rules for the use of survey research include:

- be sure that the items flow from the research design
- use language that your subjects will understand
- keep the items short and to the point
- keep each item focused on one concept or issue
- allow subjects a chance to respond to open-ended items
- select a response scale that best fits the item
- avoid overlapping response categories
- triangulate response with multiple items for each concept
- conduct a pilot test before finalizing and sending the survey instrument
- consider offering an incentive or reward for completion of the survey, such as money.

Figure 1.1 in Chapter 1 provided some examples of survey-research response forms. Likert scales or Likert-type scales are often used as a survey response format. Participants are forced to select one of a limited number of options that may describe behaviors, facts, opinions, or attitudes. These are often the variables in survey research. Surveys are used to measure either the incidence or the distribution of participants when measured against these selected variables.

Behaviors are characteristics of individuals and how they react to, or in, specified circumstances. Dynamics like time-on-task, teaming, problem-solving techniques, or other personal or professional conduct being studied may be self-reported in surveys. *Facts* are attributes described by participants regarding their own circumstances or the situations around them—gender, income, or work environment, for example. *Opinions* and *attitudes* are psychological variables that represent participants' beliefs, which may be interrelated with facts to determine significant characteristics of selected groups of participants.

Response formats for surveys vary and are determined by the type of information sought or the variables under consideration. Some common traits measured, and a sample response format for each, include:

- *value* (or performance level): unsatisfactory—needs improvement—satisfactory
- *concern*: unimportant—important—very important
- *frequency*: never—seldom—sometimes—often—always
- *agreement*: strongly disagree—disagree—neutral—agree—strongly agree
- *role/rule*: must not—should not—may or may not—should—must
- *discrepancy evaluation*: real or actual—ideal or desired
- *influence*: highly negative—negative—neutral—positive—highly positive
- *ranking*: forced choice from high to low priority.

Often, survey respondents select one response and use it consistently throughout the survey (use only the "agree" response for all items, for instance). The use of a discrepancy evaluation or ranking scale helps to provide a better distribution of response and may guard against this type of response behavior. The discrepancy evaluation uses two scales, one for what is real or actual, and one for what is ideal or desired. The ranking scale requires participants to set a priority for the items listed so that the same response for each cannot be used.

Another often-used response scale is the semantic differential. In the semantic differential technique, paired adjective descriptors that are bipolar are put opposite one another on a seven-point response scale. This format is used with three separate types of descriptors:

- *evaluative*: good-bad/best-worst/clean-dirty
- *potency*: strong-weak/large-small/heavy-light
- *activity*: fast-slow/lethargic-sharp/calm-frantic.

Researchers should be concerned that their data are representative of the population being studied, and that the data collected do, in fact, measure the characteristics under scrutiny. That is, the collection must provide reliable and valid data. Much has been written about reliability and validity of data, and several of the source books in the annotated bibliography in Chapter 14 should be referenced for more information on these topics. Validity and reliability were discussed in Chapter 2 in their general form, but they will be expounded on here to deal with interview and survey data.

Validity

As outlined in Chapter 2, validity in measurement and data-collection means that the instrument, device, or technique used to collect evidence actually measures what it was designed to measure. The first concern with the data is a concern of interpretation. The data collected must have an internal validity that represents a confidence that the responses do, in fact, describe the phenomena being studied. Questions asked about working conditions, for example, describe actual situations in the workplace and the responses received can be interpreted to capture actual information about the workplace being studied. Internal validity provides confidence that the measurement taken is appropriate and may be used to explain the phenomena.

Validity also is concerned with the generalizability of the data. This is the external validity of the measurement. The need for a representative sample drawn randomly from the population is a basic condition for the determination of external validity. Samples drawn with a purposive or other nonrandom method often do not allow the researcher to generalize to a broader population, or even across factors within a given population. Just because the results of the research cannot be generalized beyond the research group, however, does not mean that the research is not valid. One or more of the types of validity discussed in Chapter 2 may be applied with good effect to a research sample that is not randomly drawn. In general, there are two approaches to determining the validity of a measurement device:

- *Judgmental analysis*: a logical analysis of the content of the instrument (internal validity), or a logical analysis of the conditions that make up the trait, construct, or characteristic being measured (study the nature and meaning of the variables). A jury review by individuals who are knowledgeable in the subject but not part of the research group can provide this analysis for the researcher.

- *Empirical analysis*: use of a criterion measurement that is accepted as a standard or benchmark for the trait or characteristic and determining the association or correlation of the measurement instrument with that standard (external validity). The researcher can use the literature review to determine the basic criteria and make a case for validity based on a comparison of the instrument items with the established criteria.

Reliability

Data collected in a research project must be accurate and dependable if good decisions are to be made in relation to the basic questions or research hypotheses. This is the reliability of the data. Chapter 2 provided several methods for determining the reliability in a research project. Survey research most often uses three of these basic techniques:

- *Test-retest*: A reliability sample not to be part of the research group may be selected and administered two iterations of the survey instrument. Then results of the two data collections are compared to ensure the survey provides dependable information.

- *Split-half*: Just one application of the survey is applied to a sample, and questions that are measuring the same construct are compared to determine accuracy within the survey instrument.
- *Coefficient alpha*: Also known as Cronbach's coefficient alpha, after Lee Cronbach, who first published the formula in 1951 (Cronbach, 1951), the alpha coefficient compares individual responses on an instrument or test to all of the other items—often referred to as an average of all split-half comparisons.

Reliability is a necessary, but not sufficient, condition for validity. That is, a measuring device or survey could be reliable, but not valid; however, in order to be valid, it needs to be reliable. Reliability and validity can be thought of as aiming and shooting at a target. Figure 8.1 is a pictorial of the relationship between reliability and validity. A device that does not result in similar findings upon repeated iterations is neither reliable nor valid, just like a shooter who is all over the target. If the shots are grouped on the target but miss the mark, then the device is reliable but not valid. Finally, if the shots are grouped and hit the mark, the device is both valid and reliable.

Figure 8.1. Reliability and validity considered together.

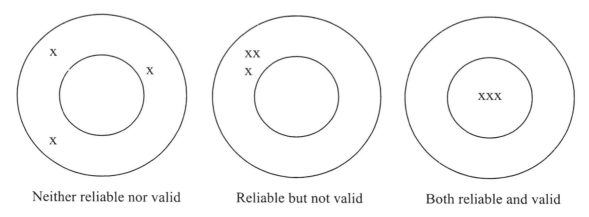

Neither reliable nor valid   Reliable but not valid   Both reliable and valid

Reliability and Validity Considered Together

If repeated iterations of the same instrument result in widely varying data, then the instrument is neither valid nor reliable. That is, they are neither dependable nor accurate, and they do not consistently measure the phenomena being studied. If repeated measures result in the same or very similar data, there is reliability of measurement, but if those data do not accurately measure the phenomena, there is no validity. In order for both to occur, there must be accurate measurements in the data that remain consistent over different uses.

Ethnographic research, research that often generates qualitative data, also should be concerned with the reliability of measures. Two types of reliability are discussed in relation to qualitative data:

- *External reliability*: Independent researchers working in the same or in similar contexts obtain consistent results from their research. A comprehensive description of the research methodology is essential so that both the replicability of procedures and the replicability of findings can be measured. External reliability is achieved when a replication of a study results in the same or very similar conclusions.

- *Internal reliability*: Different researchers studying the same data and constructs are consistent in matching data with constructs. Internal reliability means that two or more researchers agree on what they saw and how they interpret what they saw.

Selection in Action

Once the source of information is identified in a general way, the researcher must home in on the exact location of the data that will be used to answer the research question. In the continuing example on reading instruction, the published researchers used the classroom students as the data source. While this is a very common occurrence in education research, care must be taken with this type of data gathering and participant selection. This is especially true when there is an intervention, or experiment, that is conducted using human subjects. The researchers in the reading example needed to assure themselves, and the public, that no harm would come to the first-grade students who were part of the project.

When human subjects are used in research, agencies have specific protocols in place that need to be met. Care must be taken that no harm—physical, emotional, educational, psychological, or social—befall the participants. While this is especially true for school-aged children and youth, the same rules apply for adults who become sources of information or data in a research project.

The survey and interview examples previously given fall into the adult category of human participants in research. Care must be taken when selecting the individuals who will participate to ensure that no adverse outcomes result from their participation. One way to assure this result is to follow the strict guidelines for anonymity for all participants.

Data may also come from existing sources. Historical research, financial research, or education-program research projects are areas in which existing data are often used to complete a research design. One very current example of using existing data for research in the schools is the requirement for the testing of content knowledge for all students. These test scores may become the data to help answer questions about curriculum or instructional techniques in the schools. Existing school financial data can be used to answer questions about the cost benefit of certain programs when viewed over time.

Many sources of data are available to the researcher in answering research questions. The trick is to identify exactly the information source and the best technique to get it.

The sixth step in the process is outlined here. In one word, this step, or rule, can be thought of as *collect*. Linked together here, the pieces include:

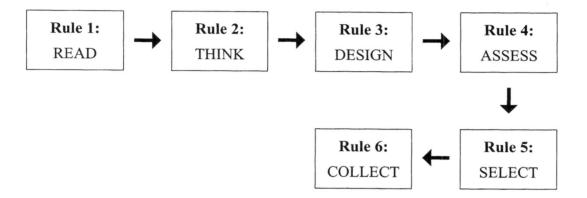

Exercise for Chapter 8

1. Why do many researchers have low response rates to surveys?

2. What issues are encountered if a researcher sends a survey to 200 randomly selected participants and only 25 respond?

3. Why is an interview sometimes a better way to collect data than a survey?

4. When is a survey more efficient than interviews?

5. How can a measuring instrument be reliable but not valid?

6. What data-collection technique could be used to measure student behavior in the class-room?

7. What are the benefits of having respondents rank-order a set of variables rather than provide numerical-value responses for each?

8. Why is a random selection of participants less important for qualitative research?

REFERENCES FOR CHAPTER 8

American Statistical Association. (1998). *What is a survey?* Alexandria, VA: ASA Section on Survey Research Methods. http://gill.amstat.org/sections/srms/whatsurvey.html

Cronbach, L. J. (1951). Coefficient alpha and the internal structure of tests. *Psychometrika, 16*(3), 297–334.

Eckstein, S. (Ed.). (2003). *Manual for research ethics committees: Centre of medical law and ethics, Kings College London.* (6th ed.). London: Cambridge University Press.

Fowler, F. (2002). *Survey research methods* (3rd ed.). Thousand Oaks, CA: Sage Publications.

Fowler, F. J. (1995). *Improving survey questions: Design and evaluation.* Thousand Oaks, CA: Sage Publications.

Houtkoop-Steenstra, H. (2000). *Interaction and the standardized survey interview: The living questionnaire.* New York: Cambridge University Press.

Kvale, S. (1996). *Interviews: An introduction to qualitative research interviewing.* Thousand Oaks, CA: Sage Publications.

Miles, M. B., & Huberman, A. M. (1994). *Qualitative data analysis: An expanded sourcebook of new methods* (2nd ed.). Thousand Oaks, CA: Sage Publications.

National Academy of Sciences (1995). *On being a scientist: Responsible conduct in research* (2nd ed.). Washington, DC: National Academy Press.

Patton, M. Q. (2002). *Qualitative research and evaluation methods* (3rd ed.). Thousand Oaks, CA: Sage Publications.

Seidman, I. E. (1991*). Interviewing as qualitative research: A guide for researchers in education and the social sciences.* New York: Teachers College Press.

Chapter 9

Review the Evidence

Rule 7: Organize and Analyze the Data

Data from research projects may be in the form of numbers, words, images, impressions, gestures, or tones that represent actual phenomena or events, or at least a current perception of that reality. Data analysis is the categorizing, ordering, manipulating, or summarizing of the information collected in the project. Numbers, or quantitative data, are subject to researcher-selected statistical tests. Remember that statistics are simple mathematical computations using the numerical data collected. Quantitative statistics are data manipulations generated for the purpose of answering the basic questions or testing the research hypotheses. Textual information creates data of another sort, qualitative data, and analysis of qualitative data follows specific conventions as well. Both categories of data and their treatment are covered in this chapter.

Quantitative Measures

Recall that Chapter 1 contained a description of the different types of numbers that may be generated in a research project. These included nominal (numbers as names), ordinal (numbers that have a sequential order), interval (numbers that have equal space between values), and ratio data (those with an absolute-zero point). Numbers that are used as names and that have no comparative values were referred to as nominal values. Measurement of nominal or other categorical values is most often done through frequency counts in which percentages of responses may be compared for analytical purposes. As the data set includes more sophisticated numbers, the tools for analysis become more sophisticated as well.

The type of statistics used in analyzing the data depends on the type of numbers collected in the research project. The most basic data in a research project are referred to as summary statistics. Summary statistics are a compilation of the numerical data that gives a collective or general meaning to the data set. The two most-used summary statistics are measures of central tendency and dispersion. Central tendency simply means a single-unit (one number) description of the data set that provides a common label (number) to all of the responses. They are measures of how scores or values in the data set cluster or collect around one value or score. Measures of central tendency are used with one variable only, or with subcategories within one variable.

Three basic measures of central tendency are:

- *mode*: the most frequently occurring number in the data set (may be used with nominal data)
- *median*: the true midpoint of the data set, where half of the numbers are above the median number and half are below (requires at least ordinal data)
- *mean*: the arithmetic average of the numbers in the data set (requires at least interval data).

Measures of dispersion using numerical data are used to provide information about how the numbers are spread out over the entire data set. Used in combination with measures of central tendency, these statistics provide a good summary of the elements in the data set, variable by variable.

Common measures of dispersion using numerical data include:

- *percentages*: the ratio of data points in a subcategory compared to 100 (e.g., 45% female means that 45 out of 100 participants were female)
- *range*: the spread of the numbers from the lowest value to the highest (e.g., salaries ranged from $33,000 to $99,000)
- *interquartile range*: dividing the numbers in the data set into fourths (much like percentages divide the set into hundredths), the interquartile range is the difference between the first and the third quartiles
- *stanine scores*: category scores based on nine classes of individual scores, rather than four as in interquartile range
- *standard deviation*: a statistical computation using a mean value (arithmetic average) and measuring and averaging the spread of each data point from the mean
- *variance*: the average squared deviation from the mean for all items; the standard deviation is the square root of the variance. Variance is used as a basic statistic in many of the formulas designed for data analysis.

In addition to summary statistics for numerical data, there are test statistics that are used to examine the data more thoroughly with regard to answering the basic questions or testing the hypotheses. Researchers use common test statistics that are established to report specific values that may be used to summarize the data and draw appropriate conclusions. Different test statistics exist for the different types of numbers that may be present in the data set (e.g., ordinal, interval, etc.; see Chapter 1 and this chapter).

Basic characteristics regarding the population and sample (population parameters estimated through sample statistics) must be measurable in order for statistical tests to be used, and most tests are based on the assumption that the population has a normal distribution, that the sample is drawn randomly from that normal population, and that the sample is representative of the research population. Usual test statistics applied to numerical data include:

- *Chi-square*: a nonparametric statistic that measures any significant difference in a set of data cells that contain frequency counts (bivariate tabular analysis). Karl Pearson published chi-square in 1900 as a criterion that could measure the goodness of fit (Plackett, 1983). Using the assumption that all cells are proportionate, the chi-square test measures any significant deviations of the observed frequencies from the expected frequencies.

- *t-test*: also known as the Student's *t*, since W. S. Gosset (Student, 1908) originally published it under the pseudonym of "Student," the *t*-test measures the difference between two mean values in a data set, or can be used to measure the difference of the mean value computed from a selected scale-score value. The higher the *t* score, the more likely it is that a significant difference exists between the means, or between the mean value and the selected scale-score value.

- *F-ratio*: the resultant statistic from a test known as *analysis of variance*, or by the acronym ANOVA. The F-ratio, named for R. A. Fisher, who created the statistic in 1925 (Fisher, 1950), gives a measure of any difference between groups by using the variance (a measure of dispersion calculated by using each data score and comparing it to the sample mean value) that can be calculated *within* each research group or category and comparing it to the variance that exists *between* the groups in a ratio. Computed F values have a corresponding table of significance, dependent on sample size, which gives a measure of confidence to any conclusions drawn based on the F statistic.

- *Correlation*: either a Spearman *rho* or a Pearson product-moment correlation coefficient (Pearson *r*, or simply *r*). The Spearman rho, invented by Charles Spearman and first published in 1904 (Spearman, 1904), is most often used to correlate rank-order (ordinal) data. The Pearson *r* is the standard correlation coefficient, first published by Karl Pearson in 1896 (Plackett, 1983), and a common statistic used for interval data to compare the association between two data sets. Both correlation coefficients vary between the values −1 and +1. When close to −1, the scores in the two data sets would appear to be distinctly different. That is, when one value is low, the compared value is high. When close to +1, the relationship is one of great similarity. That is, low values compare with other low values, and high values compare with other high values from the second data set.

- *Factor analysis*: a method for determining the number and nature of the underlying variables among larger numbers of measures in a data set. Factors, which are constructs (concepts specifically generated for research purposes), are generated using common-factor variances (similar trends in the data) from sets of measures. Given a survey instrument with multiple items aimed at measuring the same construct, a factor analysis can statistically confirm that the common items do, in fact, represent a similar trait.

- *Regression analysis*: another technique that uses common-factor variance but in a causal-comparative research paradigm. Regression uses a combination of regression (r values) and ANOVA to have one or more independent variables predict the selected dependent variable. The resultant statistic, or R^2 value, is the square of the correlation coefficient, and it is subjected to a significance test through the analysis of variance technique. The R^2 value is the percent of variation in the dependent variable that can be predicted by the selected independent variables.

- *Time-series analysis*: the use of regression analysis over time. The predictive capability of regression is used with time as a variable, and repeated measures over time are used to predict future events.

- *Hierarchical linear modeling (HLM)*: a multilevel analysis technique that is an advanced form of regression that allows for analysis at multiple levels such as classroom, school, or district.

Other statistical techniques used by researchers who generate quantitative data in their work are variations of these basic formulas. Most often, the variations are used due to anomalies in the data set that contradict the basic assumptions, and more rigorous statistics are needed to correct for these deficiencies in the data. Problems may occur with use of statistical-analysis techniques if the researcher does not have direct control over the situation, if manipulation of the data is not possible or feasible, if random selection of participants is not possible (participants self-select or volunteer), or if too many uncontrolled influences exist that make causation difficult to ascertain.

When one or more of the issues noted above are present, researchers often rely on reporting and analyzing data in a textual rather than a numerical fashion. Qualitative data have similar analysis structures, but words, rather than numbers, are the basis for the analysis.

Qualitative Measures

Analysis of textual data is much different from the statistical analyses used for numerical data, but there are basic and rigorous structures for the review and appraisal of qualitative data derived from carefully structured research projects. Qualitative data are usually the result of a field-based study in which behaviors or phenomena that are observed may not be quantifiable. The data collected are to be summarized in order that inferences may be made about the target population being studied. Direct observations that are recorded, interviews that are audio- or videotaped, historical or other archival documents that are uncovered, or other textual materials become the information resource that must be analyzed. These data most often do not have measurable characteristics (parameters) that are necessary for numerical analysis. Different methods of analysis are needed.

Qualitative analytical methods used to organize and report textual data include text coding, content analysis, phenomenology, case study, grounded theory, member checking, and triangulation. A researcher must have a good understanding of the research topic (*comprehending* the phenomena being studied), an ability to distinguish salient features of the data (*synthesizing* the data, looking for relations or linkage), the skill to appraise the uncovered relations (*theorizing* about the connections of data pieces), and the opportunity to reassemble the data pieces into a coherent argument in order to reach conclusions about the research topic (*recontextualizing* to help knowledge of the topic to grow). The researcher sorts and separates the data, organizes selected data pieces or points according to the research questions, conceptualizes how the pieces fit together to provide a succinct argument for the phenomena, refines the argument based on further data analysis, and draws conclusions about the data based on the interpretation of the reorganized data set.

Qualitative data sets usually have ample quotations, narrations, field notes, questionnaire results, and other details that allow the researcher the opportunity to understand the context being studied from the research subjects' frame of reference or point of view. The analysis of the data is carried out to explain human behavior or a specific phenomenon and, perhaps, to provide for causation of that observed behavior. As researchers consider the data and work to organize it in an appropriate array, issues of data congruence (accuracy and creditability), applicability to other settings (transferability), comparability to other research (dependability), trustworthiness with a lack of bias (confirmability), and rigor (authenticity) must be considered.

Unlike statistical data-analysis techniques, where most formulas are named for their author, qualitative data-analysis techniques are the product of continual refinement. In the beginning, textual data-treatment techniques were patterned after traditional quantitative methods, but they have since grown to encompass characteristics of their own. Some of the basic data-treatment techniques for qualitative data include:

- *Text coding*: the researcher has interview transcripts, field notes, transcribed dictation from the field, oral histories, or other documents as the data source, the data need to be coded in order for analysis to be performed. Text coding is the technique of marking the text in some way with a series of codes that separate or identify segments of text that are linked together. Typical manual techniques for text coding include marking the documents with preestablished code words, highlighting segments of data in different colors that represent different codes, manually separating the data pieces into distinct piles or groups that represent a code, or using electronic (computer) resources for the segmentation and coding.

- *Content analysis*: the technique used for historical, narrative, or interpretive data inspection. Content analysis is a systematic description of participant or research-subject behavior that is done to understand the basic meaning or foundation structure of the research topic. Researchers often separate the data to respond to the basic who, when, what, where, or how questions that may lead to research conclusions. Sometimes referred to as "deconstruction," it involves taking the data apart to get at the basic essence of the information.

- *Phenomenological analysis*: the extensive and thorough study of individual cases used to uncover or discover the basic essence of a phenomenon under scrutiny. Participant experiences are drawn out of the data and then compared and analyzed to describe or clarify the research topic as a phenomenon.

- *Case study*: analysis in a case-study approach to research is characterized by its focus on the case, or selected cases, as the unit of analysis rather than the research topic collectively. Carefully selected categories that are created to describe a limited number of details or a specific dynamic are used to separate and analyze the data.

- *Grounded theory*: the analysis of the research data is an attempt to create a specific theory about the research topic. The theory proposed is grounded in the data and developed through use of a systematic set of procedures, including intuition and inductive reasoning, by the researcher. The theory developed is most often a general pattern or theme that describes the behavior observed and is the product of constant comparison analysis of significant data pieces.

- *Triangulation*: strictly interpreted, a third-party review (thus the triangle), but basically, the concept is to have separate data pieces point to the same end or research conclusion. In some cases, a combination of quantitative data analysis along with the qualitative results may be used for triangulation; in other cases, multiple raters, different cases, or peer theme interpreters are used.

- *Member checking*: information that is provided by research participants is returned to them for confirmation. Part of the analysis is to select quotes or references from research subjects and then confirm with the subjects that the selected data is accurate.

Most, if not all, of the analysis techniques used for qualitative data are for the purpose of making summary statements about the research topic that are carefully drawn from individual bits of data. This is the inductive method, which is reasoning from the part to the whole or from particulars to the general. Data are collected in qualitative research in order to build theoretical concepts, test existing hypotheses, create new hypotheses, or challenge existing theories using intuitive understanding of observed events or recorded information. The researcher, much more than the method, is key in the data analysis in qualitative research.

Implementation

Many tools exist for the collection of research information. The example involving first-graders used test scores from the students and the results of interviews or surveys from colleagues. The published researchers used a pretest-posttest design to gather their research data. This means that the same tools (Quality Reading Inventory, for example) were used before and after the intervention of the different types of reading instruction. In order to compare apples to apples, the researcher must take care that the same information is collected in the same way from the same children. These are the things that make the comparison valid.

If the researcher conducting the survey has used a numerical response, then the surveys are collected and the responses are combined in a meaningful way. The number of responses to each item may be reviewed. Or all of the responses to each item may be added together and averaged to create a measure of central tendency for analysis. Often, statistical analyses are planned and carried out on numerical data. If respondents were asked to answer "yes" or "no" items, then the researcher may use a chi-square analysis to determine whether or not the observed yes and no answers were significantly different from expected (equal cell) values. If a five-, six-, or seven-point Likert-type scale was used, the researcher may use t-tests or analysis of variance (ANOVA) to determine if significant differences appear between or within groups.

If interviews were done, then the tape-recorded responses need to be transcribed and analyzed, either through an online method or by hand. Trends in the data or categories of response should be established, and meaning applied to them by the researcher. The researcher may need to check with the participants to clarify responses or to delve deeper into the meaning of the responses.

Other types of data call for the use of other sources of information. Test scores may be housed in a district office and made available to an individual or committee interested in studying the results and making judgments for the curriculum or instructional plan. Financial data, too, may be housed centrally and be available for use in a research project. In most research, the questions asked lead to the identification of, first, the type of information needed to answer the question, and second, to the actual source of that information.

Seven rules, or steps, in the inquiry process have been covered at this point, and the most recent step could be referred to as *analyze*. One important part of the analysis stage for data review is to determine which data are usable and which are not. Too often, researchers see data collected as data necessary to use. Sometimes, the data do not respond well to the basic question, or the data may be tainted as far as the method or timing of collection, making the information unreliable and unusable. It is essential for the researcher to keep accurate and complete notes regarding the data-collection process and to dismiss any information that is not relevant or valuable.

Linked together at this juncture, the steps in the process include:

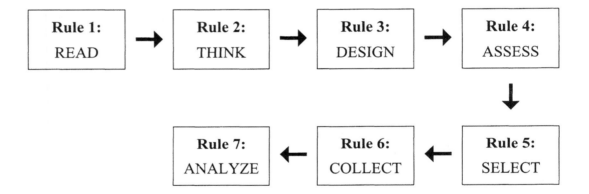

Exercise for Chapter 9

1. Suppose a researcher received responses to a 5-point value inventory (1 = strongly disagree; 2 = disagree; 3 = neutral; 4 = agree; 5 = strongly agree) in which the difference between the mean for women (3.8) and that for men (4.1) was statistically significant. Would that be a substantial (professional) difference?

2. In a research report on salaries, if the mean value (average) reported was $145,000 and the median (midpoint of the range of values) was $35,000, what conclusion could you reach regarding the sample?

3. If a data set contains "yes" and "no" answers from 50 men and 50 women, what would be the expected frequencies in the cells of a chi-square test? Why would a researcher use a chi-square test on this data set?

4. What is triangulation of the data, and why is it important?

5. Why is member checking an important tool for the ethnographer?

REFERENCES FOR CHAPTER 9

Cramer, D. (2003). *Advanced quantitative data analysis*. New York: Open University Press.

Cronbach, L. J. (1951). Coefficient alpha and the internal structure of tests. *Psychometrika*, 16(3), 297–334.

Fisher, R. A. (1950). *Statistical methods for research workers* (11th ed.). New York: Hafner.

Freebody, P. (2003). *Qualitative research in education: Interaction and practice*. Thousand Oaks, CA: Sage Publications.

Hopkins, D. K., Hopkins, B. R., & Glass, G. V. (1996). *Basic statistics for the behavioral sciences* (3rd ed.). Boston: Allyn & Bacon.

Manly, B. F. J. (2004). *Multivariate statistical analysis: A primer* (3rd ed.). London: Taylor & Francis.

Paulson, D. S. (2003). *Applied statistical designs for the researcher*. London: Taylor & Francis.

Plackett, R. L. (1983). Karl Pearson and the chi-squared test. *International Statistical Review*, *51*(1), 59–72.

Spearman, C. (1904). The proof and measurement of association between two things. *American Journal of Psychology*, *15*, 72–101.

Student (W. S. Gosset) (1908). The probable error of a mean. *Biometrika*, 6(1), 1–25.

Williams, F., & Monge, P. (2001). *Reasoning with statistics: How to read quantitative research* (5th ed.). London: Harcourt College Publishers.

Notes

Chapter 10

Display the Findings

Rule 8: Present the Data

Once the data in a research project have been collected and analyzed by the researcher, it is time to prepare data displays that provide the substance of the project. As in the analysis phase, different types of displays are used for different types of data. The data analysis was conducted to test research hypotheses or to answer basic research questions. The data displays are offered in a research report to communicate that analysis to a larger audience. Numerical data are usually displayed through the use of tables, charts, or graphs; statistical results from analyses have a traditional format of presentation; and textual data are often summarized with selected quotations from research participants or other annotations from the data to confirm traits or phenomena.

The presentation of the data in a research project is a bridge between the research questions or hypotheses and the conclusions and recommendations. The data selected for display must be those that are logically linked to the basic questions. The style of presentation is often to select data for each question or hypothesis and to display those elements of data that are clearly connected to the topic. The presentation should also prepare the reader for the conclusions to be drawn. The researcher should be able to draw on the data presented and refer to those data in the final part of the report, in which conclusions, recommendations, and implications of the study are discussed.

Not all data collected for a research project need to be presented in a research report. In fact, the true meaning of research is to ferret out those quintessential elements that shed light on the subject under scrutiny, then to use those elements as evidence leading to a conclusion. It is imperative that researchers take all safeguards available for the collection and analysis of data, then use standard methods of display to make the points or draw the conclusions warranted. General methods of data display for numerical and textual data are provided in the rest of this chapter.

Quantitative Data

Quantitative data are numbers and, for the researcher, are the easiest data to display since there are basic conventions to use. The most rudimentary method of displaying numerical data is in the form of frequency counts or frequency distributions. Numbers and percentages can be reported in the text of the report or they can be displayed through the use of tables and cross-tabulations. Research variables or categories may be divided by subject or by the different levels of subject response.

Graphs or charts provide another method of displaying research data. The data must have the capacity for a two-dimensional representation, and then selected research constructs are chosen for the horizontal and vertical axes of the presentation. Line graphs are used to connect the data points on a display, and bar graphs are either horizontal or vertical rows, or columns that provide summaries of the data.

Measures of central tendency for data displays can be placed in graphs or charts as well, or they may serve as part of the written analysis of the display. If statistics are used to measure similarities or differences of the measures of central tendency (mean, median, and mode) or of dispersion (range, standard deviation, and variance), then the actual computed statistics need to be presented, along with the usual statistical table for the type of measurement selected. The data in the tables for numerical analyses are, in all cases, manipulations of the raw data collected by the researcher. Statistics are computations performed using the data derived from the study.

When including research data in tabular form or with graphs or charts, the researcher should be aware of the common structure for presenting condensed data in reports. There are three steps in the process:

- introduce the table, graph, or chart in the text ("Table 1 contains....")
- present the table, graph, or chart (consult the APA style manual on how to create tables)
- discuss the salient features of the table, graph, or chart in the text (pick out the highlights).

The researcher should keep in mind two guidelines in the discussion of data in the condensed form. First, not all data need to be discussed. Point out the highlights or salient features of the data displayed. Items on the fringe, the highest or lowest numbers or scores, or the outliers in the data set may be selected for special attention. The second guideline is to try not to draw conclusions from the data in the presentation stage. The discussion should be simply to point out facts from the data in the table, not to offer an interpretation as to why those special features occur. The interpretation is to be presented in the discussion of the findings.

Qualitative Data

Summary tables and charts, along with figures designed by the researcher to help the reader follow the interpretation lines created by the researcher, are the basic techniques for displaying textual data. Concepts such as thick description or rich attribution serve as foundation tools for the researcher. This means that the reporting is replete with quotations, narrations, or other details that come from the data sources.

Just as with the numerical data, textual data form a bridge between the research questions and the summary discussion at the end of the report. Information in the data is separated into cogent pieces, categorized according to the research topics or questions, combined along those category or question lines to give strength to the argument, then reported by category or question.

The researcher should focus on the questions and use them as an advanced organizer for the arrangement and display of the data. Subheadings in the data set should be directly linked to the research questions, and the report should follow the lines of reporting the data pieces that were deconstructed and then reorganized to respond to those questions. For instance, if survey questions were part of the data collection, then the report should include responses to each question that has pertinence to the topic (e.g., "In response to Question A, Group Z said....").

When the data are anecdotal, the researcher should provide ample evidence from the situations described to support any conclusions that may be drawn. It is incumbent upon researchers reporting on qualitative work to include those items or data pieces that do not fit with the majority direction and, in the end, to discuss why that might have occurred. Data that do not conform to the direction of most should not be hidden, but rather explained.

Analysis in Action

Once the data are collected, the researcher needs to step back from the data set and begin to scrutinize it—the researcher must *analyze* the data. Analysis, or the evaluation, appraisal, and questioning of the information collected, is essential. Are the data linked to the questions or hypotheses? Do the data relate well to the sources? What are the reasons for contradictory data? Are more data needed? What are the connections of the different data pieces? These are all questions that should be answered in the analysis phase.

Included in the analysis phase in the research process is the need to *organize* the information—the data—for display and to answer the basic questions. Research means summarizing the information into comprehensible packets that are directly related to the questions or hypotheses. What statistics are appropriate for the quantitative data? What quotes or passages are appropriate for the qualitative data? How can the data be organized to ensure a logical connection between the data source and the research outcomes? Organization is a necessary step in the creation of an acceptable and logical argument from a research project.

The results of a survey that has numerical data should be combined in tables that provide an overview of the responses. These might be the actual tally counts of responses, or they might be the average, with a measure of spread like the range of scores, the standard deviation, or some other technique for presenting the analyzed data. Experimental and quasi-experimental research have accepted conventions for the display of data, including the display of statistical tests applied to the data. The researcher should follow the existing conventions rather than attempt to be creative. The format of these presentation tools can be found in the literature read in preparation for the research project, or they are described in detail in the *Publication Manual of the American Psychological Association* (APA, 2001).

If textual data are involved, the researcher should be judicious in the selection of quotes, or in the combination of thoughts from several sources, then present that information in a meaningful way. Often, the best evidence from textual data is the careful selection of the respondents' own words to make the researcher's intended point. Information from several sources is good, but the researcher should be careful not to overdo the inclusion of participant quotes.

In either case, be it numerical data or textual data, the information collected must be read, reviewed, and combined or separated in order to be applied to the research question. Plans for the dissemination of the information should be made in advance of outlining and then writing the final report.

The eighth step in the process, or the eighth rule of inquiry, can be summarized as *present*. Linked together, the steps thus far include:

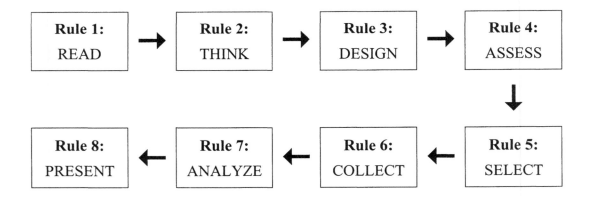

Exercise for Chapter 10

1. Why are tables or charts more effective in the presentation of numerical data than writing numbers in the text?

2. When are pie charts more effective than tables for a data display?

3. When the researcher is reviewing transcripts of interview data, what other sources of information are helpful to her or him?

4. Why is it important to reference data that do not support the basic premise of the study?

5. How are the data displays helpful when drawing conclusions about the project?

6. How should a researcher handle data that call for the need for further research?

7. What selection conventions could a researcher use when choosing quotations from textual data?

REFERENCES FOR CHAPTER 10

American Psychological Association (2001). *Publication manual of the American Psychological Association* (5th ed.). Washington, DC: American Psychological Association.

Day, R. A. (1998). *How to write & publish a scientific paper* (5th ed.). Phoenix, AZ: Oryx Press.

Gall, J. P., Gall, M. D., & Borg, W. R. (2005). *Applying educational research: A practical guide.* Boston: Allyn & Bacon.

Pyrczak, F., & Bruce, R. R. (2005). *Writing empirical research reports: A basic guide for students of the social and behavioral sciences* (5th ed.). Glendale, CA: Pyrczak Publishing.

Rubens, P. (1995). *Science and technical writing: A manual of style.* New York: Henry Holt & Co., Inc.

Notes

Chapter 11

Answer the Question

Rule 9: Interpret the Data

While organizing the data for display, the researcher should keep in mind the directions in which the data take the project and should begin a list of things found and things not found. That is, while analyzing the data and preparing it for display, the researcher should keep a list of potential conclusions and possible recommendations or implications that flow from the data set. The categories or headings for this list of potential final statements should be the research hypothesis or the basic questions. After all, the research is conducted in order to answer the questions. By keeping track of what the data say, the researcher will find it much easier to report the research findings.

Three basic categories of discussion are used in writing the concluding remarks for a research project: conclusions, implications (from speculation), and recommendations. The category of conclusions should be in every research report, and the other two categories may or may not be present. Once again, the data from the findings section will direct whether or not discussion is warranted beyond the conclusions drawn.

Answering the research questions or making judgmental statements about the hypotheses must be logically and solidly linked to the data. The reporting of the data must provide a direct link to any conclusions drawn. The researcher should make it clear that any interpretations are from the point of view of the researcher and may not be the same ones another reviewer of the data may make. Complementary to the drawing of conclusions is the need to rule out other potential interpretations. Data should not be suppressed in this endeavor. If multiple interpretations or questionable causation are possible, the researcher should make the reader aware of those circumstances.

Because any research that is to be published should go through a peer-review process, as discussed in Chapter 1, researchers should be constantly vigilant to the problems of acting on premature findings or of publishing prematurely. Conclusions, implications, and recommendations need a direct and logical link to the data, and the data must be inclusive so that other potentially contradictory results that may be warranted can be explained. Conclusions should be a category of results present in all research because that is the appropriate way to enter and expand the knowledge base for the topic researched.

Conclusions

Conclusions are summary statements about the research topic that are linked to the basic questions or hypotheses, and to the data. The data analysis is most often a study of similarities or differences, or an attempt to describe and explain situations, circumstances, or phenomena. The concluding remarks are the result of the researcher's inductive leap from the data, or the researcher's deductive statements about the data. In either case, there must be a logical connection to the data, and the concluding statements must be related to the questions asked or the hypotheses posed.

Conclusions are the informed opinions or judgments of the researcher that are formed after careful examination of the research data. Research conclusions should serve a purpose. Theories or ideas may be confirmed or denied, problems may be solved, questions may be answered, hypotheses may be accepted or rejected, interrelationships between or among individuals or things may be explained, or new theories or ideas may be created or tested. Conclusions are an interpretation and discussion of what was found in the research. Interpretations that may result in data-driven decisions are conclusions that are helpful to readers.

When researchers are drawing conclusions about the work they have completed, the needs of the field or of the locus of the research should be taken into account. If substantiation of the status quo results from the research, or if a direction for change is recommended, the researcher must state those conclusions with credibility and in a way that can be understood by the public the research is addressing. Brevity and simplicity in language are a plus for reaching the right audience with the research conclusions.

Not all statistically significant findings result in a solid conclusion for the research. As mentioned in Chapter 6, there may be a distinct difference between statistical significance (i.e., the confidence in observed similarities or differences) and practical significance (i.e., the importance for program or policy decisions). The same may be true for qualitative data. One quote from one individual may not lead to an appropriate conclusion, but if that one quote does the job of explaining or describing what the data say overall, it is appropriate in leading or substantiating a conclusion.

Implications

Data implications are speculations made by the researcher when the data do not necessarily confirm the result, but do have a strong connection to a potential finding. The researcher implies that there may be a connection, without "proving" it with the data collected. Implications may also be stated for concepts that are outside the basic research design. Results that provide a description of a construct that is not part of a basic question or hypothesis may lead the researcher to state an implication of the study.

Implications may lead to further study or to using the same database to answer questions not posed in the original research. It is incumbent on the researcher to offer these speculations so that the research can be understood in context and so they can broaden the horizon of potential research in the topic. Implications may lead to recommendations for future research, are a common result of dissertation research, and are a very good tool for designing another project and for adding to the knowledge base in the topic area.

Recommendations

Research recommendations have two uses. The first is to suggest further research. Much like the speculation that the research may have implications in other areas, the recommendation may be for further research. The recommendation, however, may provide a more concise structure for a future researcher to use. The interacting variables or a new design for a research project may be recommended.

The second use of a recommendation section in a research report is to speak directly to the audience most closely connected to the research topic. Once conclusions are logically designed and stated, then the use of the research becomes the subject of recommendations for the research locus. The agency, group, or phenomena being studied may be given direction for future action based on the conclusions drawn in the research.

Once again, the recommendations for redirected action or behavior should be succinct and focused directly on the audience. Based on the information gleaned from the research, the researcher provides a roadmap for future action with a prediction of consequences for action taken or avoided.

Pulling It Together

Once the data are analyzed and organized for display, it is time for the researcher to *write* about the project. This step starts with a summary of the basic literature from the *read* step, progresses through a description of the paradigm being used from the *think* and *design* steps, includes data displays from the *analyze* and *collect* steps, and moves forward with the researcher's conclusions, recommendations, and implications.

The write-up of a research project should follow the questions asked in the research. If survey items are used, then the responses to each item should be captured by the writer and explained with a connection to the basic question. It is in the writing of a research report that the reference text mentioned at the beginning of this book, *The Elements of Style,* becomes a valuable tool. The research writer should follow the basic conventions of language use and research rhetoric. Remember, good writing is rewriting. Read what is written and revise to make the meaning crystal clear.

It is always important to *review* what has been written. This review step involves more than the researcher taking a critical look at her or his own work for editorial corrections. Crucial to this step is the review of the conclusions drawn by others. Peer review is essential to every research project. Whether as an internal guide to implementation of results, or as a jury review for publication, every report should be scrutinized and critiqued to assure reliability.

Researchers may want help from the participant audience for the review stage, particularly when interview data are used. *Member checking* is the technique used for this purpose. For example, the researcher may send a copy of the write-up to the participant whose quotes are used, and ask, "Is this accurate?" or "Does this capture what you said?" Once the report is written and the author is confident that the results are both reliable and valid, then the application phase begins.

The step added to the sequence by Rule 9 may be termed *interpret*. Linked together at this juncture, the pieces include:

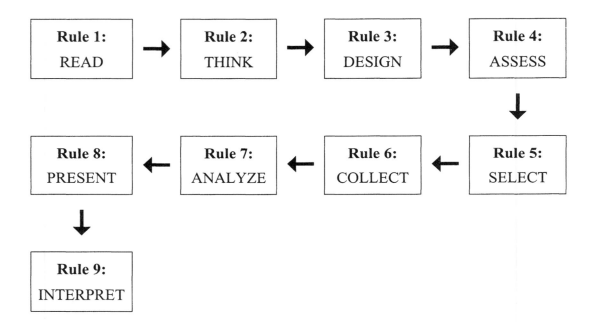

Exercise for Chapter 11

1. Why is it important to have data with which to drive educational decisions?

2. What is wrong with using data to make decisions before the research questions have been posed?

3. What can a researcher do if the data at hand are not adequate to the purpose?

4. What should a researcher do if the data from one hypothesis or question help to respond to another one?

5. How can a researcher assure that conclusions drawn from the data are warranted?

6. Are all statistical conclusions meaningful for professional decisions? Why or why not?

REFERENCES FOR CHAPTER 11

Box, G. E. P., Hunter, J. S., & Hunter, W. G. (2005*). Statistics for experimenters: Design, innovation, and discovery* (2nd ed.). Hoboken, NJ: Wiley-Interscience.

Eisner, E. (1991). *The enlightened eye: Qualitative inquiry and the enhancement of educational practice.* New York: Macmillan Publishing Company.

Farmer, E. L., & Rojewski, J. W. (2001). *Research pathways: Writing research papers, theses, and dissertations in workforce development.* Lanham, MD: University Press of America.

Larose, D. T. (2004). *Discovering knowledge in data: An introduction to data mining.* Hoboken, NJ: Wiley-Interscience.

Merriam, S. B. (2002). *Qualitative research in practice: Examples for discussion and analysis.* San Francisco: Jossey-Bass.

Shavelson, R. J., & Towne, L. (Eds.). (2002). *Scientific research in education.* Washington, DC: National Academy Press.

Notes

Chapter 12

Determine Closure

Rule 10: Synthesize the Findings

The final rule for completing a data-based inquiry project is to summarize the findings for quick retrieval and briefing. The abstract as a summary statement was outlined in Chapter 2. Rather than reading abstracts as a preparation for the project, now the researcher is responsible for writing one. The subjects or variables in the research, the type of research used, the basic questions or hypotheses used as a foundation, the key conclusions drawn from the data, and the important implications or recommendations from the study are included in the abstract.

Another helpful summary document is a research brief, or a synthesis of the research project. Longer than an abstract, but shorter by far than the complete report, the research brief has the same content pieces as the abstract, but each is handled in a more inclusive way. The research brief may go into more detail regarding conclusions and recommendations if the intended audience will be implementing program change based on the reported data.

Research as inquiry, for the most part, is connected by theory to other inquisitive endeavors. The synthesis of the project needs to make the link to former and future research so that the reader may see the work in the context of the broader picture. In this regard, very select items from the report's bibliography may be cited, especially as the citations link previous research to the new work. A reference to the need for the next step in the research process— that is, recommendations for future research—is always a good way to end a synopsis of the project.

Researchers' Responsibilities

The consumer who is not interested in the design and completion of an authentic research project may reenter the discussion at this stage. After reading several of the reports identified through the ERIC search used previously as an example, the reader may decide to use the little-books approach for a group of challenging students in her or his classroom. The confidence gained by comparing the subjects in the research project with students in the classroom may help in the application of the results of the research.

The No Child Left Behind (NCLB) legislation mentioned at the beginning of this book directed educational change to be based on scientific research. So if the school is planning to use money from the Title I fund available through NCLB to incorporate a new reading technique, such as the little-books approach, the fact that research was used to make this determination is essential.

It might be that the plan is to replicate the published project in one's own circumstance before making an implementation decision. This may be due to a different student population from that used in the original research, a different structure for the instructional day, or any other deviation that may lead to spurious conclusions if the design of the original research was implemented. In this case, the application of the findings of the primary research is in the replication at another school.

Whether one is using the research to make program adjustments or conducting original research to test new ideas, any changes made can be considered data-based and substantiated by research. Data-driven decisions are those most often resulting in successful programs, in education as well as in other walks of life.

Success or failure of program plans needs to be confirmed and reported to the appropriate audiences. These reports can take on many different forms. There are the formal research articles, such as those mentioned from the ERIC search. There are also oral presentations of results to colleagues, staff, managers, board members, or other audiences. The selection of the type of report is directly related to both the audience and the configuration of the setting for the report.

Reporting

The final step in the process is to *report* the findings in an appropriate way. Once completed, most research is reported for the review and acceptance of others. Coworkers, other researchers, other professionals in the field, or other consumers all represent individuals or groups who become the recipients of the researcher's work. The length, style, and language of the reports written must recognize and be prepared for the appropriate audience.

The audience for the example of testing different methods of reading instruction may be a small group of colleagues or a wider audience through publications. If the researcher intends to publish the results, care must be given from the very beginning to review the journal or other publication for which the manuscript is intended. Topic, type of research (quantitative or qualitative), format of writing (scientific or expository), and other considerations must be borne in mind throughout the design, data, and writing stages.

Often, the data-analysis stage of the research sequence provides the proper tools for the reporting stage. The charts, graphs, figures, or tables constructed by the researcher or found in the research literature may be used as visual tools in the reporting stage. Projecting the summary data on a screen through a PowerPoint® presentation, or through other means, gives life to the presentation and realism to the data. Form follows function in the reporting of research information, so the size and makeup of the audience most often dictate the type of presentation to be used.

In the reading-instruction method example used throughout this book, the interested individual might want to share the results of the original research with colleagues. This might entail a brief presentation of the summarized results in a faculty meeting. Copies of the original research may be the best vehicle for that discussion. If there were other supportive or contradictory research articles, they, too, could be used. If a committee has read the research and intends to present the findings to an administrative committee or to a school board, then a summary with combined visuals may be the best route.

For those who replicate a study, or who create an original research project based on existing literature, the report should include the basis for the design and the verified results of the research. The reason for conducting research is to add to the knowledge base of the subject being studied, and this addition is certified through the publication of the results according to accepted research protocols. The final element in the sequence of actions that lead to a research project's completion is to *synthesize* the findings. This final step completes the logical train of thought that represents the steps in any inquiry endeavor. As mentioned earlier, not all rules apply to all situations, but the steps provided here should help the consumer or researcher to make sense of the inquiry process.

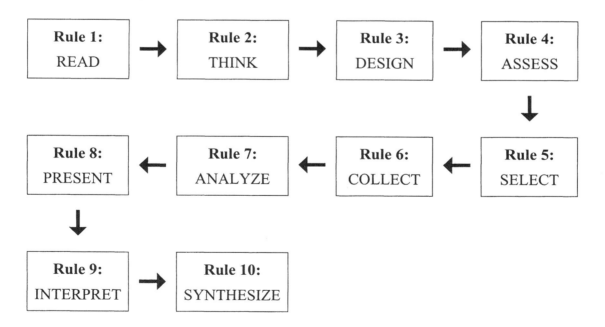

Summary

As a consumer examines completed research, or as a researcher begins, proceeds with, and finalizes a project, the following rules may serve as a checklist for tasks that must be accomplished. These rules apply to all kinds of research in many different professions and settings.

1. Rule 1: *READ*—Identify the existing theoretical basis of the research concept, then read and summarize the pertinent research literature.
2. Rule 2: *THINK*—Isolate the purpose of the study and identify the research topic and basic research questions.
3. Rule 3: *DESIGN*—Choose a research methodology that becomes the design of the study.
4. Rule 4: *ASSESS*—Recognize the evidence needed to answer the research questions and identify the data sources from which the answers can be found.
5. Rule 5: *SELECT*—Ascertain the appropriate evidence source and identify the data sources, subjects, or research participants.
6. Rule 6: *COLLECT*—Gather the needed evidence by collecting the research data.
7. Rule 7: *ANALYZE*—Review the evidence by organizing and analyzing the data.
8. Rule 8: *PRESENT*—Display the research findings through a formal presentation of the data.
9. Rule 9: *INTERPRET*—Answer the research question by thoroughly interpreting the data.
10. Rule 10: *SYNTHESIZE*—Determine closure of the project by *s*ynthesizing the findings.

Exercise for Chapter 12

1. Which parts of the final report are crucial for the abstract?

2. How may graphs and charts be valuable as communication tools for research presentations?

3. How does peer review enhance the reliability of findings?

4. Why is it important to link the results of an individual research project to the research conducted in the past?

5. Why is it important to suggest new research needed in the future in a report?

REFERENCES FOR CHAPTER 12

Berry, R. (2004). *The research project: How to write it* (5th ed.). London and New York: Routledge, a Taylor & Francis Group.

Day, R. A. (1998). *How to write & publish a scientific paper* (5th ed.). Phoenix, AZ: Oryx Press.

Farmer, E. L., & Rojewski, J. W. (2001). *Research pathways: Writing research papers, theses, and dissertations in workforce development.* Lanham, MD: University Press of America.

Pyrczak, F., & Bruce, R. R. (2005). *Writing empirical research reports: A basic guide for students of the social and behavioral sciences* (5th ed.). Glendale, CA: Pyrczak Publishing.

Tashakkori, A., & Teddlie, C. (Eds.). (2003). *Handbook of mixed methods in social and behavioral research.* Thousand Oaks, CA: Sage Publications.

Notes

Part III

Resources

Notes

Chapter 13

Research in Action

Research is a human endeavor that has its foundation in natural inquisitiveness and a person's basic need to know. Curiosity about how things work or fit together, why phenomena occur, why individuals act as they do, and the need for substantiation to credit or discredit what common sense tells a person, continue to fuel the need for research. It all starts with a knowledge base regarding a topic that is ripe for study. The researcher needs to ask the right questions, contemplate how answers might be found, and design a method to find and report the answers to the questions posed.

Inquisitiveness has always led to inquiry, and repeated inquiry has led to structured forms of research. Formal research began as a scientific endeavor, and science has been honing the methods of research ever since. Conceptual schemes have been designed to conduct empirical testing of theoretical structures, to take a systematic look at relationships, or to attempt to explain observed phenomena. Science relies on measurement, and on the control of the objects or subjects of the research, in order to be accepted by the public.

Specific paradigms exist for the framework in order to carry out the research. These patterns exist for both number-based (quantitative) and text-based (qualitative) research. Information collected is usually categorized, ordered, manipulated, analyzed, summarized, and reported to support answers to the basic questions asked. The researcher makes inferences or draws conclusions based on the analysis of the information collected. Sometimes, statistical analysis—the numbers generated from the research data using accepted formulas—is used to make the researcher's point. Test statistics are numbers calculated from the research data, used to verify decisions about the basic questions, or to test the hypotheses, depending on what paradigm is being used by the researcher. Statistics rely on having good numerical (quantitative) data.

Textual interpretations of data have similar rules to follow. When the information collected is in the form of words rather than numbers, or when the researcher does not change or attempt to influence conditions in the research, care must be taken to validate findings and substantiate conclusions drawn from the data. Replications of the research or meta-analyses of past and present research help with this validation. Repeated case studies, taken together, provide both potential solutions to problems and potential new questions to be considered.

Realistic research settings, such as those that occur in education, often do not provide the researcher with the desired control to complete a valid scientific experiment. However, field-based projects allow for the study of more complex circumstances. They can be used to seek solutions to practical problems, can help a researcher to design and develop new theories, and, finally, field-based research allows for a broader, though less documented, discussion of the topic or phenomenon.

The following sections use the rules presented in Part II of this book and provide examples of the stages implied by the rules when used in research projects in education. Much research can be carried out, and can be valid for the consumer, without using all the steps in the rules. As mentioned in the beginning, these rules are there as a checklist of what typical research contains—the steps in a traditional research project. The separate rules should be considered, then used or omitted, as dictated by the design being implemented. Many of the examples provided are from dissertations written by students in the Edgewood College doctoral program. While the examples are just pieces of larger and complete research projects, they do serve as examples of how each stated rule may be considered in the context of a larger research project.

Rule 1: *READ*

Identify the existing theoretical basis of the research concept, then read and summarize the pertinent research literature.

A graduate student in education often comes to a research course with a problem or issue in mind. Such was the case for a student in the doctoral program at Edgewood College. This student studied the prevalence of minority superintendents in the Midwest and the issues that both sitting and prospective administrators of color faced in achieving their jobs and aspiring to higher levels of administration. Because there was a dearth of research on the specific topic, he needed to outline a literature search that would provide a foundation for the topic. His outline included literature from the broad category of leadership, including an empirical section on traditional styles and another on nontraditional leadership. Added to this foundation were publications focused directly on the topic of African American school superintendents. The author of this study reviewed the theoretical and empirical literature foundation on three interrelated variables associated with the chief school-officer position as a basis for a conceptual framework. Those three variables were:

- leadership theory
- nontraditional leadership theory
- African American sitting and aspiring superintendents.

His review of literature was developed from a systematic search for books, studies, and articles concerning the broad topic of traditional and nontraditional leadership theories, the specific role of the superintendent, and the plight of African American superintendents. He located books, studies, and articles using World Cat, ERIC, ProQuest Information and Learning Education Journals, Academic Search Premier Database, Interlibrary Loans, and other databases and online catalog files about the selected topics. Keywords used in the search included underrepresentation, unrealistic expectations, unequal treatment, cultural congruence, and the particular needs of African American sitting and aspiring superintendents (Bates, 2006).

Another approach to conceptualizing the research project through the review and assimilation of the literature is to create a theoretical model of the research project. A pictorial model can represent the connection and interaction of the disparate pieces of information gleaned from the literature into a mosaic that pictures the work the researcher is hoping to accomplish. A theoretical model can also serve as a categorization of the concepts that need further study through reading research.

One example of a theoretical model used in research comes from a study that connected the Interstate School Leaders Licensure Consortium (ISLLC) standards and the requirements of the No Child Left Behind (NCLB) legislation with the leadership behaviors of school superintendents (Smolek, 2005). Figure 13.1 on the next page provided the researcher with categories that led to the selection and study of existing research and literature. The categories of research on the ISLLC standards, the literature on NCLB, and qualities of effective superintendents were generated to provide a theoretical base for the research. A first premise for this researcher was that leadership related to the policy and standards. Each box in the model provided a category to study, and the overlap in the model provided a construct for the research (Smolek, 2005).

Figure 13.1. Theoretical components of quality leadership.

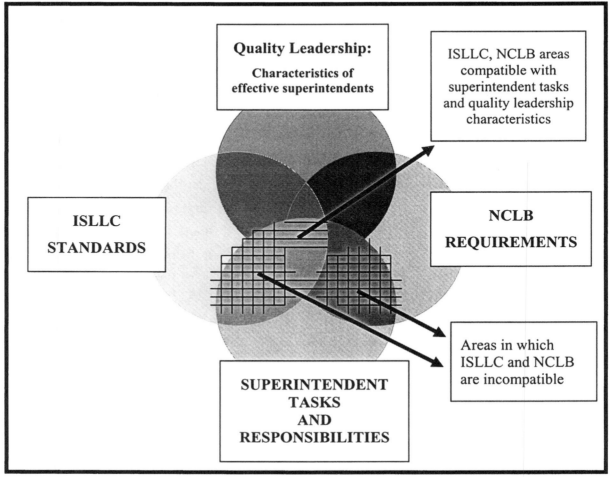

Quality Leadership:
Characteristics of effective superintendents

ISLLC, NCLB areas compatible with superintendent tasks and quality leadership characteristics

ISLLC STANDARDS

NCLB REQUIREMENTS

Areas in which ISLLC and NCLB are incompatible

SUPERINTENDENT TASKS AND RESPONSIBILITIES

Rule 2: *THINK*

Isolate the purpose of the study and identify the research topic and basic research questions.

The topic of the research project must flow from the existing literature, and from the concepts and constructs that exist in that literature. Especially important are those references that are bona fide research studies either directly or tangentially connected to the prospective topic. Once the topic is isolated based on what has been read, the researcher must carefully state the actual problem or issue in a way that it can be solved or answered through use of new information—new data—to add to the literature.

Another research student at Edgewood College began her study with two issues. She read what emerged for researchers and policy shapers regarding the supply and demand of teachers, especially hiring a sufficient number of teachers for every classroom, then ensuring maintenance of the quality of teachers in every classroom. An added variable was that the focus of the research would be high-poverty urban schools. Thinking about these concepts, this researcher decided to focus on the teacher-retention component and to isolate one aspect of a retention program in an urban school district—mentoring.

The hypothesis of the study was that a mentoring program would increase teacher retention in high-poverty urban schools because the literature pointed out that mentoring programs should decrease teacher attrition. Three basic questions were designed and proposed for the study:

- Do beginning teachers perceive that a teacher-mentoring program increases their desire to remain in a high-poverty school in an urban school district?

- What factors are seen as significant by beginning teachers in determining the effectiveness of a teacher-mentoring program to assist with their preparation to become a quality teacher?

- Do beginning teachers perceive that a teacher-mentoring program increases their desire to remain in the teaching profession? (Florian, 2005)

These basic research questions provide the direction for not only the data collection for the project, but also for the analysis and subsequent reporting of the results. It is important to ask questions that are not in the "yes" or "no" style, so that discussion and debate can occur from the reported results and conclusions drawn. These are the mechanisms for knowledge to grow through research.

Rule 3: *DESIGN*

Choose a research methodology that becomes the design of the study.

Throughout this text, readers have been made aware of the distinctions in the research tradition among the basic designs of qualitative research, quantitative research, and a project that combines qualitative with quantitative in a mixed-methods approach. Once the research questions have been formalized, the next step for the researcher is to determine how to go about getting the information pertinent to answering those questions. The location and type of data available for the research help to determine the research methodology to be used. Quantitative scientific research usually connotes numerical data and statistical analysis of those data. Qualitative research includes an analysis of textual data. Mixed methodology combines the use of numerical data with textual confirmation of the findings in a triangulation assessment. Examples from three student dissertations follow, each illustrating a different design paradigm.

Quantitative Design

In education, as with many fields of study, there is a great amount of numerical data available to help researchers answer questions. The use of existing data sets or sources is often the methodology for graduate students interested in specific aspects of an educational event or endeavor. One example of the type of data generated recently, due to the demands of federal legislation in the No Child Left Behind Act, is that of student test scores. Schools are required to test students at various grades and to report the results of those tests to the public. Many state departments collect the test scores for all districts and schools in the state and provide those data to the public through online access.

Another data source available to the public regarding public schools is the budget of the schools and the per-pupil expenditures of each school district. A recent research project of a graduate student used these two data sources to design a quantitative study regarding the spending levels of schools and the results of the test scores over time. The research question looked into the change in test scores for low-spending districts as compared to high-spending districts. The quantitative design of the study took advantage of the state database to identify both low and high per-pupil expenditure districts and to compare the test scores of the same class of students in different years.

The statistical analysis used was an analysis of variance (ANOVA) that measured and compared the combined student test scores within districts from one grade to another and the scores between the high- and low-spending districts. Using the existing data sources and traditional methods of statistical measurement, the researcher was able to draw conclusions regarding the interaction of spending and student success (Hoese, 2006).

Qualitative Design

Most textual data used in education research come from interviews or other interactions that provide answers to questions or responses to prompts dealing with the research topic. The interview questions or research prompts flow naturally from the basic questions, and they often include opportunities to expand upon the information directly related to the research topic. The usual design of a qualitative study using textual data begins with the preparation and vetting of interview items. Subjects are chosen for the study based on identified knowledge or experience with the subject, and data collected are subjected to some form of categorization.

An example of a qualitative research design used in a case-study approach is the analysis of team interaction in a middle school teaching team. The researcher, as a participant-observer, used observation methods and interviews to explore the team dynamics in formal team meetings. Interview questions were structured and the interviews were conducted for each teacher separately from the team. The researcher asked additional questions that arose during the interview to further explore the interviewee's comments. Each of the interviews was tape-recorded and then transcribed.

The researcher also took notes during each of the interviews to facilitate careful attention to each response by the interviewee, to flag important items, and to look for themes. The researcher completed a debriefing form after each interview. The results of each interview were made available to each subject for member checking. Further verification of interview data was made by observation. Notes were taken during the observation, and a checklist was used to mark the specific collaborative behaviors observed. The checklist was intended to facilitate the careful observation of measurable behaviors by the researcher. It was also intended to reduce researcher bias by looking for specific actions while still being able to note interesting observations. Notes did include important interactions that took place and other interesting observations. The researcher also completed a debriefing form after each observation. In addition to interviewing, surveying, and observing, each teacher answered three journal prompts about her or his teaming experiences. The journal prompts were intended to be a method of hearing the teacher's voice in a different format and to help the researcher to learn about the team's collaboration through a different medium (Rugotska, 2005).

Mixed Methods

Many education research projects combine numerical data with textual data to ferret out the answers to the research questions. These mixed-methods designs are intended to use the best information available and to make the case for reliable data by triangulation of the information received. Often, the design is to survey a broad range of participants and to then select subjects from the database to conduct more in-depth interviews. The interview questions come from the same categories of items in the survey, and the purpose of the researcher is to confirm or question the survey results through the interviews.

A mixed-methods design was used to conduct a recent study of alternatively certified teachers. The research design employed a quantitative survey followed by a qualitative interview. The two methods were conducted sequentially, first with a deductive instrument and analysis, followed by an inductive process and analysis. The intent was to describe the experiences and perceptions of teachers who received their training through different certification programs. A survey that included first-year teachers' perceptions of essential teacher competencies was created and used to gather baseline data. Each participant selected 10 essential behaviors she or he believed were the most critical to perform as beginning teachers. Then a semistructured interview was individually scheduled with each of the 10 participants. Interviewing to find out about the experiences of a particular group was the essence of the research design.

During the interview, the beginning educators rated their preparation in terms of how well their program prepared them to perform the 10 competencies they rated as the most important. More specifically, this study was an in-depth phenomenological-based survey and interview process. The rationale for conducting a study using the tradition of phenomenology was that its intent was to describe the experiences and perceptions of educators who received their teaching license through an alternative program. The survey provided the essential components of the interview through the participants' quantitative rating of competencies. The interview process guided the research throughout the course of the study as the group of participants reflected on their journey through an alternative certification program. Thus, the mixed-methods approach provided a quantitative foundation for the qualitative collection of textual data used to answer the research question (Wade, 2005).

Rule 4: *ASSESS*

Recognize the evidence needed to answer the research questions, and identify the data sources through which the answers can be found.

Once again, data sources abound for education research projects—from the classroom, the school, the district, the state, and even from the federal level. These data are a valid and reliable source for research information. Many research projects are designed to collect new data from the appropriate sources in order to answer the research questions. If the question is on funding, then budget data are used. If the question is on student performance, then test scores are most often the data used. If the questions deal with professional perceptions, attitudes, or knowledge, then the evidence needed may come in several forms.

Most research reports contain a section that outlines the potential sources of data, especially if the previous research used similar sources. The issues of population and samples play an important role in the identification of data sources. Research tradition has allowed for carefully selected samples from a well-constituted research population to offer a technique or procedure to legitimately answer questions for the entire population. A more recent phenomenon in education research, as well as in research in other disciplines, is to use the case-study approach to provide the evidence required to answer the questions.

Stratification of the research population is a technique often used to separate and distinguish the categories that may naturally exist in the population or that are meaningful to the research questions. Potential evidence sources are divided into groups for the collection and analysis of data. Comparisons or contrasts are made between the groups rather than between individuals. Researchers may use already established stratification of populations (race, gender, income, or location are a few), or they may create their own for the purpose of the research.

An example of one common subdivision for the purpose of analysis deals with the size of a community. A nine-item coding scheme for a rural-urban continuum was originated in 1975 by members of the U.S. Economic Research Service for the report titled *Social and Economic Characteristics of the Population in Metro and Nonmetro Counties: 1970*. This coding scheme was updated after both the 1980 and the 1990 censuses, with a somewhat more restrictive procedure for determining metro adjacency. The breakdown is as follows (Brown, 2006):

Metro counties:

Counties in metro areas of 1 million population or more.

Counties in metro areas of 250,000 to 1 million population.

Counties in metro areas of fewer than 250,000 population.

Nonmetro counties:

Urban population of 20,000 or more, adjacent to a metro area.

Urban population of 20,000 or more, not adjacent to a metro area.

Urban population of 2,500 to 19,999, adjacent to a metro area.

Urban population of 2,500 to 19,999, not adjacent to a metro area.

Completely rural or less than 2,500 urban population, adjacent to a metro area.

Completely rural or less than 2,500 urban population, not adjacent to a metro area.

This coding is used often when researchers are interested in the data from one or more specific sizes of community. Obviously, many researchers use the school size or pupil enrollment as a determining factor in selecting a research sample as well. The previous examples used per-pupil expenditures and test scores as other distinguishing factors in establishing evidence sources for a research project. The key element to keep in mind is that the evidence sources must match the questions asked.

In many cases in educational research, a convenience sample is used for a specific purpose. Schools within a district, or districts within a specified geographic area, often an athletic conference, are used for comparison purposes. The rationale for these purposive samples is not to generalize research findings to all schools, but rather to make informed decisions about the local condition based on local or area measurements.

Rule 5: *SELECT*

Ascertain the appropriate evidence source and identify the data sources, subjects, or the research participants.

In some cases, the source of the evidence for the research project is readily at hand. Many case studies are completed by participant observers who are integrally involved in the circumstance or process being studied. If that is the case, the data sources are a known quantity, and access is available to the researcher in her or his capacity as a trusted member of the group. More often, the researcher needs access to the appropriate data source and must rely on the participants' willingness to contribute to the project. The guarantee of anonymity and confidentiality is important when one is judging data sources. Participants in research projects are often more willing to be involved when they feel comfortable that their input will be part of a larger picture. That is, there is an understanding that the responses will be reported in aggregate, not in individual and attributable forms.

A recent study that employed qualitative research in an attempt to understand how principal behaviors and actions influence the successful implementation of accountability practices may serve as an example of the careful selection of research participants. In the end, the research was a case study of two principals within the same large metropolitan school district, utilizing a purposive sample. The district was purposely selected for several reasons. First, it was nationally recognized for its improvements in student achievement, and second, it had implemented the model the researcher desired to study—a holistic accountability system, including the development of district power standards. A third reason for the selection was that the district was recommended by an external consultant who knew of the success the model being studied provided.

An important criterion for the selection of the schools was that every single school in the district had made gains in mathematics and language arts as reported on its state test scores. These gains exceeded 20 percent in the case of several schools within the district. Although every school displayed significant growth, those schools with the highest poverty levels displayed the greatest growth in academic achievement. The two principals studied were from two of these schools. So the evidence source for this research was the principal, but the selection of the principals was based on the performance of the students in the schools.

For the purposes of triangulation, the researcher interviewed a total of four teachers, two at each of the schools led by the two principals. Teachers interviewed were identified by each of the two principals: one teacher who "came on board" very quickly, and another who was at first neutral or hesitant but eventually "came on board." The teachers were selected as sources to shed light on and corroborate the actions and behaviors of the school principals (Koehler, 2006).

Rule 6: *COLLECT*

Gather the needed evidence by collecting the research data.

Once the data sources are known, the collection of the research data begins. The researcher has a list of individuals to interview, a group of participants to survey, numerical data sources to collect and organize, or other information sources to identify to help answer the research questions. Form follows function with the collection of research data. The research design, if carefully thought out and organized, should give direction to the data collection.

In some cases, the researcher may be too close to the subjects to allow for a fair and unbiased response. Such was the case for a superintendent researcher interested in determining parents' rationale for transferring their children to a different school district while continuing to live in the resident district attendance area (known as open enrollment). This study was conducted in two phases. In Phase I, surveys were administered to all families who had elected to attend a nonresident school district or private school, or who home schooled their child or children and still continued to live in this study's district.

Because the researcher was the current superintendent of the school district involved in this study, and to aid in the reduction of respondent bias, an independent educational consultant was contracted to administer the survey. A letter was sent to the entire sampling of open-enrollment-participation families explaining the purpose of the survey and asking for their participation in this study. Participants were encouraged to take the survey online via the district's Web site homepage. If families did not have access to the technology needed, alternative access options were made available and explained in the survey introductory letter. A second letter along with a hard copy of the survey was mailed to the nonrespondents after two weeks. Again, the group was asked to complete the survey online, but if it was more convenient, they were allowed to submit a hard copy of the survey to the independent educational consultant in an included self-addressed stamped envelope. By mailing the survey directly to the independent consultant, the respondents assured the confidentiality of their responses. Confidentiality was emphasized in the cover letters that were mailed to all participants. After another two weeks, a third and final letter and survey were mailed to those in the sample who had not responded.

Phase II involved face-to-face interviews of the survey respondents that self-identified their willingness to be interviewed to supply more detailed information. The interviewees were self-selected from a specific Phase I survey question and asked if they would participate in an interview. Building rapport and asking effective questions during the interview was crucial to gathering good data. It was important to have a certain level of trust and a good understanding between the researcher and the participant. This rapport was developed by good, effective communication. The participants needed to be assured that confidentiality would be upheld and they could withdraw from the study at any time (Richey, 2006).

In addition to developing effective questions designed to solicit responses focused on the central issue of this study, the interviewer also contributed to the overall results with notes and observations. The interviewer's notes are a valuable method for recording impressions, reactions, and nonverbal information. This example provides evidence of different methods of data collection in one study. First, a survey was administered through both electronic and paper-and-pencil (hard-copy) formats. Reminders and encouragements were sent to elicit the best response. Part of the survey was to solicit potential participants for the interview stage. Data were collected through recording the participants' responses to the interview items, but also through the interviewer making notes about pertinent nonverbal information that may be used to further describe and explain voiced responses.

Rule 7: *ANALYZE*

Review the evidence by organizing and analyzing the data.

The presentation of data is driven by the research design. By reviewing all of the information collected in a research project, then organizing those data into a framework aligned with the research questions, the researcher is able to begin to find the answers to the questions posed. Some of the data will be important to the research results; other data may not have the direct relationship the researcher needs for proof. The review stage is for the researcher to select the wheat and discard the chaff accumulated through the data-collection stage. There are different conventions for the different modes of research. Basic illustrations of the qualitative and quantitative approaches are provided below.

Qualitative Data Analysis

Organizing data from a qualitative study usually does not include tabular displays. The researcher must review the textual data for themes or categories of responses and select the quotes or attributions that best represent the accumulated response of the participants. Sometimes, the number of times the same or similar concepts are quoted is tallied, and the concepts may be listed with their respective totals.

The researcher mentioned previously (Richey, 2006), who studied school choice, used a data-organization technique that listed the basic responses to interview questions for three categories of parents in order to make judgments about the research questions. This tabular analysis of data is presented in Table 13.1 on the next page. The three categories were used as the column headings for the table, and the qualitative survey data were summarized in separate lists for the three categories of respondents.

Table 13.1

Top Reasons Parents Chose an Alternative Educational Option for their Children

Private-school families (33)	Open-enrollment families (29)	Home-school families (15)
Religious beliefs and values	Quality of teaching staff	Beliefs and values
Quality of former dist. admin.	Curriculum concerns	Quality of teaching staff
Quality of teaching staff	Location of schools	Location of schools
Quality of former board members	Quality of support staff	Block scheduling
Block scheduling	Quality of former dist. admin.	Quality of former dist. admin.
Facility concern	Quality of building principal	Quality of former building prin.
Lack of materials and resources	Quality of former board members	Quality of former board members
Budget/Finance Issues	Quality of current board members	Facility concerns
	Quality of coaches	Quality of food service
	Facility concerns	

(Richey, 2006, p. 79.)

Grounded Theory. A valuable mechanism for the organization and review of research information is a constant comparative method, also known as grounded theory. A researcher who studied the implementation of democratic principles in post-communist Romanian schools used the grounded-theory approach. Romanian teachers were interviewed, and the transcribed interviews became the data for the study. The study used semistructured interviews coordinated by a key informant on a similar topic, and the interviews gave voice to Romanian teachers' understandings of the promotion of democratic processes within their schools and the effect on students and society. Observational field notes were kept by the researcher as well. Grounded theory was employed during data analysis.

This researcher did not come to either the interviews or the analysis with a predetermined, unchangeable framework. Instead, the data were used to develop theory at both the time of collection and afterwards, during reflection. However, the researcher did attempt to become sensitized to the possible ways in which interviewees may understand and communicate their thoughts as members of Romanian society. The nonlinear model for assessing teacher perceptions of democratic principles within public schools in Romania was contemplated throughout the process. The themes or categories of policy, practice, and societal influences were taken into consideration as perceptions were revealed (Decker, 2007).

A second example of a data guide for qualitative research is from a study of early intervention for primary-age students. In this case, parent, teacher, and student interviews were organized through use of a systematic approach required in the grounded-theory application.

The researcher used a conditional relationship guide to transfer data into a reflective coding matrix.

All staff, parent, and student interview questions were placed into the conditional relationship guide individually, as separate categories, due to the nature and connectedness of the questions to the study. The purpose of the guide was to identify relationships and interactions among the categories while contextualizing the interview responses. Once the questions were placed in the category column, responses were organized in the relationship guide as what, when, where, why, how, and, finally, with what consequence. The completion of the conditional relationship guide was reviewed and double-checked against the actual audio and written responses to ensure that all perspectives were captured in the formatted process.

The statements within each consequence category were individually conceptualized and, when combined, formed a core category (of links and relationships) for the reflective coding matrix and further analysis. The concepts identified in the staff-interview conditional relationship guide were problem solving, interdisciplinary, belief, change, and progress. Table 13.2 below is an example of a more complex data organization in which teacher interview data were organized in the conditional relationship guide for the purpose of analysis.

Table 13.2

Staff Conditional Relationship Guide

Category	What	When	Where	Why	How	Consequence
Evidence used to construct the problem	Teacher concern brought forward to the BCT members	Twice a month	Building Consultancy Team meetings	Teacher has tried basic classroom intervention but concerns continue to exist	Teacher has prepared ahead of time any logs of the tried intervention	Gain support from the BCT members
Evidence used to evaluate the intervention	Discussion of the teacher's tried intervention	During the BCT meeting but the teachers are not present	One BCT member usually talks ahead of time with the teacher	To gain a better understanding of the teacher's efforts	May or may not have well-documented efforts, but if so, 2 to 3 weeks of intervening is common	Not always sure the intervention matches the concern
Resolve differences in perceptions	Teacher may disagree with the team, team members discuss why they feel the way they do and often use supported research	When trying to come to agreement on an intervention, much discussion happens; time may hinder further discussion due to the number of children	During meeting time	The BCT members want to see progress, therefore try to be sure the intervention matches the concern	Observe between BCT sessions	May have to make adjustments

Continued →

Table 13.2 (*continued*)

Category	What	When	Where	Why	How	Consequence
Types of intervention when problem occurs	If a behavior intervention is needed, the social worker or school psychologist assists most; if academic, the reading or math specialist offers recommendations	When enough of a concern to disrupt the educational process of the student or others	Interventions are carried out within the classroom or during unstructured times	The members believe this is the best intervention for the child at the time	The members often support the teacher in implementing the intervention throughout the day, stopping in the classroom or meeting with the child individually	Student shows progress or has further behavioral or academic concerns
Perception of effectiveness of the interventions	By the mere fact the behavior may decrease or increase	When the staff are observing	In the appropriate setting	Natural context of where the behavior occurs	Gather 2–3 weeks' worth of data	If staff are not focused on specific outcomes, it can be difficult to know
Perceived effectiveness differences within	At times, one staff person may have a better relationship than others, so the problems are perceived differently	When student is in multiple environments	Often unstructured times during lunchroom, recess, music, art, or physical education	It appears there is less structure during these instructional times	Each person has a time to voice any differences during the meeting	The team tries to come to an agreement in choosing the appropriate interventions
Factors during the intervention process that influence the referral for special-education evaluation	Frustration of the staff. Continued behavior or academic concerns; staff insist the student needs help	When they feel the student would benefit from small-group or one-on-one instruction	Student will benefit from small-group instruction within the special education classroom	Student is not showing any gains in behavior and/or academics	Accumulated data indicate a disability may exist	A referral for special-education evaluation is made

(Kelly, 2007, p. 35.)

Quantitative Data Analysis

Quantitative data have a commonly accepted method of display. Summary statistics and formal reports of test statistics follow a prescribed pattern. Summary statistics are most often reported by one or more measures of central tendency (mean, median, and mode) and a measure of dispersion (range, standard deviation, or variance). The subjects or categories are listed on the left side of tables, and the numerical data are placed in the table itself under the appropriate heading. One example of a table with summary data is presented in Table 13.3 on the next page. In this presentation of findings from a study of teacher incentives, a 5-point Likert scale was used (Jorgensen, 2006). Scale scores for items with a mean of 3.5 or greater were considered "high" scores, while those at 2.5 or lower were considered "low." Scores with a mean between 2.6 and 3.4 were considered "neutral." If a researcher is interested in comparing two of the mean values generated in the study, a *t*-test could be used. The *t*-test is a statistical test of a hypothesis that two mean values are relatively (statistically) equal. A significant finding indicates that the two values are "statistically significantly different."

Table 13.3
Summary Statistics for Elements of Teacher Incentives

Structural questions	Mean	Standard deviation
Instructional paperwork	2.57	0.65
Length of school day	3.00	0.33
Length of lunch/prep periods	3.24	0.44
Freedom to act in the class	3.22	0.67
Collaboration opportunities	3.89	0.74
Leadership roles	3.65	0.60
Committee work	2.47	0.85
Length of the school year	3.11	0.31
Involvement in curriculum development	3.41	0.60
Support services	3.76	0.55
Professional development	3.92	0.64
Team teaching	3.67	0.68

(Jorgensen, 2006, p. 47.)

Statistical analyses of data also have prescribed presentation formats. For example, the analysis of variance (ANOVA) tables usually contain the degrees of freedom (df), the sum of squares (SS), the mean square term (MS), and the F ratio, with its probability of being statistically significant. The degrees of freedom value measures the number of independent pieces of information on which the precision of the test statistic is based. The degrees of freedom for an estimate equals the number of observations (values) minus the number of additional parameters estimated for that calculation. In most cases where there is one measurement being made, the degrees of freedom is one less than the total number of observations or participants ($N - 1$). Think of it as anchoring one piece of information, and the rest are free to fluctuate around that selected number. Another way to consider the concept of degrees of freedom is to think about the opportunities for change. Given one value, the opportunity to select a different value from your set is one less than the total, therefore $N - 1$.

The sum of squares is computed by first subtracting each scale score value from the average (mean) value, then squaring that difference (multiplying the number by itself), and then adding (summing) all of the squared values. The mean square is the quotient of the two sum of square values divided by their respective degrees of freedom, and the F ratio is the quotient of the two mean square values. Another statistic commonly used and reported in research reports is regression analysis. Regression begins with an ANOVA test, then uses a least squares method to align data points in order to produce a predictive value, the R-squared term.

An example of an ANOVA table and the result of a regression analysis on the data are presented in Table 13.4 below. Modern statistical-analysis packages on most computers are able to take the raw data, calculate the statistics, and produce tables like the examples here. It is not essential that researchers know how to calculate the statistics, but rather they must know what each measurement or formula means.

In this example, the ANOVA comparing overall GPA with composite ACT for 102 students was statistically significant. The R-squared adjusted value was 40%, indicating that approximately 2/5 of the variation of the composite ACT scores could be attributed to the overall GPA of each student (McCarthy, 2007). In other words, a student's GPA is a good predictor of how she or he will score on the ACT, but it is not a perfect predictor. A researcher might conclude that there are other factors influencing how well students do on the ACT or that grade inflation masks the reliability of GPA as a measure across high school students.

Table 13.4

Regression Analysis of Overall Composite GPA on ACT

Analysis of variance

Source	df	SS	MS	F	p
Regression	1	566.45	566.45	68.96	0.000
Residual error	101	829.61	8.21		
Total	102	1396.06			

R-squared value = 40.6%

R-squared (adjusted) = 40%

(McCarthy, 2007, p. 36.)

Another research example of the use of ANOVA and regression is taken from a project that compared attitudes of superintendents and curriculum directors in districts where technology integration had been implemented according to a formulaic procedure. The final step in this process was to determine the type of relationship, if any, that existed between superintendents' responses and curriculum leaders' responses (Peterson, 2006).

When combining all the data collected from both groups, Table 13.5 on the next page shows the results of the ANOVA. ANOVA compares the variation between groups to the variation within each group by using the statistical variance. Looking at the ANOVA results for the combined group in Table 13.5, one notes that the null hypothesis (that states that there is no difference between the groups) is rejected because the observed F value is much greater than the computed critical F value; the p-value (the level of significance) is very small. Thus, in the end, there was a statistical difference when comparing the attitudes of superintendents to those of curriculum leaders in the same districts regarding the status of technology integration in the district.

Table 13.5
ANOVA Combined Scores

Source of variation	Sum of squares	df	Mean sum of squares	p-value	Observed F	F critical
Between groups	37.8812	1	37.8812	6.208×10^{-15}	92.9421	3.9634
Within groups	31.7911	78	0.4075			
Total	69.9724	79				

(Peterson, 2006.)

Note that in Table 13.5, the probability (*p*) value is written in scientific, or exponential, notation. Often, the *p*-value is well below the selected test level (.01 or .05), but is reported as an actual value. The exponent (10^{-15}) provides the number of decimal places that are zeros prior to the computed value. Many software products that perform statistical analysis, such as Microsoft® Excel, use this type of notation. In this example, the *p*-value is not 6.208, which would not be significant, but rather the number 0.000000000000006208, which is highly significant.

Using a different part of this study as a further example, Table 13.6 below presents the results of a regression analysis using different data. In a linear regression formula, the correlation coefficient is multiplied by itself (squared) to generate the test statistic *R*-squared. The statistic represents the amount of variation in one variable that can be attributed to the other variable.

Table 13.6
Superintendent and Curriculum Directors' Combined Scores

Statistic	Calculated value
R	0.4877
R-squared	0.2378
Adjusted *R*-squared	0.2178
Standard error	0.4255
Observations	40

(Peterson, 2006.)

The *R*-squared term, also called the coefficient of determination, measures the amount of shared variation between the two variables. It is often used to determine a level of influence or predict future events. In the example, the *R*-squared value represents a 23.8% (an adjusted

21.8%) overlap in attitudes of superintendents and curriculum directors (Peterson, 2006). In regression analysis, the standard error of the statistical estimate is calculated through use of the residual mean square; that is, the combination of the difference of individual scores from the regression model. Suffice it to say that the smaller the standard error, the better or more precise the predictions from the model.

In the end, the type of data collected predicts the type of analysis to be used. The main link to keep in mind is the relationship of the data to the basic questions. The researcher must study the data, rearrange it, or combine it in several ways so that a logical conclusion may be drawn to the investigation. Too often, a researcher gets lost in the individual pieces of data, such as one quote or one statistic. It is essential to step back from the individual pieces and gain a broad overview of what is there in order to make sense of the whole.

Rule 8: *PRESENT*

Display the research findings through a formal presentation of the data.

The beginning of the data presentation comes from the review and selection of the charts, tables, and graphs generated in the data-review stage. The researcher must select those that best respond to the research questions, determine how best to present the data, then create the medium with which to relay that presentation.

Some of the display will be just like those tables used as examples earlier in the chapter. Not all tables generated in the data-analysis phase will be part of the final presentation, but many will be. Additionally, the researcher will combine results for data-generated tables to make summary points or judgments about the research questions. These basic questions become the organizing vehicle for the presentation of data. What pieces of information best represent the answer to the question? Those are the pieces that need to be displayed for the reader.

Several data-display techniques can be used by researchers. Bar graphs offer an opportunity to provide a visual comparison of the difference between concepts or categories. Figure 13.2 on the next page is an example of a bar graph on teacher characteristics taken from a study of highly qualified teachers. Classroom teachers who were identified as highly qualified by administrators participated in this research project. The intrinsic qualities listed by the respondents were varied, and the researcher combined the various responses in the category "intrinsic qualities" for data display. The researcher identified the various characteristics mentioned by the participants and labeled the category for analysis purposes.

These characteristics included many different qualities, from sense of humor to strong work ethic, and from confidence in their teaching ability to being compassionate to others, with a final result of more than 16 different intrinsic characteristics listed. The same was true for the category of pedagogy. The researcher combined responses that included items such as knowledge of teaching strategies, knowledge of assessment strategies, and knowledge of child development for the pedagogy category (Plunkett, 2004).

Figure 13.2. Characteristics of highly qualified teachers.

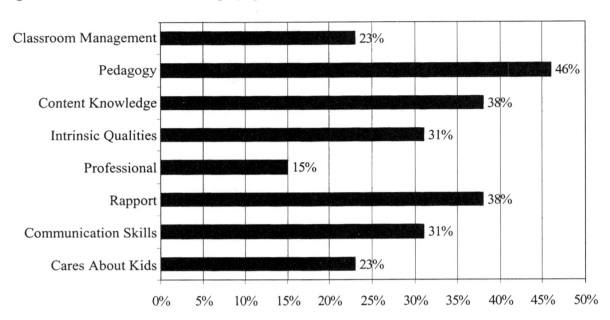

(Plunkett, 2004, p. 67.)

The value of using bar graphs, especially those that combine several individual responses into a category, is that they provide both an individual summary and a comparison of responses between categories in one visual representation.

Line graphs are another data-display technique that provide a visual comparison for the reader. Figure 13.3 on the next page provides an example selected from a dissertation referenced previously, showing the use of a line graph to depict data from two sources; in this case, superintendents and curriculum leaders in the same districts.

Figure 13.3. Comparison of construct means for superintendents and curriculum leaders.

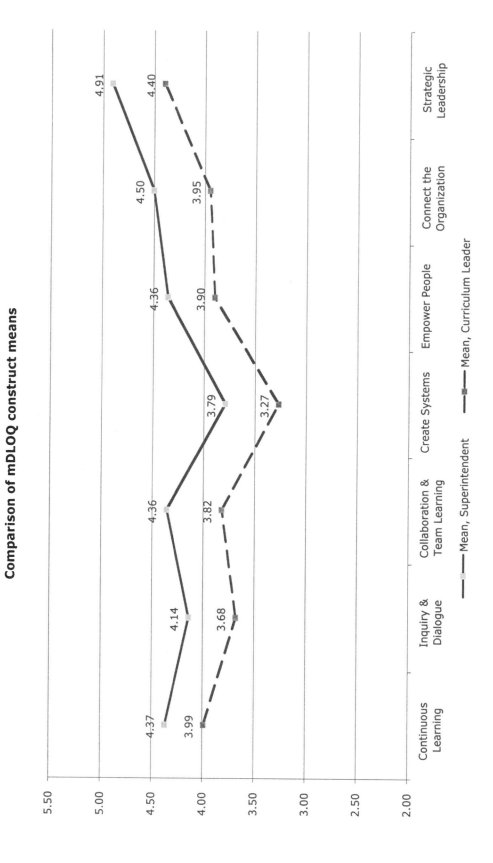

Comparison of mDLOQ construct means

(Peterson, 2006.)

Circle graphs, also known as pie charts, offer a third visual display for research data. A pie chart is a circular graph that represents all of the data in a data set (100% of the data) in a single picture, and it is so named because of the resemblance to a pie with unequal slices. The circle is divided into sections emanating from the circle's center to its rim, and each section is proportional to the quantity it represents. Together, the sections create a full circle. Figure 13.4 below is an example of a pie chart from a Wikipedia file.

Figure 13.4. Pie chart of English-speaking countries.

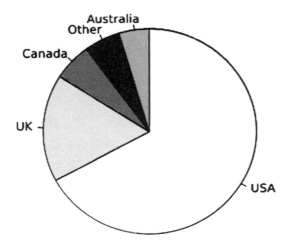

(Wikipedia, 2007.)

Scatterplots may be a helpful data-display technique, especially when correlation coefficients or regression analysis (referred to as *regression plots*) are used for testing the data. An example of a regression line in a scatterplot is provided in Figure 13.5 on the next page. This plot is from a research project that compared the results of the overall GPA and composite ACT scores for individual students. One advantage of a scatterplot of quantitative data is that it provides a visual image of what the statistic measures. A reader can see the actual trend in the data, and that trend is substantiated by the statistical test. The scatterplot also provides a reminder of the outliers in the data, those data points that do not necessarily conform to the trend. An example for the plot in Figure 13.5 on the next page would be those students who have a high GPA but score low on the ACT, or, conversely, those who have a GPA below 3.0 but score above 20 on the ACT. It allows the researcher to ask the question, "Why does that happen?"

Figure 13.5. Regression analysis of overall GPA and composite ACT.

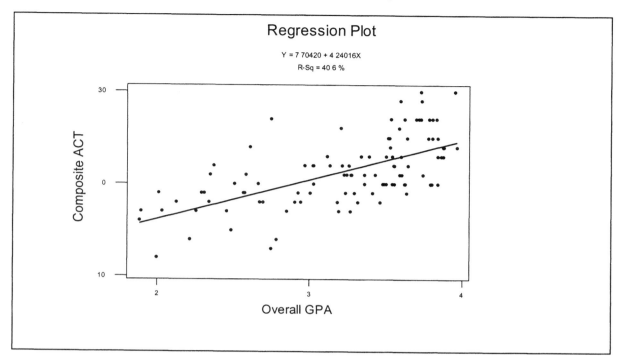

(McCarthy, 2007.)

Rule 9: *INTERPRET*

Answer the research question by thoroughly interpreting the data.

Data interpretation is the most fundamental and significant activity for a researcher in any project. The research question has been posed, the information that was identified to help answer the question has been collected or generated, and now it is time to make sense of those data in order to answer the question.

Data interpretation is talking about the data in research terms, with the research question or problem as the organizing vehicle. The researcher needs to allow the data to talk by way of creating categories or themes that emerge from the data and relate to the construct or concepts that have been created for the research design. These categories or themes flow from the analysis phase.

An example of data interpretation may be provided from a study of the impact of the standards movement on school districts and the accompanying accountability to standards imposed by local, state, and federal policy. Perceptions of teachers and administrators were collected from surveys and interviews, then were used to determine a number of strands of the standards movement in order to gauge its effectiveness. Data interpretation pointed to possible strengths and weaknesses in the implementation process regarding standards-based education and the communications systems that guided its implementation. The categories or themes that emerged from this interpretation stage included the impact on curriculum, equity, resources, assessment, accountability, time, and communication.

Presented below are the researcher's thoughts on each of these themes as she carried out her data interpretation (Fondell, 2004).

Impact on Curriculum. According to the survey respondents, the quality of the standards and benchmarks in the targeted district was acceptable. At least 75% of teachers and administrators responded that they agreed or strongly agreed with every statement that addressed the clarity of the standards and benchmarks, the teachers' and administrators' ability to understand the performance standards associated with the standards and benchmarks, and the quality of the standards and benchmarks in terms of addressing thinking skills and problem solving. In addition, both groups perceived the alignment process as successful.

Equity. The issue of equity brought a different perception. When it came to assessing student achievement levels according to standards, a greater number of teacher respondents perceived that the achievement gap (because of race, poverty, language, background, or gender) was closing, as evidenced in their classroom assessments, than did teachers who perceived that gap closing when it came to state assessments. The perceptions of the administrators likewise differed in regard to the achievement gap, with more than half of the administrators believing the narrowing of the gap to be evident in classroom assessment.

Resources. The teachers in this study seemed to feel the lack of resources more strongly than administrators in every area except that of time for collaboration. Whereas administrators expressed a positive view of the availability of resources, the percentage of administrators expressing more negative perceptions regarding time for collaboration was larger than the percentage of teachers responding negatively.

Assessment. The teachers surveyed expressed between 25% and 42% disagreement in several key statements concerning assessment and accountability. Respondents did not know if state assessments measured what was taught in the district schools, nor if state, district, and classroom assessments collectively provided an adequate profile of student, school, and district performance. A major concern for administrators regarding assessment and accountability was that state assessments were not measuring what was taught in the district schools. The lack of confidence in the district's assessment and accountability system was highlighted in the survey results. The results indicate a strong need for staff development in the area of assessment so that teachers and administrators in the district would become more knowledgeable of state and district assessment practices and more capable of using test data to plan for curriculum and instruction.

Accountability. According to respondent perceptions, two additional needs in the district were for teachers to meet regularly with other teachers in their content area and grade level to discuss students' progress and adjust instruction as needed, and also for the school to provide adequate remediation for students who need extra support to meet high standards. These seem to be two very critical pieces of the process for full implementation of standards-based education in any district, and the issues that could make or break standards-based education in general.

Time. If roadblocks to full implementation of standards-based education in a district are to be avoided, attention needs to be directed to those perceptions of teachers and administrators which cause the most discontent and frustration. Most of the key frustrations seemed to center on the element of time and stress: time involved in implementation that was an infringement on already overworked teachers; trying to teach too much with too little time; and the stress of accountability.

Communication. A 10% minority responded with "I don't know" to many key items in the survey. That type of response would indicate the need for more information or better communication within the district. One example is communication about the use of the standards and benchmark documents and how the curriculum is aligned with the standards and benchmarks. Responsibility for teaching to the standards and shared accountability also need to be communicated to all staff (pp. 45–54).

In this example, the researcher separated the survey and interview results that dealt with one or more of the issue areas, and those areas became the themes for interpretation. By outlining the interpretive results, the researcher is able to move to the final stage of the research process: the determination of the conclusions and recommendations. Interpretation is a middle stage between presenting the data and either drawing conclusions or answering the research question. Interpretation is very dependent on the data, and it is important for the researcher to make informed, data-driven assumptions about themes or categories prior to reaching conclusions.

Rule 10: *SYNTHESIZE*

Determine closure to the project by synthesizing the findings.

Synthesis is the process of combining different ideas, concepts, phenomena, or objects into a new structure. The purpose of synthesizing research data is to answer the research question and to provide thoughtful recommendations for future research. The categories for data synthesis include conclusions, implications, recommendations, and conjectures. The conclusions are the primary synthesis results because they should be direct responses to the research questions.

A dissertation studying beginning teachers' preparation in classroom management was conducted by way of a survey of all beginning teachers in a selected geographical area. Conclusions drawn from the data that answered the research question and provided closure to the project were as follows (Burhop, 2004):

> The data received to analyze how beginning teachers spend a majority of their time came from a rank-order survey to which beginning teachers responded. Beginning teachers were asked to rank instruction, classroom management, staff development, school organization, and general duties. Classroom management, by the data received in this study, has solidified itself as a major component of a beginning teacher's school day. (p. 105).... With the data supporting that beginning teachers spend adequate and important time dealing with classroom management issues, it is then important that teachers receive adequate training in that area. (p. 108).... The message sent by the respondents on this issue is relatively clear. The need for better curriculum in the area of classroom management is needed, especially in the development of a class or classes that teach students about classroom management, its styles, and how it fits to the subject area that they teach at the middle and high school levels. Observations of veteran teachers and practical field experiences were also identified by a small portion of the sample group as a vital element to teacher training. Beginning teachers responding to this survey were split among the strengths and weaknesses of their teacher education programs. Although some strengths were identified, such as hands-on experience or classroom instruction, the respondents stated there needs to be improvement in those areas in preparing preservice teachers for the classroom (p. 120).

Conclusions for a study are often followed by recommendations for action on the part of the researcher. In the study quoted above, a recommendation for teacher preparation institutions was: "Classroom management as it relates to time use and teacher effectiveness, which then relates to better student learning…must be a priority in our teacher education programs. The recommendation of this research is a call for a stronger review of the curriculum of teacher education programs" (Burhop, 2004, p. 123).

Summary

In summary, in any research project, the basic steps for a researcher to consider and check off the list include:

Rule 1: *READ*—Identify the existing theoretical basis of the research concept, then read and summarize the pertinent research literature.

Rule 2: *THINK*—Isolate the purpose of the study and identify the research topic and basic research questions.

Rule 3: *DESIGN*—Choose a research methodology that becomes the design of the study.

Rule 4: *ASSESS*—Recognize the evidence needed to answer the research questions, and identify the data sources through which the answers can be found.

Rule 5: *SELECT*—Ascertain the appropriate evidence source and identify the data sources, subjects, or research participants.

Rule 6: *COLLECT*—Gather the needed evidence by collecting the research data.

Rule 7: *ANALYZE*—Review the evidence by organizing and analyzing the data.

Rule 8: *PRESENT*—Display the research findings through a formal presentation of the data.

Rule 9: *INTERPRET*—Answer the research question by thoroughly interpreting the data.

Rule 10: *SYNTHESIZE*—Determine closure to the project by synthesizing the findings.

The annotated bibliography in Chapter 14 provides references and resources that the reader may use to expand her or his knowledge of any of the identified research topics, and will be helpful in expanding a researcher's knowledge of a particular aspect of research selected for further study.

Exercise for Chapter 13

1. What are some potential data sources for the following topics?
   - teacher mentoring
   - administrative contracts
   - student test scores
   - policy requirements for classrooms

2. Design comparative studies for the following pairs of constructs:
   - job satisfaction and salary
   - time on task and pupil learning
   - class size and student reading scores
   - student teaching and first-year teachers

3. Describe the contents of a research report based on:
   - interview data
   - survey data
   - budget analysis
   - federal and state policy

4. Describe how data analysis may be used to support informed conclusions, and discuss how researchers may abuse data to reach unwarranted conclusions.

REFERENCES FOR CHAPTER 13

Bates, R. T. (2006). *The perceptions of sitting and aspiring African American superintendents: Their motivations and barriers.* Unpublished doctoral dissertation, Edgewood College, Madison, WI.

Brown, S. R. (2006). *The rural Wisconsin school district superintendent and school business management: A study of knowledge, training and essential job skill acquisition.* Unpublished doctoral dissertation, Edgewood College, Madison, WI.

Burhop, K. T. (2004). *Beginning teachers' perceptions in southwest Wisconsin of their classroom management training by institutions of higher education.* Unpublished doctoral dissertation, Edgewood College, Madison, WI.

Decker, R. G. (2007). *Teacher perceptions of democratic principles in Romanian schools.* Unpublished doctoral dissertation, Edgewood College, Madison, WI.

Draper, N. R., & Smith, H. (1966). *Applied regression analysis.* New York: John Wiley & Sons, Inc.

Florian, G. (2005). *The effects of a teacher mentoring program on teacher retention in high-poverty, urban schools.* Unpublished doctoral dissertation, Edgewood College, Madison, WI.

Fondell, J. A. (2004). *Teachers' and administrators' perceptions of the standards movement in a Wisconsin school district.* Unpublished doctoral dissertation, Edgewood College, Madison, WI.

Hoese, J. (2006). *Is there a difference in achievement scores between high-spending and low-spending school districts on the Wisconsin knowledge and concepts exam?* Unpublished doctoral dissertation, Edgewood College, Madison, WI.

Jorgensen, L. A. (2006). *Rural high school principals' perceptions of organizational changes needed to retain rural teachers in North Dakota.* Unpublished doctoral dissertation, Edgewood College, Madison, WI.

Kelly, B. E. (2007). *Factors that influence the referral of elementary African American males to special education: A reflection of the pre-referral process.* Unpublished doctoral dissertation, Edgewood College, Madison, WI.

Koehler, A. J. (2006). *Principal behaviors and actions that influence the successful implementation of accountability practices in public schools.* Unpublished doctoral dissertation, Edgewood College, Madison, WI.

McCarthy, D. P., Jr. (2007). *The relationships among traditional college predictive indicators and the tenth grade Wisconsin knowledge and concepts examination.* Unpublished doctoral dissertation, Edgewood College, Madison, WI.

Peterson, T. J. (2006). *Leading forward, thinking forward: Systems thinking and 21st century skill implementation.* Unpublished doctoral dissertation, Edgewood College, Madison, WI.

Plunkett, C. E. (2004). *What are the characteristics of a highly qualified teacher and how do we help maintain that status?* Unpublished doctoral dissertation, Edgewood College, Madison, WI.

Richey, M. A. (2006). *How open enrollment affects a medium sized school district in northern Wisconsin.* Unpublished doctoral dissertation, Edgewood College, Madison, WI.

Rugotska, L. (2005). *A case study of teacher collaboration in the middle grades.* Unpublished doctoral dissertation, Edgewood College, Madison, WI.

Smolek, S. (2005). *The impact of no child left behind on rural superintendents' abilities to implement the Wisconsin administrative standards.* Unpublished doctoral dissertation, Edgewood College, Madison, WI.

Wade, J. H. (2005). *Perceptions of participants in alternative certification programs.* Unpublished doctoral dissertation, Edgewood College, Madison, WI.

Wikipedia (2007). *English speaking dialects.* http://en.wikipedia.org/wiki/Image:English_dialects1997.svg

Notes

Chapter 14

Annotated Bibliography

The books that are referenced and summarized in this annotated bibliography represent some of the more current and complete works in the specialized areas of research. The entries are divided into the following categories:

- Research Foundations
- Behavioral Research
- Library Research
- Statistical Analysis
- Quantitative Research
- Qualitative Research
- Survey Research
- Interview Research
- Case-Study Research
- Reading and Writing Research Reports
- Educational Research
- Research Ethics
- Action Research
- Dissertation Research

While not an exhaustive bibliography of research techniques, this brief annotated list should provide the reader with a beginning set of resources for reading and conducting research. Most of the listed texts have a bibliography of their own that may be used to expand the reader's reference list on the specific topic.

Resources used to identify and select references for this chapter include:

- The *Research Bibliography* prepared by the Research Resources Committee, Library Research Section, MLA, updated in 2002 by Jana Allcock, Alice Edwards, Mary Gillaspy, and Eileen Stanley. The URL for this list, which is periodically updated, is http://research.mlanet.org/resbib.html#books. This resource contains many more research references that may be of interest or use to the reader.
- Action Research and Evaluation Online (AREOL), a Web site that contains a listing of recent books on action research and related topics along with brief summaries.

The URL for AREOL is http://www.scu.edu.au/schools/gcm/ar/areol/areolhome. html. This is a resource file housed at Southern Cross University in Australia that supports a regular public program for action research and evaluation online, offered twice a year, in mid-February and mid-July. For details, email Bob Dick at bdick@scu.edu.au or bd@uq.net.au.

- Publishers' Web sites that contain brief summaries of the textbooks published by different publishing houses. Readers looking for textbooks on specific research topics would do well to visit the Web sites of the major publishers, on which the current texts in the annotated list presented here may be found, along with other references.

- The author's professional analysis of textbooks used for various research courses at the college and graduate school levels. (For format and length consistency, the authors edited some of the data obtained from the sources listed above.)

Research Foundations

Campbell, D. T., & Stanley, J. C. (1963). *Experimental and quasi-experimental designs for research*. Boston: Houghton Mifflin Company.

> This 71-page book is a classic and a standard reference for research design. It is the foundation of the quasi-experimental approach. The authors outline 16 basic experimental designs for research and provide 12 common threats to valid inference that all researchers should know.

Creswell, J. W. (2002). *Research design: Qualitative, quantitative, and mixed methods approaches* (2nd ed.). Thousand Oaks, CA: Sage Publications.

> Every chapter shows how to implement a mixed-method design as well as how to tackle quantitative and qualitative approaches; ethical issues have been added to a new section in Chapter 3; writing tips and considerations have been expanded and moved to the first part of the book to ensure that research plans and proposals start in the right direction; and the latest developments in qualitative inquiry (advocacy, participatory, and emancipatory approaches) have been added to Chapter 10.

Eden, C., & Spender, J. C. (Eds.) (1998). *Managerial and organizational cognition: Theory, methods, and research*. London: Sage Publications.

> Readers get a good understanding of the important theoretical and methodological challenges of cognitive research. Examples of research questions that

can be pursued from a cognitive perspective are provided. The book chapters cover causal mapping for organizational and managerial decision-making.

Fawcett, J., & Downs, F. S. (1999). *The relationship of theory and research* (3rd ed.). Philadelphia: F.A. Davis.

The relationship between conceptual models, middle-range theories, and empirical research methods is provided. The authors discuss how to integrate research findings and present guidelines for writing research reports. Appends several sample research papers with Fawcett's analyses.

Gall, M. D., Borg, W. R., & Gall, J. P. (2003). *Educational research: An introduction* (7th ed.). Boston: Allyn & Bacon.

A comprehensive introduction to the major research methods and types of data analysis used today, this text provides in-depth coverage of all facets of research, from the epistemology of scientific inquiry to research design, data collection, analysis, and reporting of the completed study.

Huck, S. W. (2004). *Reading statistics and research* (4th ed.). Boston: Allyn & Bacon.

This text shows consumers of research how to read, understand, and critically evaluate the statistical information and research results contained in technical research reports. The text is also useful for applied researchers who need advice on how to analyze their own data and summarize their empirical findings. Students in education and other disciplines need to learn how to interpret and use statistics and research, but often, they do not have any way to begin this process. This text clearly and methodically presents basic statistical and research concepts and illustrates how to employ them in making sound educational decisions.

Isaac, S., & Michael, W. B. (1995). *Handbook in research and evaluation* (3rd ed.). San Diego: EdITS Publishers.

This book provides an overview of major methods of research, statistical analysis, and measurement instruments. It provides an overview of alternative approaches, exhibits of reference models, and listings of strengths and weaknesses of different models of research. There are some very useful summaries of common problems and solutions in designing, conducting, analyzing, and communicating the results of research projects.

Kerlinger, F. N. (1992). *Foundations of behavioral research* (4th ed.). New York: Holt, Rinehart and Winston.

This volume includes everything a researcher needs to know about the methods and principles of behavioral research. The examples are extremely useful in facilitating the understanding of research methods and the analysis of data. This comprehensive guide can be used for work in psychology, nursing, sociology, market research, and other areas.

Lattal, K., & Perone, M. (Eds.). (1998). *Handbook of research methods in human operant behavior*. New York: Plenum Press.

Methodological issues arise in any discussion of research on human behavior. This book addresses many of these questions with 19 experts in the field. It is a valuable resource for researchers who want to bridge laboratory developments with applied study.

Leedy, P. D., & Ormrod, J. E. (2005). *Practical research: Planning and design* (8th ed.). Upper Saddle River, NJ: Pearson-Prentice Hall.

Excerpts from actual research projects guide the reader through all phases of the research process in this book. It is a manual designed to help research students in any discipline to understand the fundamental structure of quality research and the methodical process that leads to genuinely significant results. It guides the reader, step-by-step, from the selection of a problem to study, through the process of conducting authentic research, to the preparation of a completed report, with practical suggestions based on a solid theoretical framework and sound pedagogy. This text shows two things: (1) that quality research demands planning and design; and (2) how the reader's own research projects can be executed effectively and professionally.

Newman, I. (1998). *Qualitative-quantitative research methodology: Exploring the interactive continuum*. Carbondale, IL: Southern Illinois University Press.

The centerpiece of this book is the author's graphic representation of inquiry as a cycle of steps that each type of method takes in a different order and manner. Quantitative inquiry is depicted as beginning with a theory to be tested, while qualitative inquiry is shown as starting with data collection and proceeding to the construction of new theory.

Patten, M. (2005). *Understanding research methods: An overview of the essentials* (5th ed.). Glendale, CA: Pyrczak Publishing.

> Good reading for the beginner in research. Patten introduces 13 different topics, such as theory, hypotheses, variables, experimental and nonexperimental studies; differentiates between quantitative and qualitative research; and discusses ethical issues in research. Of special interest are the 13 topics on understanding statistics.

Behavioral Research

Ader, H., & Mellenbergh, G. (Eds.). (1999). *Research methodology in the social, behavioural, and life sciences.* London: Sage Publications.

> An overview of behavioral research, including social sciences and life sciences, is provided. This text is a good introduction to behavioral research. Chapters include information on metadata, experimental design, measurement models, meta-analysis, graphs, well-defined models of data sets, causality and structural equation models, and more.

Babbie, E. R. (1998). *The basis of social research* (8th ed.). Belmont, CA: Wadsworth.

> Behavioral research is carried out in the world of social sciences. This is a good general text on the fundamental logic and skill of this type of research. It includes easy-to-understand discussions of elementary statistics and a comprehensive glossary of terms.

Eichler, M. (1991). *Nonsexist research methods: A practical guide.* New York: Routledge.

> Researchers must take care to eliminate bias in their work. This book provides a systematic approach to identifying and eliminating sexist bias in social science research. Chapters are problem defined. The book includes a Nonsexist Research Checklist designed for use in the research process.

Orcher, L. T. (2005). *Conducting research: Social and behavioral science methods.* Glendale, CA: Pyrczak Publishing.

> This book takes students through the steps from selecting a research topic to writing the final research report. Balanced coverage of quantitative and qualitative methods makes this book appropriate for all students.

Paul, J. (2005). *Introduction to the philosophies of research and criticism in education and the social sciences.* Upper Saddle River, NJ: Pearson-Merrill-Prentice Hall.

> Intended both for education students who aspire to become researchers and for those who simply need to read and understand research literature, this book focuses on the underlying perspectives justifying the major approaches currently being used in educational research. Introductory chapters lay the foundation for exploring varying research perspectives. Nine specific perspectives on research are examined, through discussions written by senior scholars known for their expertise in the perspective. A guided tour of criticism is given in which these same scholars demonstrate the use of the critical method by critiquing six studies selected as exemplars of different research approaches.

Somekh, B., & Lewin, C. (Eds.). (2005). *Research methods in the social sciences.* Thousand Oaks, CA: Sage Publications.

> Both qualitative and quantitative research methodologies are introduced, and readers are encouraged to become members of a community of researchers engaged in reflection on the research process. Researching in the postmodern context is covered, including deconstruction, hermeneutics, poststructuralism, feminism, and virtual realities, among other topics.

Tashakkori, A., & Teddlie, C. (Eds.). (2003). *Handbook of mixed methods in social and behavioral research.* Thousand Oaks, CA: Sage Publications.

> This handbook is a collection of articles by leading scholars on what has come to be known as the third methodological movement in social research. Aimed at surveying the differing viewpoints and disciplinary approaches of mixed methods, this book examines mixed methods from the research enterprise, to paradigmatic issues, to application. The book also discusses the strengths and weaknesses of mixed-methods designs and provides an array of specific examples in a variety of disciplines, from psychology to nursing. It can be used either as a pedagogical tool or as a reference for researchers because it is rich in examples and includes a glossary, easy-to-follow diagrams, and tables to help readers become more familiar with the language and controversies in this evolving area.

Trochim, W., & Donnelly, J. P. (2006). *The research methods knowledge base* (3rd ed.). Stamford, CT: Atomic Dog Publishing.

This third edition provides coverage of quantitative methods and enhanced coverage of qualitative methods. It can be used in a variety of disciplines and is ideal for a comprehensive introductory undergraduate or graduate-level course. Through its conversational, informal style, it makes material that is often challenging for students both accessible and understandable. The book covers everything from the development of a research question to the writing of a final report, describing both practical and technical issues of sampling, measurement, design, and analysis.

Library Research

Badke, W. B. (2004). *Research strategies: Finding your way through the information fog* (2nd ed.). New York: iUniverse, Inc.

The author covers aspects of research, including finding a topic, searching databases, using a computerized periodical index, using the Internet, taking and organizing notes, and writing the paper. Formats for papers are provided in an appendix. The author covers most of the basics and procedures of doing research, and two research case studies are presented, including reference sources, topical analysis, book searches, and periodical literature.

Beasley, D. (2000). *Beasley's guide to library research.* Toronto: University of Toronto Press.

An invaluable "how to" resource for library-based research, Beasley includes useful information on the many services of research libraries and includes computer databases and online computer searches.

Gebhard, P. (1997). *The reference realist in library academia.* Jefferson, NC: McFarland & Company, Inc.

Search strategies and identification of reference sources are covered. Making use of information sources and the responsibility of professional librarians in working with clients are included.

Hacker, D., & Fister, B. (2002). *Research and documentation in the Electronic Age* (3rd ed.). Boston: Bedford/St. Martins.

The first part of the book lays out how to pose a research question and determine a search strategy. Part two covers how to find and evaluate resources. The authors offer a good general introduction, explaining what databases are and the types of resources found within them. The authors also supply strong advice and tools for previewing articles and Web sites to determine if they are sources worth using. The third part covers the academic areas of humanities, social science, and science. Each of these broad topics is broken down into specific academic areas listing important print and electronic resources. Part four covers the major citation styles of MLA, APA, Chicago, and CBE. One great feature of the documentation section is that a sample paper (including in-text citation and a list of works cited) is included for each of the styles.

List, C. (2002). *Information research* (2nd ed.). Dubuque, IA: Kendall/Hunt Publishing Company.

The updated and expanded second edition of this book is a well-organized introduction to the research process. The chapters cover how information is organized and presented, the terminology of information technology and the place of technology in the process, and the research process itself—from analyzing a research topic and choosing appropriate tools to constructing a search strategy and evaluating and citing the information retrieved from both print and electronic sources.

Statistical Analysis

Aron, A., Aron, E. N., & Coups, E. (2005). *Statistics for the behavioral and social sciences: A brief course* (3rd ed.). Upper Saddle River, NJ: Pearson.

This unique text capitalizes on a successful approach of using definitional formulas to emphasize concepts of statistics rather than rote memorization. This conceptual approach constantly reminds readers of the logic behind what they are learning. Procedures are taught verbally, numerically, and visually, which appeals to individuals with different learning styles. Focusing on understanding, the text emphasizes the intuitive, de-emphasizes the mathematical, and explains everything in clear, simple language. This text not only teaches statistics, but also prepares users to read and understand research articles.

Batavia, M. (2001). *Clinical research for health professionals: A user-friendly guide.* Boston: Butterworth-Heinemann.

This text offers a nontechnical, coherent summary of research concepts and methods, focusing on the features of good research and common mistakes. The book uses metaphors, visual images, and examples to simplify complex research concepts, and it provides computer exercises to help readers understand statistical concepts.

Box, G. E. P., Hunter, J. S., & Hunter, W. G. (2005*). Statistics for experimenters: Design, innovation, and discovery* (2nd ed.). Hoboken, NJ: Wiley-Interscience.

> A premier guide and reference for the application of statistical methods, especially as applied to experimental design, the second edition adopts the same approach as the first edition by demonstrating through worked examples, readily understood graphics, and the appropriate use of computers. Catalyzing innovation, problem solving, and discovery, the text provides experimenters with the scientific and statistical tools needed to maximize the knowledge gained from investigation and research. The authors' practical approach starts with a problem that needs to be solved, then illustrates the statistical methods best utilized in all stages of design and analysis.

Coolidge, F. L. (2006). *Statistics: A gentle introduction* (2nd ed.). Thousand Oaks, CA: Sage Publications.

> Basic statistical operations are presented in a conversational tone. The text shows how statistics do not need to be difficult or dull. Parametric and non-parametric topics are covered, including standard scores, correlation, regression analysis of variance, *t*-tests, and other statistical tests.

Cramer, D. (2003). *Advanced quantitative data analysis*. New York: Open University Press.

> A variety of statistical techniques are used to analyze quantitative data that master's students, advanced undergraduates, and researchers in the social sciences are expected to understand and undertake. This book explains these techniques, when it is appropriate to use them, how to carry them out, and how to write up the results.

Hopkins, D. K., Hopkins, B. R., & Glass, G. V. (1996). *Basic statistics for the behavioral sciences* (3rd ed.). Boston: Allyn & Bacon.

> The approach in this book is conceptual rather than mathematical. The authors stress the understanding, application, and interpretation of concepts rather than derivation and proof or hand computation. The book provides clear definitions, examples, and problem sets, and makes the reader feel better about statistics.

Keller, D. K. (2006). *The Tao of statistics: A path to understanding (with no math)*. Thousand Oaks, CA: Sage Publications.

> Statistics are provided in plain English. The text provides explanations of how statistics are used and what they mean, rather than exercises in computing statistical formulas. Both basic concepts and complex statistical models are covered.

Larose, D. T. (2004). *Discovering knowledge in data: An introduction to data mining*. Hoboken, NJ: Wiley-Interscience.

> Data preprocessing and classification, exploratory analysis, decision trees, association rules, model evaluation techniques, and other data-mining topics are covered. The powerful black-box data-mining software now available can produce disastrously misleading results unless applied by a skilled and knowledgeable analyst. This book provides both the practical experience and the theoretical insight needed to reveal valuable information hidden in large data sets. Employing a "white box" methodology with real-world case studies, this step-by-step guide walks readers through the various algorithms and statistical structures that underlie the software and presents examples of their operation on actual large data sets.

Lohninger, H. (1999). *Teach/me: Data analysis*. Berlin-New York-Tokyo: Springer-Verlag.

> This resource is a multimedia tool on the analysis of complex data in research. It includes a comprehensive, hyperlinked textbook on data analysis. Additional highlights include an open architecture for use with any teaching material, interactive examples, a course and exam designer, protection of resources by encryption, and a data laboratory with sample data sets and import function for hands-on experience. Definition of basic statistical terms, precision, linear and nonlinear models, data types, and statistical tests for parametric and nonparametric data are covered.

Lomax, R. G. (2007). *Statistical concepts: A second course* (3rd ed.). New York: Psychology Press.

> Designed for a second course in statistics, this text includes topics not ordinarily covered in basic textbooks. Examples from education and behavioral sciences are included, and tables of statistical assumptions and the effects of their violations are provided.

Maier, M. H. (1995). *The data game: Controversies in social science statistics* (2nd ed.). Armonk, NY: M. E. Sharpe.

This work provides an excellent overview of the problems of relying on statistics to provide information and solutions and gives examples of incorrect sampling, misinterpretation of data, and other interesting controversies.

Manly, B. F. J. (2004). *Multivariate statistical analysis: A primer* (3rd ed.). London: Taylor & Francis.

Multivariate methods are now widely used in the quantitative sciences as well as in statistics because of the ready availability of computer packages for performing the calculations. While access to suitable computer software is essential to using multivariate methods, using the software still requires a working knowledge of these methods and how they can be used. This text provides a concise, accessible introduction to multivariate techniques ideal for research across the range of quantitative sciences. It includes recent ideas about multivariate analyses, important new material, and updated references. It also compares and contrasts the major statistical software packages, and it provides all the data used in the book on a companion Web site.

Paulson, D. S. (2003). *Applied statistical designs for the researcher*. London: Taylor & Francis.

Showcasing a discussion of the experimental process and a review of basic statistics, this volume provides methodologies to identify general data distribution, skewness, and outliers. It features a unique classification of the nonparametric analogs of their parametric counterparts according to the strength of the collected data. It includes three varieties of the student *t* test and a comparison of two different groups with different variances, two groups with the same variance, and a matched-paired group. It introduces the analysis of variance and Latin square designs, presents screening approaches to comparing two factors and their interactions, and meta-analysis and regression analysis are considered.

Rountree, D. (2004). *Statistics without tears: A primer for nonmathematicians*. Boston: Allyn & Bacon.

This text uses words and diagrams, rather than formulas and equations, to help students from all subject areas to understand what statistics are and how to think statistically.

Sheskin, D. J. (2003). *Handbook of parametric and nonparametric statistical procedures* (3rd ed.). London: Taylor & Francis.

> The third edition provides unparalleled up-to-date coverage of more than 130 parametric and nonparametric statistical procedures, as well as many practical and theoretical issues relevant to statistical analysis. It helps the reader to decide what method of analysis to use, how to use a particular test for the first time, how to distinguish acceptable from unacceptable research, and how to interpret and better understand the results of published studies.

Sprent, P., & Smeeton, N. C. (2000). *Applied nonparametric statistical methods* (3rd ed.). London: Taylor & Francis.

> This text emphasizes better use of significance tests and explains the rationale of procedures with a minimum of mathematical detail, making it not only an outstanding textbook, but also an up-to-date reference for professionals who conduct their own statistical analyses. There is expanded coverage of topics such as ethical considerations, calculation of power and of sample sizes needed, statistical packages, and sections on the analysis of angular data, the use of capture-recapture methods, and the measurement of agreement between observers, runs tests, and regression diagnostics.

Sprinthall, R. C. (2003). *Basic statistical analysis* (7th ed.). Boston: Allyn & Bacon.

> The goal of this book is to demystify and present statistics in a clear, cohesive manner. The reader is presented with rules of evidence and the logic behind those rules. The book is divided into three major units: Descriptive Statistics, Inferential Statistics, and Advanced Topics in Inferential Statistics.

Urdan, T. C. (2005). *Statistics in plain English* (2nd ed.). New York: Psychology Press.

> This text is a brief and simple overview of statistics. How the statistical tests and formulas work and how they are interpreted is covered. Statistics are described, with explanations of how they work, and examples are provided for each statistical process.

Quantitative Research

Black, T. R. (1999). *Doing quantitative research in the social sciences: An integrated approach to research design, measurement, and statistics.* Thousand Oaks, CA: Sage Publications.

This text provides a comprehensive and integrated approach to using quantitative methods in the social sciences. The author's method focuses on designing and executing research so that issues such as planning, sampling, designing measurement instruments, choosing statistical tests, and interpreting results are integrated into the research process. Research design issues are introduced along with statistical procedures necessary for data analysis that develop analytical skills and decision-making powers. It includes a wide range of examples and activities, providing the student with a solid foundation in research design, measurement, and statistics.

Chiulli, R. M. (1999). *Quantitative analysis: An introduction.* London: Taylor & Francis.

Written in a lecture format with solved problems at the end of each chapter, this book surveys quantitative modeling and decision-analysis techniques. It serves to familiarize readers who need quantitative techniques utilized in planning and optimizing complex systems, as well as students experiencing the subject for the first time. A background in calculus is not required because the book allows the reader to comprehend the material through examples and problems, and also demonstrates the value and shortcomings of many methods.

Morgan, S. E., Reichert, T., & Harrison, T. R. (2002). *From numbers to words: Reporting statistical results for the social sciences.* Boston: Allyn & Bacon.

This text is a valuable reference tool that guides students through drafting the results of quantitative experiments and investigations. Everyone who conducts quantitative social science research writes up the results of her or his experiments and investigations, but most texts offer little guidance on how to do so. This supplemental text teaches students how to draft the results of statistical experiments and investigations in text or visual format. This how-to book is designed to be used in combination with primary statistics or research methods texts and also serves as an effective reference for students new to statistics and for experienced researchers.

Schwab, D. (1999). *Research methods for organizational behavior*. Mahwah, NJ: Lawrence Erlbaum Associates.

> While the focus of this book is on quantitative research, readers with various levels of research knowledge can use it successfully. The first 15 chapters introduce basic research topics. The final section contains four short chapters that extend the discussion of a basic topic. This book covers applied issues usually missing in research texts, such as cleaning data, handling missing data, coding data, and transforming data.

Tabachnick, B. G., & Fidell, L. S. (2006). *Using multivariate statistics* (5th ed.). Boston: Allyn & Bacon.

> This text takes a practical approach to multivariate data analysis, with an introduction to the most commonly encountered statistical and multivariate techniques. It provides practical guidelines for conducting numerous types of multivariate statistical analyses and it gives syntax and output for accomplishing many analyses through the most recent releases of SAS and SPSS. The book maintains its practical approach, focusing on the benefits and limitations of applications of a technique to a data set—when, why, and how to do it. Overall, it provides a timely and comprehensive introduction to today's most commonly encountered statistical and multivariate techniques while assuming only a limited knowledge of higher-level mathematics.

Williams, F., & Monge, P. (2001). *Reasoning with statistics: How to read quantitative research* (5th ed.) London: Harcourt College Publishers.

> This text is designed to help readers become knowledgeable of cross-curriculum quantitative research literature. It provides a clear, inviting view of quantitative research strategies for those who may not have a mathematical background. The authors impart a conceptual understanding rather than teach calculation methods. Examples are cross-curriculum and generic. Its strength is that it is very brief and does not overwhelm with too much detail.

Qualitative Research

Berg, B. L. (2000). *Qualitative research methods for the social sciences* (4th ed.). Boston: Allyn & Bacon.

> With considerable breadth, this practical book covers a variety of qualitative techniques, including ethnography, historiography, action research, grounded

theory, and case study. It examines interviewing and focus groups. It discusses such topics as ethics, content analysis, and the writing of research papers.

Bogdan, R., & Bilen, S. K. (2003). *Qualitative research in education: An introduction to theory and methods* (4th ed.). Boston: Allyn & Bacon.

The purpose of this introductory-level text is to provide the reader with a background for understanding the uses of qualitative research in education (and other professions), to examine its theoretical and historical underpinnings, and to provide the how-to's of conducting qualitative research. This edition places qualitative research within current debates about research methods and alternative ways of gathering knowledge.

Briguela, B. M., Stewart, J. D., Carrillo, R. G., & Berger, J. G. (2000). *Acts of inquiry in qualitative research.* Cambridge, MA: Harvard Education Press.

This comprehensive book from the editors of the *Harvard Educational Review* examines the nature and uses of qualitative research. Researchers, practitioners, participants, and scholars address the proliferation of methodologies, ethical and disciplinary concerns, and issues of equity and diversity such research raises from a wide variety of viewpoints. *Acts of Inquiry in Qualitative Research* also presents a broad assortment of articles by authors from several academic disciplines who examine their own fields' contribution to qualitative research in the past, as well as future trends. The book is divided into six sections reflecting different acts of inquiry in qualitative research habits of thought and work, ethics and validity, the relationships of the researcher and the participants, data collection, data analysis and interpretations, and the uses of research. *Acts of Inquiry in Qualitative Research* is unique in bringing together a rich collection of theoretical arguments and case studies, which makes it an invaluable resource for teaching, learning, and practicing qualitative research.

Bryman, A. (1992). *Quantity and quality in social research.* London–New York: Routledge.

This text is relevant to any social science and is an excellent beginning point for learning about qualitative research and mixed methodologies. The author provides excellent research examples of every point made and includes a comprehensive 20-page bibliography for readers to further their study.

Creswell, J. (1998). *Qualitative inquiry and research design: Choosing among five traditions.* Thousand Oaks, CA: Sage Publications.

> Creswell focuses on five separate types of qualitative research in this book. They include biography, phenomenology, ethnography, case study, and grounded theory. Methods and criteria of selecting an appropriate technique and the values of each method are provided.

Denzin, N. K., & Lincoln, Y. S. (Eds.). (2005). *The SAGE handbook of qualitative research* (3rd ed.). Thousand Oaks, CA: Sage Publications.

> Once again, the editors have put together a volume that represents the state of the art for the theory and practice of qualitative inquiry. Built on the considerable foundations of the landmark first two editions, the third edition moves qualitative research boldly into the 21st century. The editors and authors ask how the practices of qualitative inquiry can be used to address issues of social justice in this century. There are 14 totally new topics, including indigenous research, institutional review boards and human-subject research, critical and performance ethnography, arts-based inquiry, narrative inquiry, Foucault, the ethics and strategies of online research, cultural and investigative poetics, and the politics of evaluation.

Glesne, C. (2006). *Becoming qualitative researchers: An introduction* (3rd ed.). New York: Allyn & Bacon.

> The third edition of this basic text provides an understanding of qualitative research methods and explores the diverse possibilities within this inquiry approach. This text covers the range of possibilities along with numerous exercises that offer beginning students the opportunity to practice and refine the skills of a qualitative researcher. The wealth of examples in the text is exceptional, as is the accessible writing style.

Gummesson, E. (2000). *Qualitative methods in management research* (2nd ed.). Thousand Oaks, CA: Sage Publications.

> This is the second edition of a book noted for its wide-ranging examination of qualitative research and its philosophy and practice, with reference to management research. The book takes into account issues of both management consultancy and applied research and effectively integrates the two traditions.

Lee, T. W. (1999). *Using qualitative methods in organizational research.* Thousand Oaks, CA: Sage Publications.

> The concepts of reliability and validity in qualitative research are examined, and exemplary methods of generating and testing theory are presented. The use of focus groups, case studies, and interviews is included.

Lichtman, M. (2006). *Qualitative research in education.* Thousand Oaks, CA: Sage Publications.

> By blending history and tradition with some practical ideas, the book looks at the past and toward the future to give readers a sense of the field and how it has changed. It aims to help education students become savvy qualitative researchers and includes group and individual activities that provide practical suggestions for building the required skills. The major topics of gathering, organizing, and analyzing results are examined to provide practical information on conducting qualitative research. Actual examples and illustrations help the user to translate abstract ideas into concrete suggestions.

Marshall, C., & Rossman, G. B. (1999). *Designing qualitative research* (3rd ed.). Thousand Oaks, CA: Sage Publications.

> This book takes the reader through the qualitative process, including building the conceptual framework; setting up the research design; data-collection methods; recording, managing, and analyzing data; as well as planning time and resources.

Merriam, S. B. (2002). *Qualitative research in practice: Examples for discussion and analysis.* San Francisco: Jossey-Bass.

> Examples of qualitative research are provided, with comments and reflections from the researcher. The different types of qualitative research are discussed.

Miles, M. B., & Huberman, A. M. (1994). *Qualitative data analysis: An expanded sourcebook of new methods* (2nd ed.). Thousand Oaks, CA: Sage Publications.

> Bringing the art of qualitative analysis up-to-date, this edition adds hundreds of new techniques, ideas, and references developed in the past decade to the corpus contained in the first. The increase in the use of computers in qualitative analysis is also reflected in this volume. There is an extensive appendix on criteria to choose from among the currently available analysis packages. Through examples from a host of social science and professional disciplines, this text

remains the most comprehensive and complete treatment of this topic currently available to scholars and applied researchers.

Patton, M. Q. (2002). *Qualitative research and evaluation methods* (3rd ed.). Thousand Oaks, CA: Sage Publications.

> An expanded version of what was already a valuable resource, this is an entertaining and practical account of qualitative research methods in general, including qualitative evaluation. The book presents a compelling defense of the use of qualitative data in some research and evaluation situations. This revision takes account of recent development in qualitative research and evaluation in the breadth of its coverage.

Willis, J. W. (2007). *Foundations of qualitative research: Interpretive and critical approaches.* Thousand Oaks, CA: Sage Publications.

> Key theoretical and epistemological concepts are introduced through use of historical and real-world examples. General guidelines for seven qualitative research frameworks are covered, together with the conceptual foundations of interpretive, critical, and postpositivist paradigms.

Survey Research

American Statistical Association (1998). *What is a survey?* Alexandria, VA: ASA Section on Survey Research Methods. http://gill.amstat.org/sections/srms/whatsurvey.html.

> This is a series of 10 brochures on survey topics including quality of surveys, focus groups, telephone surveys, margin of error, and other topics. The American Statistical Association offers these brochures online, and they are free to the public.

Fowler, F. (2002). *Survey research methods* (3rd ed.). Thousand Oaks, CA: Sage Publications.

> Researchers who want to collect and analyze survey data are provided a foundation for evaluating how each aspect of a survey can affect its precision, accuracy, and credibility. Includes the latest options available to researchers in using the computer and Internet for surveys. Emphasizes the importance of minimizing sampling errors through superior question design.

Fowler, F. J. (1995). *Improving survey questions: Design and evaluation.* Thousand Oaks, CA: Sage Publications.

> This book is part of the SAGE applied social research methods series. It de-

scribes the development of a survey interview form, focusing on how to structure questions that lead to the responses desired. It includes procedures to improve the quality of survey data for quantitative analysis and techniques of evaluation to use when analyzing and interpreting the data.

Thomas, S. J. (2004). *Using Web and paper questionnaires for data-based decision-making.* Thousand Oaks, CA: Corwin Press.

This practical handbook provides suggestions for using both Web-based and paper-based questionnaires for data gathering. There is good guidance for planning a survey research project and for communicating the results to a variety of audiences.

Interview Research

Holstein, J. A., & Gubrium, J. F. (1995). *The active interview.* Thousand Oaks, CA: Sage Publications.

Those who use field interviews as a research method often have limited access to their survey participants, so they must make the most of the time spent together. This text includes suggestions on language to use during interviewing and hints for conducting better field interviews.

Houtkoop-Steenstra, H. (2000). *Interaction and the standardized survey interview: The living questionnaire.* New York: Cambridge University Press.

Through the use of in-depth qualitative conversation analysis (CA), the author provides a strong voice that illustrates the weaknesses in the assumptions and practices of standardized interviews. Survey interviewing is an important source of social science data, and the state of survey interviewing is reliant on standardization. The author advocates administering survey questions via flexible interviewing.

Kvale, S. (1996). *Interviews: An introduction to qualitative research interviewing.* Thousand Oaks, CA: Sage Publications.

Originally a Swedish publication, this covers theoretical aspects of interviewing, ethical issues involved, and improving interview reports.

Seidman, I. E. (1991). *Interviewing as qualitative research: A guide for researchers in education and the social sciences.* New York: Teachers College Press.

Much of the research conducted in education is through interviews and surveys. This book provides a step-by-step introduction to the research process using in-depth interviewing in research. It also discusses specific interviewing skills and links them to important issues in interviewing and qualitative research.

Case-Study Research

Bassey, M. (1999). *Case study research in educational settings*. Philadelphia: Open University Press.

> The case study has long been a research tool. This book offers new insights into the case study as a tool of educational research and suggests how it can be a prime research strategy for developing educational theory that illuminates policy and enhances practice. Structured, narrative, and descriptive approaches to writing case-study reports are also discussed, and the value of conducting an audit is considered.

Gomm, R., Hammersley, M., & Foster, P. (Eds.) (2000). *Case study method: Key issues, key texts*. Thousand Oaks, CA: Sage Publications.

> The authors of the collected papers in this text include Robert Stake, Yvonna Lincoln, Egon Guba, Ralph Turner, and Howard Becker. The papers are grouped into two categories: intrinsic case study and generalizability, and case study and theory. Both instances offer a variety of views and are summarized at the end of each section by the editors. There is an annotated bibliography that is valuable to researchers.

Stake, R. E. (1995). *The art of case study research: Perspectives on practice*. Thousand Oaks, CA: Sage Publications.

> The title is well chosen. This is a clearly written account that deals with the style and culture of research as well as the pragmatic details. It is a practical and readable overview from an experienced researcher.

Yin, R. K. (2003). *Case study research design and methods* (3rd ed.). Thousand Oaks, CA: Sage Publications.

> This comprehensive presentation covers all aspects of the case-study method—from problem definition, design, data collection to data analysis, composition, and reporting. It also traces the uses and importance of case studies to a wide range of disciplines—from sociology, psychology, and history to management, planning, social work, and education. There are references to examples of actual case studies that appear in the companion volume, *Applications of Case Study Research*, Second Edition (Sage, 2003).

Yin, R. K. (2003). *Applications of case study research* (2nd ed.). Thousand Oaks, CA: Sage Publications.

> Written to augment the author's earlier, extremely successful volume, this applications book presents and discusses new case studies from a wide array of topics offering a variety of examples or applications of case-study research methods. These applications demonstrate specific techniques or principles that are integral to the case-study method. Through these practical applications, the reader is able to identify solutions to problems encountered during this type of research.

Reading and Writing Research Reports

American Psychological Association. (2001). *Publication manual of the American Psychological Association* (5th ed.). Washington, DC: American Psychological Association.

> Rules for writing research reports are provided. They are drawn from extensive reviews of existing literature and provide an extensive guide for writing research reports. The fifth edition adds formats of electronic and legal references, along with content on methods and case-study reports.

Berry, R. (2004). *The research project: How to write it* (5th ed.). London and New York: Routledge, a Taylor & Francis Group.

> Now in its fifth edition, this guide to project work continues to be an indispensable resource for all students undertaking research. Guiding the reader from preliminary stages to completion, the book sets out in clear and concise terms the main tasks involved in conducting a research project; covering choice of topic; using the library effectively; taking notes; shaping and composing the project; providing footnotes, documentation, a bibliography; and avoiding common pitfalls. This edition features a chapter on making the most out of the Internet by knowing where to start assessing the quality of the material found there. Other features include a model example of a well-researched, clearly written paper with notes and bibliography, and a chapter on getting published in a learned journal for more advanced researchers.

Bracey, G. W. (2006). *Reading educational research: How to avoid getting statistically snookered.* Portsmouth, NH: Heinemann.

> The advent of the No Child Left Behind legislation led to the need for educators to be able to read and use educational research. This text covers understanding data use, the construction of scientifically based research, how vari-

ables are used, determining whether a study is meaningful for use, and assessing the data derived from standardized tests.

Day, R. A. (1998). *How to write & publish a scientific paper* (5th ed.). Phoenix, AZ: Oryx Press.

A clearly written guide, this publication presents a brief history of scientific writing, then succinctly takes the reader through a series of how-to chapters—from preparing a title to keyboarding the manuscript. Includes details on writing book reviews, theses, conference reports, and review papers, as well as how to prepare poster sessions. Appendices of unique value cover abbreviations that may be used without definition in table headings, common errors in style and spelling, and words and expressions to avoid.

Farmer, E. L., & Rojewski, J. W. (2001). *Research pathways: Writing research papers, theses, and dissertations in workforce development.* Lanham, MD: University Press of America.

This handbook provides a practical approach to writing research papers. Both quantitative and qualitative research methods are covered, and examples are provided for both practitioners and researchers.

Galvan, J. L. (2006). *Writing literature reviews: A guide for students of the social and behavioral sciences* (3rd ed.). Glendale, CA: Pyrczak Publishing.

A practical guide to writing literature reviews in behavioral and social sciences, this book focuses on reviewing academic journal resources to find relevant research literature. A systematic, multistep process for writing critical reviews of original research is provided. Analyzing both quantitative and qualitative research is covered, along with guidelines for style, mechanics, and language use.

Pyrczak, F. (2008). *Evaluating research in academic journals: A practical guide to realistic evaluation* (4th ed.). Glendale, CA: Pyrczak Publishing.

This supplementary guide is for students who are learning how to evaluate published reports of empirical research. Numerous excerpts from journals in the social and behavioral sciences provide examples that allow students to learn the practical aspects of evaluating research. By deemphasizing jargon, this book allows students to begin evaluating research with confidence.

Pyrczak, F., & Bruce, R. R. (2005). *Writing empirical research reports: A basic guide for students of the social and behavioral sciences* (5th ed.). Glendale, CA: Pyrczak Publishing.

> This is a classic book that shows students how to follow the traditions in scientific writing. The 12 chapters cover 119 guidelines with updated examples throughout. This title now has an instructor's answer key, which can be shipped with an examination copy.

Rubens, P. (1995). *Science and technical writing: A manual of style.* New York: Henry Holt & Co., Inc.

> This style manual covers many aspects of scientific writing. It is particularly strong on creating usable data displays and illustrations, and designing useful documents.

Educational Research

Ary, D., Jacobs, L. C., & Razavich, A. (1985). *Introduction to educational research* (3rd ed.). New York: Holt, Rinehart & Winston.

> The stated purpose of this text is to help readers understand and evaluate the research of others and to carry out basic research with minimal support or assistance. The various types of research prevalent in education are covered, and the advantages and disadvantages of each are discussed. Guidelines for writing research proposals and ethical considerations are covered.

Best, J. W., & Kahn, J. V. (2006). *Research in education* (10th ed.). Boston: Pearson Education, Inc.

> Designed as a research reference or as a text in an introductory research methods course, this book covers all of the basic aspects of research methods and statistics. A variety of methods are covered, and a complete range of research tools, such as the use of inferential statistics, is included. One chapter is devoted to qualitative research.

Bogdan, R. C., & Biklin, S. K. (2003). *Qualitative research in education: An introduction to theory and methods* (4th ed.). Boston: Allyn & Bacon.

> The intent of this textbook is to provide a background for understanding the use of qualitative research in education. The authors emphasize the use of descriptive data, grounded theory, participant observation, and the study of individual comprehension of the entire field of education. The organization of the book parallels the process of conducting qualitative research, which enables

the reader to use the text as a step-by-step guide in carrying out a research plan.

Borg, W. R., Gall, J. P., & Gall, M. D. (1993). *Applying educational research: A practical guide* (3rd ed.). New York: Longman.

> The intent of this book is to make educational research as accessible as possible to the educational practitioner. Examples of research studies that focus on school improvement are included, and the use of research in data-based decision-making is covered. Chapters on analyzing and synthesizing research in education are intended to support the collection of diverse research on a particular topic or problem. Education research methods, including experimental, correlational, causal-comparative, descriptive, and quantitative studies, are described and explained.

Burton, D. (2004). *Practitioner research for teachers.* Thousand Oaks, CA: Corwin Press.

> This book is a significant text for teachers involved in practitioner research. It includes the notion of classroom research as evolving from previous movements based upon school effectiveness and action research. It shows how being able to conduct and understand research is vital for the professional development of teachers. The practical issues of the design and carrying out of classroom-based research are covered with practical examples to illustrate points where appropriate. Each chapter includes recommended further reading and practical tasks.

Clandinin, D. J., & Connelly, F. M. (2000). *Narrative inquiry: Experience and story in qualitative research.* San Francisco: Jossey-Bass.

> The use of narrative inquiry, that is, the understanding of experience as lived and told through stories, is related to educational settings. New and practical ideas for conducting field work, composing field notes, and conveying research results are provided.

Coladarci, T., Cobb, C. D., Minium, E. W., & Clarke, R. C. (2003). *Fundamentals of statistical reasoning in education.* New York: Wiley.

> This is a statistics book specifically geared toward the education community. It gives educators the statistical knowledge and skills necessary for everyday classroom teaching, for running schools, and for professional development pursuits. It emphasizes conceptual development with an engaging style and clear exposition, and it provides an emphasis on statistics common to local and

large-scale assessment using a case-study approach, which models the process of data analysis, conceptualizes the learning of challenging statistical concepts, and addresses high-stakes testing.

Conrad, C. F., & Serlin, R. C. (Eds.). (2006). *The SAGE handbook for research in education: Engaging ideas and enriching inquiry.* Thousand Oaks, CA: Sage Publications.

Selected scholars from K-12 and higher education were invited to advance a research agenda that would result in self-reflective practitioners. Narratives, vignettes, and examples are used to provide emerging approaches to research in education.

Eisner, E. (1991). *The enlightened eye: Qualitative inquiry and the enhancement of educational practice.* New York: Macmillan Publishing Company.

Qualitative research is viewed from the perspective of the arts and humanities in this book. With the premise that knowledge is made, not merely discovered, the author argues that research should be a reflection of the human mind as well as a reflection of nature. Generalizability, validity, interpretive writing, and the role of theory in educational research form the central notions of this book.

Firestone, W. A., & Riehl, C. (Eds.) (2005). *A new agenda for research in educational leadership.* New York: Teachers College Press.

The University Council for Educational Administration partnered with the American Educational Research Association to cosponsor the writing and publication of this book. Prominent scholars in the field review current knowledge about leadership, frame new questions to generate important research in the field, and direct researchers and policymakers to rethink how educational administration, leadership, and policy should be understood. Covering a broad range of topics, from accountability systems and school-community relationships to the education of students from diverse backgrounds, the authors submit current research to critical scrutiny in order to develop frameworks for new research that can have a significant impact on policy and practice.

Freebody, P. (2003). *Qualitative research in education: Interaction and practice.* Thousand Oaks, CA: Sage Publications.

A broad range of real-life examples is used to describe the different qualitative methods available to analyze educational data. The author focuses on research that documents observations that are conceptually informative, professionally useful, and ideologically productive. The complexities of educational research, including how the qualitative method works and how the outcomes may be interpreted, are covered.

Gall, J. P., Gall, M. D., & Borg, W. R. (2005). *Applying educational research: A practical guide.* Boston: Allyn & Bacon.

> The text includes numerous recently published research articles involving high-interest problems of educational practice. The chapters treat quantitative, qualitative, and applied forms of educational research, and the text brings research alive for educators by introducing readers to people who actually do research. The book makes no assumptions about readers' prior knowledge of research or statistics. The text builds the readers' confidence so that they are able to successfully read research reports and conduct research.

Gall, M. D., Borg, W. R., & Gall, J. P. (2003). *Educational research: An introduction* (7th ed.). New York: Allyn & Bacon.

> As one of the most highly used and respected textbooks in educational research, this edition provides the student of research methods a broad overview of research techniques used in the field of education. It is a comprehensive introduction to the major research methods and types of data analysis used today. It provides in-depth coverage of all facets of research, from the epistemology of scientific inquiry to research design, data collection, analysis, and reporting of the completed study.

Gay, L. R., Mills, G. E., & Airasian, P. W. (2006). *Educational research: Competencies for analysis and applications.* Upper Saddle River, NJ: Merrill/Prentice Hall.

> This book is a practical text focused on the skills and procedures students need in order to become competent consumers and producers of educational research. The text uses a direct, step-by-step approach to the research process and incorporates tasks and articles throughout to provide students with the practice they need to master research steps and evaluation. This comprehensive instructional resource encompasses the full spectrum of the field, making it appropriate as a core text for an introductory course in educational research.

Glanz, J. (2006). *Fundamentals of educational research: A guide to completing a master's thesis.* Norwood, MA: Christopher-Gordon Publishers, Inc.

> Written to support the understanding of basic research principles in order to complete a research task, or to be a consumer of research writings, this text

separates the various components of educational research into fundamental topics for review. The style is comfortable and in a workbook format for easy reading and use in the application of research in education.

Glass, G. V., & Hopkins, K. D. (1996). *Statistical methods in education and psychology* (3rd ed.). Boston: Allyn & Bacon.

> The approach of this text is conceptual rather than mathematical. The authors stress the understanding, applications, and interpretation of concepts rather than derivation and proof of hand computation. Selection of topics in the book was guided by three considerations: (1) What are the most useful statistical methods? (2) Which statistical methods are the most widely used in journals in the behavioral and social sciences? and (3) Which statistical methods are fundamental to further study?

Green, J. L., Camilli, G., & Elmore, P. B. (Eds.) (2006). *Handbook of complementary methods in education research.* Mahwah, NJ: Lawrence Erlbaum Associates, Inc.

> Authors of the 46 different entries in this book bring together the wide range of research methods used to study education and make the logic of inquiry for each method clear and accessible. The history of the methodology, the specific research designs used, what questions can be addressed by the particular method, and ways to analyze and report outcomes are provided. Philosophical, epistemological, and ethical issues facing researchers are examined.

Johnson, B., & Christensen, L. (2004). *Educational research: Quantitative, qualitative, and mixed methods* (2nd ed.). Boston: Pearson.

> The second edition of this book is an informal and highly readable text that provides a clear and in-depth understanding of the different kinds of research—including technology-based—that are used in education today. It introduces the fundamental logic of empirical research and explores the sources of research ideas. There is a balanced examination of quantitative, qualitative, and mixed research, one of the book's strongest features. While quantitative research strategies are covered extensively, the text also discusses various qualitative approaches, such as ethnography, historical methods, phenomenology, grounded theory, and case studies. Sampling techniques, ethical considerations, data-collection methods, measurement, judging validity, experimental and nonexperimental methods, descriptive and inferential statistics, qualitative data analysis, and report preparation are also covered.

Lichtman, M. (2006). *Qualitative research in education: A user's guide.* Thousand Oaks, CA: Sage Publications.

Key features of this text are that it introduces traditions and major influences in the field of qualitative research in education, it focuses on specific aspects of qualitative methodology, and it addresses issues related to meaning and communication leading to judgment from the research. Group and individual activities are provided to help education students plan and conduct qualitative research.

Lodico, M. G., Spaulding, D. T., & Voegtle, K. H. (2006). *Methods in educational research: From theory to practice.* San Francisco: Jossey-Bass.

Written for students, educators, and researchers, this text offers a refreshing introduction to the principles of educational research. Designed for the real world of educational research, the book's approach focuses on the types of problems likely to be encountered in professional experiences. Reflecting the importance of the No Child Left Behind Act, "scientifically based" educational research, school accountability, and the professional demands of the 21st century, it empowers educational researchers to take an active role in conducting research in their classrooms, districts, and the greater educational community—activities that are now not only expected but also required of all teachers.

McMillan, J., & Schumacher, S. (2006). *Research in education: Evidence-based inquiry* (6th ed.). New York: Pearson-Longman.

This text provides a balanced combination of quantitative and qualitative methods and enables students to master skills in reading, understanding, critiquing, and conducting research. Many examples and article excerpts are used throughout the text to demonstrate and highlight the best practices in educational research. Evidence-based inquiry is emphasized in two ways: (1) introductory chapters focus on the added importance of data-driven decision-making, and (2) methodological instructions provide explicit guidelines for conducting empirical studies.

Robinson, V., & Lai, M. K. (2005). *Practitioner research for educators.* Thousand Oaks, CA: Corwin Press.

Practitioner research is a method whereby educators learn, through their own inquiry, how to adjust their practices in ways that will improve teaching and learning. This book explains how practitioner inquiry can be used by educators to solve instructional problems and improve student achievement. The authors include step-by-step instructions, ready-to-use tools, and examples of successful practitioner research projects. Focusing on the pragmatic aspects of embedding research into everyday practice, the authors demonstrate how to develop a manageable research question, select research methods appropriate to the question, plan and conduct a research project that is both practical and rigorous, use evidence to check the accuracy of claims about what works, and communicate the results of the research to a range of professional audiences.

Shavelson, R. J., & Towne, L. (Eds.) (2002). *Scientific research in education.* Washington, DC: National Academy Press.

The National Research Council produces reports that synthesize scientific knowledge over a wide range of areas. This report offers a comprehensive perspective of scientifically based research in education. It also shows the diversity of philosophical bases and methodological structures within education research. Suggestions for how the federal government can best support high-quality education research are provided.

Slavin, R. E. (2007). *Educational research in an age of accountability.* Boston: Allyn & Bacon.

Written in a very clear and user-friendly style, this text focuses on understanding the intent of the researcher, the procedures, and the results so that students can use appropriate research findings to inform school change. This text emphasizes how responses to the accountability movement in schools can be focused around using and understanding scientific inquiry. It balances quantitative and qualitative research methodology and discusses action research and mixed methods in detail.

Vierra, A., Pollock, J., & Golez, F. (1998). *Reading educational research* (3rd ed.). Upper Saddle River, NJ: Merrill.

Written in a highly readable, nonintimidating style, this text is designed for graduate students enrolled in an introductory educational research course. It prepares them to read educational research reports and to understand and evaluate what they read. This book introduces students to the role of research in science and instructs them in how to locate and read research reports. It provides extensive coverage of qualitative and quantitative research methods and describes how researchers collect and analyze data. It then discusses practical limitations on the ways in which research is used.

Research Ethics

Council of Biology Editors EPC. (1990). *Ethics and policy in scientific publication.* Bethesda, MD: The Council.

> An informative and useful book that discusses issues pertinent to the ethics of publication in science. Includes topics such as fraud, redundant publication, the peer-review process, and lying with statistics.

Eckstein, S. (Ed.). (2003). *Manual for research ethics committees: Centre of medical law and ethics, Kings College London* (6th ed.). London: Cambridge University Press.

> This text is a unique compilation of legal and ethical guidance, and, for the first time, the manual has been produced in one easy-to-search hardback volume. In this sixth edition, there are 15 new chapters covering key issues from participation in clinical trials to cloning. It is intended for members of research ethics committees; researchers involved in research with humans; members of the pharmaceutical industry; and students of law, medicine, ethics, and philosophy. Presented in a clear and authoritative form, it incorporates key legal and ethical guidelines. There are specially written chapters on major topics in bioethics by leading academic authors, practitioners, pharmaceutical industry associations, and professional bodies.

National Academy of Sciences. (1995). *On being a scientist: Responsible conduct in research* (2nd ed.). Washington, DC: National Academy Press.

> Since the first edition was published in 1988, more than 200,000 copies of this report have been distributed. Now this well-received booklet has been updated to incorporate the important developments in science ethics and includes updated examples and material from the landmark volume *Responsible Science* (National Academy Press, 1992). The revision offers several case studies in science ethics that pose provocative and realistic scenarios of ethical dilemmas and issues. It presents penetrating discussions of the social and historical context of science, the allocation of credit for discovery, the scientist's role in society, the issues revolving around publication, and many other aspects of scientific work. The booklet is written in a conversational style and explores the inevitable conflicts that arise when the black and white areas of science meet the gray areas of human values and biases.

Sales, B. (2000). *Ethics in research with human participants.* Washington, DC: American Psychological Association.

> The author presents the ethical principles that underlie the decision-making process in planning and implementing research with human participants. The author also differentiates between privacy and confidentiality and covers the needs of special populations.

Action Research

Grady, M. P. (1998). *Qualitative and action research: A practitioner handbook.* Bloomington, IN: Phi Delta Kappa International.

> This book shows how practical research can be used to alter curriculum content, instructional practices, and school policies. The author defines qualitative research and describes how to design a research project and collect data, how to analyze the data, and how to report results. He also defines action research as a specific type of qualitative research. Research in education is presented as a form of professional development for the consumer.

Greenwood, D. J., & Levin, M. (1998). *Introduction to action research: Social research for social change.* Thousand Oaks, CA: Sage Publications.

> A readable introductory overview of participative action research is provided. The three essential components of research, participation, and action are stressed within a cyclic process of action and reflection. Descriptions are also given of action science, human inquiry, and participative evaluation.

Herr, K., & Anderson, G. L. (2005). *The action research dissertation: A guide for students and faculty.* Thousand Oaks, CA: Sage Publications.

> This guide for students engaged in an action research project provides a road-map through the complexity of the action research process as it relates to theses and dissertations. Action research dissertations are contrasted with the traditional dissertation, and questions of validity, design, ethics, and defense are handled.

James, E. A., Milenkiewitz, M. T., & Bucknam, A. (2007). *Participatory action research for educational leadership.* Thousand Oaks, CA: Sage Publications.

> Designed for professional learning communities in schools, this book provides an easy-to-read overview of the participatory action-research process. Valid

and reliable data-driven outcomes are stressed. Reflective practices guide the research routines presented.

Johnson, A. P. (2002). *A short guide to action research* (revised printing). Boston: Allyn & Bacon.

An introductory overview of action research offered in sufficient detail for a novice to follow. Useful examples are given. It deals only with educational action research, from a quite traditional perspective.

Koshy, V. (2005). *Action research for improving practice: A practical guide.* Thousand Oaks, CA: Corwin Press.

Whether you are a busy teacher conducting further study or a time-pressed trainee teacher writing your dissertation, this concise guide takes you through the stages in carrying out action research. The step-by-step advice shows you how to choose your topic; plan your action; gather, review, and analyze your data; and write your report or dissertation.

Mertler, C. A. (2006). *Action research: Teachers as researchers in the classroom.* Thousand Oaks, CA: Sage Publications.

Prospective and practicing teachers are introduced to the process of conducting classroom-based action research. Research techniques are integrated into teachers' everyday instructional practices to support the improvement of student learning. Each step in the process is discussed in detail through the use of practical information for teachers to design their own action research projects.

Reason, P., & Bradbury, H. (Eds.). (2000). *Handbook of action research: Participative inquiry and practice.* Thousand Oaks, CA: Sage Publications.

This book represents an important leap forward for action research. The chapters in the book are written by an array of the best-known writers in the action research field, though newcomers have not been neglected. Many varieties of action research are represented, as are many settings. There are four sections. "Groundings" presents the foundations. "Practices" covers some of the varieties. "Exemplars," the largest section in terms of number of papers, provides a rich collection of case studies. "Skills" identifies some of the competencies upon which action researchers draw.

Sagor, R. (2000). *Guiding school improvement with action research*. Alexandria, VA: Association for Supervision and Curriculum Development.

> The version of action research here is primarily teacher research, in which a teacher uses research to understand and improve her or his own practice. It offers a variety of ways in which practitioners can research their practice, including collaborative action research. Quantitative and qualitative methods are discussed. As the author's summarized process shows, it is mostly research in the tradition of quasi-experimentation. The process is: (1) selecting a focus, (2) clarifying theories, (3) identifying research questions, (4) collecting data, (5) analyzing data, (6) reporting results, and (7) taking informed action.

Sagor, R. (2004). *The action research guide book: A four-step process for educators and school teams*. Thousand Oaks, CA: Corwin Press.

> Blending qualitative and quantitative research methods, action research is a practical tool for improvement in which the school or classroom is the laboratory. Focused on school improvement, this book outlines the steps in action research and provides tables, charts, forms, and worksheets to demystify and simplify the process. Each chapter provides concrete strategies for immediate use and allows the reader to implement an action research project after reading just a few chapters. This book provides the guidance needed by individual teachers and teacher teams, preservice teachers in teacher education courses, principals, counselors, and other educators as they work toward their goal of school improvement.

Stringer, E. (2007). *Action research* (3rd ed.). Thousand Oaks, CA: Sage Publications.

> Emphasizing community applications of action research, this clearly written book explains how to conduct action research in very practical terms yet is consistent with the theoretical literature. A series of tools to use in the process is provided to help researchers work through the political and ethical issues that frame inquiry.

Whitehead, J., & McNiff, J. (2006). *Action research: Living theory*. Thousand Oaks, CA: Sage Publications.

> The philosophy behind conducting action research and the process of carrying out a research project are defined in terms of a foundation discipline. Action research is set in an ethical yet politically engaged position for the 21st century.

Evidence, validity and legitimacy, and research implications are covered in the context of increasing educational knowledge.

Dissertation Research

Bryant, M. T. (2004). *The portable dissertation advisor.* Thousand Oaks, CA: Corwin Press.

> This dissertation guide is for students who study from a distance. It includes pragmatic advice for those students who are nontraditional graduate students and who have a required dissertation to complete. The author draws on years of experience as an advisor to provide a step-by-step approach to completing a research dissertation.

Glatthorn, A. A., & Joyner, R. L. (2005). *Writing the winning dissertation: A step-by-step guide* (2nd ed.). Thousand Oaks, CA: Corwin Press.

> This text helps to demystify the process of writing your master's thesis or doctoral dissertation. This experience-based, practical book takes you through the process using a step-by-step approach. It provides specific models and examples for the complex writing process. Included are chapters on laying the groundwork for the thesis or dissertation, organizing and scheduling the work, peer collaboration, using technology, conducting quality research and writing a winning report, defending and publishing the research, and solving problems throughout the dissertation process.

Locke, L. F., Spirduso, W. W., & Silverman, S. J. (2000). *Proposals that work* (4th ed.). Thousand Oaks, CA: Sage Publications.

> Covering all aspects of the proposal process, from the most basic questions about form and style to the task of seeking funding, this text offers clear advice backed up with excellent examples. In this edition, the authors have integrated a discussion of the effects of new technologies and the Internet on the proposal process, with URLs listed where appropriate. In addition, there is a new chapter on funding for student research and a comprehensive chapter on qualitative research. As always, the authors have included a number of specimen proposals, two of which are completely new to this edition, to shed light on the important issues surrounding the writing of proposals.

Mauch, J. E., & Birch, J. W. (1998). *Guide to the successful thesis and dissertation* (4th ed.). New York: Marcel Dekker, Inc.

> The authors provide a handbook for students and faculty reflecting the most recent trends in thesis and dissertation preparation and research.

Piantanida, M., & Garman, N. B. (1999). *The qualitative dissertation: A guide for students and faculty.* Thousand Oaks, CA: Corwin Press.

> Each step in the design of a qualitative research process is reviewed in the context of writing a dissertation. Helpful advice on handling issue areas and pressure points is provided for the entire dissertation process.

Roberts, C. M. (2004). *The dissertation journey: A practical and comprehensive guide to planning, writing, and defending your dissertation.* Thousand Oaks, CA: Corwin Press.

> This text provides concise, straightforward information on the dissertation process, from conceptualizing a topic to publishing the results. The author focuses on the practical aspects of writing and organizing a dissertation, as well as the psychological and emotional hurdles involved. Geared to the specific needs and concerns of doctoral students, this guidebook includes checklists and sample forms, organization and time-management tips, current information on using technology, suggestions for support groups, and an in-depth list of resources for further inquiry.

Thomas, R. M. (2003). *Blending qualitative and quantitative research methods in theses and dissertations.* Thousand Oaks, CA: Corwin Press.

> This comprehensive guide offers an important resource that responds to the growing trend of combining qualitative and quantitative research methods in theses and dissertations. It thoroughly discusses a wide array of methods, the strengths and limitations of each, and how they can be effectively interwoven into various research designs. Aimed at empowering students with the information necessary to choose the best approach for their needs, this user-friendly text outlines numerous research options from varying viewpoints and highlights the procedures involved in putting each method into practice.

Notes

Glossary

Abstract: A summary of a longer text, especially that of an academic record of research.

Action research: Inquiry or research that deals with issues or problems that exist in a workplace and need attention. It is usually designed and carried out by practitioners who identify the problem, collect and analyze data, and use the collected information to make data-driven decisions to improve their own practice or to improve working conditions.

ANOVA: Analysis of variance, a statistical measure of difference within and between the variance of selected variables in a quantitative data set.

Antecedent variable: Also called the independent variable, it is the variable that is not subject to treatment, but rather held constant throughout an experiment.

Applied research: Research to solve specific, practical questions. It can be exploratory, but is usually descriptive in nature, attempting to make clear the salient features of the phenomenon being studied.

Bias: Distortion in a research project caused by variables or circumstances not considered in the data collection, or in the variable itself. Also, the potential for a researcher to read results inaccurately due to a predisposed prejudice.

Blind review: An evaluation of a research report conducted by experts in the field in which the identity of the author or authors of the research is kept confidential.

Case study: One of several ways of doing social science research, a case study includes experiments, surveys, multiple histories, and analysis of archival information. Case-study methods involve an in-depth, longitudinal examination of a single instance or event.

Categorical data: Numbers used as labels for data sets, or for data that has order, although intervals between the data points may not be equal.

Causal-comparative: A correlational study in which causation is attributed to one or more variables.

Central tendency: A measurement device that gives meaning to the center or middle of a distribution of variable values; mean, median, and mode are three common examples.

Chi-square: A nonparametric statistical test that measures the difference between the observed data and the expected frequency of data.

Cluster sample: Technique used when "natural" groupings are evident in the population. The total population is divided into these groups (or clusters) and a sample of one or more entire groups is selected for research.

Coefficient alpha: Also known as Cronbach's coefficient alpha, it is a reliability check for internal consistency of a measurement instrument that is derived by computing all possible split-half correlations from the responses. Based on the average inter-item correlation among items, the usual minimum score for a reliable index is 0.700.

Concept: An abstract idea or mental general principle with a corresponding representation in language that brings together objects, phenomena, or individuals and identifies a relationship between or among them.

Conceptualization: To arrive at a generalization as a result of the study of theory, or of things seen or experienced, that creates a measurable research task using abstract ideas.

Construct: A systematic assembly of research concepts used to create or improve a theory or framework, most often using predetermined criteria or benchmarks. A research construct is the result of systematic thought about a subject in which a complex theory or subjective notion has been created and systematically put together.

Constructivism: A philosophical perspective that views all knowledge as created through iterations of systematic thought resulting in a constructed reality.

Construct validity: Assurance that a data-collection device relates appropriately to all variables within the identified area of study, and that the items in the instrument measure the targeted phenomena.

Content validity: Assurance that a data-collection device measures accurately the complete range of meanings within the area of study, or all facets of a social construct being studied.

Control variable: The variable in an experiment that is not changed in the research process, but rather is held constant in order to compare the results of any treatment or change to the experimental variable.

Correlation: The strength and direction of a linear relationship between measurable variables, often using predefined statistical tests such as the Pearson product-moment correlation coefficient or the Spearman *rho* test. Measures of correlation vary from -1 to $+1$, and a correlation near zero is an indication of a weak relationship.

Correlational study: An examination of similar trends in the data of a research project; a necessary but not sufficient finding to imply causation.

Criterion validity: Assurance that a data-collection device measures accurately the external phenomena being studied.

Data: Information in the form of text, characters, images, or numbers obtained in a research project.

Deductive: A form of reasoning in which research expectations are based on general principles and a conclusion is reached through the application of rules of logic to the premise using previously known facts. The logic moves from the general to the specific.

Delphi technique: A research method in which a panel of experts is surveyed in several iterations, each time with an anonymous summary provided of the previous round's results in order for consensus to be reached on the issue.

Dependent variable: The variable being studied in a research project that changes based on the manipulation, or is based on normal changes of other variables.

Descriptive research: A method of study that illustrates and explains specific details or characteristics of the population or phenomena being studied.

Developmental research: The study of growth or change in issues from an inter- or multidisciplinary point of view.

Dispersion: The scatter, spread, or distribution of research data around some measure of central tendency, such as the standard deviation from the mean value.

Dissertation: A formal thesis based on an authentic and independent research project, usually submitted to faculty at an institution of higher education as a requirement for an advanced degree.

Empirical: Research based on or characterized by observation and experimentation and dependent on evidence that can be observed and recorded.

Epistemology: The branch of philosophy that is the study of the nature, validity, and scope of knowledge and belief.

Ethnography: Research that presents descriptions of human social circumstances or interactions, usually in textual form or in a combination of text and quantifiable data.

Experimentation: Research that is based on scientific tests or new and untried methods in which some manipulation is used to determine the effect of the treatment on the variable being studied.

Ex post facto: Research that includes making judgments about individuals or phenomena after events have occurred or circumstances have passed.

Extraneous variables: Variables that interact in a research project, other than the selected independent variable, that have an effect on the subject of the project and that cannot be controlled or measured with any degree of accuracy.

Face validity: Assurance from one or more individuals knowledgeable in the field that a data-collection device at least looks like it accurately measures the external phenomena being studied.

Factor analysis: A statistical operation that separates a data set into dimensions (factors) based on common trends in the data.

Field study: A research technique in which the researcher is immersed in the environment being studied and records activities and events while in that environment.

Fundamental research: Also called basic research, it most often is exploratory and has the advancement of knowledge as its primary objective. Using relationships between variables to create or improve theory, results of fundamental studies may lead to additional applied research.

Grounded theory: Based on the constant comparative method of research, it is a systematic theory-generation technique using both inductive and deductive reasoning in which research hypotheses are generated based on conceptualized ideas and based more on observation than any other schema.

Historical: A research technique that draws on information or events of the past for description and analysis.

Hypothesis: A conjectural statement about the nature of individuals or phenomena that is used as a basis for investigation. It is the predicted relationship between an independent and a dependent variable.

Hypothesis testing: Determining whether the expectations in the conjectural statement about research variables exist, often through use of statistical procedures to determine the accuracy.

Independent variable: Also called predictor variables, they are the research values taken as given and used by the researcher to explain or determine the research result, which is often the dependent variable.

Inductive: A form of reasoning in which research expectations are based on general principles derived from specific observations. The logic moves from the specific to the general.

Inquiry: A planned and formal investigation or research process structured and carried out to determine the facts of a situation in order to augment knowledge, resolve doubt, or solve a problem.

Interval data: Research data in which individual data points have a rank order, and there are defined and equal intervals between each data point, so the differences between arbitrary pairs of measurements can be used in a meaningful way.

Interval sample: Also known as "systematic" sampling, the researcher uses a rotating method to select the sample: taking every other, or every 10th, subject, for instance.

Intervention: A treatment used in a research project intended to produce a measurable and positive outcome.

Interview: A data-collection technique in which the researcher interacts directly with research participants and asks a series of questions for the purpose of determining facts or opinions in order to generate research data.

Investigation: A detailed examination or inquiry into a subject being studied.

IQ: The intelligence quotient derived by dividing a test taker's mental age by her or his chronological age. Often measured through standardized intelligence tests and reported as a standardized scale score between 55 and 150, with 100 (the mean) considered average, and with a standard deviation of 15.

Jury: A select group of people knowledgeable in the research subject, used to judge the merits of the research plans or to critique the results.

Likert scale: A questionnaire response scale with standard response categories for a range of items, usually represented by numerical values, for the purpose of statistical analysis.

Literature: The body of published work concerned with a particular topic, especially including published research reports on the subject.

Measurement: Estimation, subject to error, of some physical quantity of an object, concept, or phenomenon using defined base units that make reference to specific empirical conditions.

Meta analysis: A single study that is a published research report including a summary of or the combination of several individual studies that focus on the same research question or hypothesis.

Nominal data: Research data in which individual data points are numerals, used only as names for the research constructs, and whose numerical value are irrelevant.

Nonparametric: A statistical category for research that is concerned with data sets that do not have specific quantities related to the general population being studied, but rather have flexible population parameters that are not fixed in advance.

Normal population: The assumption that the distribution of elements in a population is spread out according to the normal probability curve, also known as the bell-shaped curve (see the appendix at the end of this book).

Observation: The careful surveillance and recording of behavior, natural phenomena, or activity in a research project.

Operational: The structure of management and control of a research project that follows conceptualization from established theory.

Ordinal data: Research data in which individual data points have a rank order and comparisons of greater and less can be made, but conventional operations such as addition or subtraction are meaningless.

Panel interview: A longitudinal research project in which the same group of individuals is interviewed at specific intervals over the course of the project and multiple phenomena are observed over multiple time periods.

Paradigm: A research model of how ideas relate to one another that forms a conceptual framework and defines a scientific discipline or other epistemological context.

Parameter: A characteristic or summary value representing a general quantity that is considered to be a true measurement from an entire population being studied.

Participant-observer: A research strategy in which the researcher has an intensive involvement with individuals in their natural environment, often over an extended period of time.

Peer review: Also known as refereeing, the process of subjecting research results to the scrutiny of experts in the field, used to ensure that authors adhere to the standards of their disciplines.

Phenomenology: The philosophical study of conscious and immediate experience used to describe a body of knowledge that draws from perceptions of things as they are and as they relate to one another.

Phenomenon: An observable event or something perceived or experienced by the human senses.

Philosophy: The academic study of the systematic examination of concepts such as truth, existence, reality, causality, and freedom, using a set of basic principles underlying a particular sphere of knowledge.

Placebo: A treatment prescribed to a patient in a medical research project that contains no medicine, but is meant to create the psychological effect of taking medicine.

Positivism: The theory that knowledge can be acquired only through direct observation and experimentation, and that the only authentic knowledge is scientific knowledge.

Postpositivism: A belief that theory both shapes reality and follows it, and that the truth of science pertains to the study and description of phenomena as they are found in the real world.

Pre-posttest: A research design in which subjects are exposed to the same measurement both before and after experimental treatment.

Primary source: A document or other source of information created at or near the time of study and that relates directly to the subject of study.

Probability: A statistical theory that allows researchers to draw conclusions about the likelihood of events occurring, or the accuracy of conclusions drawn from the data.

Purposive sample: Also called "judgmental sample," the researcher selects respondents based on intimate knowledge of the population being studied and the need to ensure certain aspects of the population are represented in the research.

Qualitative: Research that uses textual and other nonnumerical data as a basis to study human behavior and the underlying patterns of relationships.

Quantitative: Research that uses numerical representations as a basis to systematically study phenomena and their relationships.

Quasi-experimental design: Research that includes experimental treatment of variables, but under less-than-controlled circumstances, and where extraneous variables may create a bias in the results.

Questionnaire: One of several methods of data collection in which a set of questions is sent to a select sample of participants for response and for combined analysis.

Random sample: A group selected for participation in a research project in which each member of the population has an equal chance of being selected for the study.

Rank order: Positioning research items from a collection of similar constructs or traits on an ordinal scale with a value relationship to one another.

Ratio data: Research data that include a true zero point, in which individual data points have rank order and meaningful intervals, in which meaningful ratios exist between arbitrary pairs of numbers, and in which arithmetic operations of multiplication and division may be used.

Regression analysis: A statistical procedure that includes a significant causal-comparative component that allows the researcher to determine the percent of variation in one variable based on other variables in the data set.

Reliability: The consistency of a measuring instrument that provides confidence that the researcher is able to derive the same results from repeated measurements of the same phenomenon.

Replication: Repeating the same experiment or carrying out the same research process in several iterations to assure that results are accurate and valid and to reduce error in findings.

Research: A human activity based on intellectual investigation into a subject and aimed at discovering facts and creating, interpreting, or revising theories in order to increase human knowledge of different aspects of life.

Research consumer: An individual who reads and interprets research reports and publications for the purpose of knowledge acquisition, or self- or professional improvement.

Research design: The plan or scheme of the overall research project in which the researcher describes the interaction of the problem or issue under consideration, the information needed to analyze the issue, and the techniques used to collect and evaluate the research data.

Research methods: A commonly accepted structure to carry out a research endeavor including, but not limited to, exploratory research that establishes and identifies new hypotheses, constructive research that develops solutions to problems, and empirical research that uses evidence to test hypotheses and derive solutions.

Sample: Units or individuals selected from a population to serve as data-collection cases or as research participants.

Scale data: Numerical data that can be applied to an interval measurement.

Science: A systematically organized body of knowledge that has been the object of careful study carried out according to accepted methodologies.

Scientific method: A specific body of techniques for investigating phenomena and acquiring new knowledge, or confirming or correcting existing knowledge, that is based on observable and measurable empirical evidence.

Secondary source: Textual or other documentary written accounts based on a collection of primary or other secondary sources.

Semantic differential: A data-collection device in which respondents are asked to record a value statement between two bipolar words or a range of words.

Split half: A technique to determine the reliability of a measurement instrument by comparing data from one half of the instrument items to the other half.

Standard deviation: A statistical measure of dispersion calculated by computing the square root of the mean of the differences of each item from the sample mean.

Standard error: The calculated difference between the estimated or measured value (statistic) and the real value (parameter). The lower the standard error, the better the estimate.

Statistic: A calculated estimate of the actual value for the whole population, usually derived from a research sample.

Statistical analysis: An applied mathematical measurement technique for numerical data that uses predetermined formulas to analyze data in order for the researcher to draw reasoned conclusions about the research questions.

Statistics: Estimates of population parameters, or a branch of mathematics that deals with the collection, analysis, interpretation, and presentation of numerical data.

Stratified sample: The division of a research population into homogenous groups, or strata, for the purpose of selecting a sample.

Substantive validity: Also known as educational validity, answers the question of whether or not the size of the research group (the sample) is adequate to the purpose of the study (i.e., is the group "substantial" enough to warrant conclusions?).

Survey: A device to collect quantitative information about items in a population, and an analysis of responses to a poll of a sample of a population to determine opinions, attitudes, or knowledge.

Survey research: A statistical study of a sample from a defined population that asks questions about selected aspects of individuals' lives, such as age, income, opinions, attitudes, or knowledge.

Test: A series of questions, problems, or practical tasks used to measure knowledge, ability, experience, or disposition.

Test-retest: A measure of reliability derived from successive iterations of the same measurement instrument over a specified period of time, usually calculated with a correlation statistic.

Theory: A conjecture, opinion, or speculation about a set of facts, propositions, or principles analyzed in relation to one another and used to explain phenomena.

Thesis: A dissertation based on original work, especially as work toward an academic degree.

Time series: A statistical procedure that studies a sequence of data points measured at successive times, spaced at uniform intervals, either to comprehend the theory of the data points or, most often, to make forecasts about the phenomenon being studied.

Treatment: The act of manipulating members of a research sample by subjecting a new process or agent to the elements in order to determine the effects of the manipulation.

Triangulation: The use of more than one method in a research study, with a goal of double-checking or triple-checking the results so that the researcher can be more confident of the results if different research methods lead to the same conclusion.

Validity: Confidence that the research method and the techniques used to collect data actually measure what they purported to measure and that the conclusions or descriptions of the subject or topic under consideration that are found or drawn by the researcher are accurate, reasonable, and justifiable.

Variable effect: A measure of the strength of the relationship of two variables in a research project. Also known as effect size, it identifies the amount or magnitude of the observed results beyond the question of significance.

Variables: A measurable attribute in a research project whose value may fluctuate over a wide range over time or over individuals, and whose change may influence or cause a change in another population parameter.

Variance: A statistical measure of the spread or variation of a group of numbers in a sample, equal to the square of the standard deviation.

Composite Bibliography

American Psychological Association. (2001). *Publication manual of the American Psychological Association* (5th ed.). Washington, DC: American Psychological Association.

Bracey, G. W. (2006). *Reading educational research: How to avoid getting statistically snookered.* Portsmouth, NH: Heinemann.

Center for Advanced Research in Phenomenology. (2006). *What is phenomenology?* Retrieved November 10, 2005, from: http://www.phenomenologycenter.org/phenom.htm.

Conant, J. (1951). *Science and common sense.* New Haven: Yale University Press.

Demetrion, G. (2004). *Postpositivist scientific philosophy: Mediating convergences.* gdemetrion@msn.com. Retrieved November 10, 2005 from: http://www.the-rathouse.com/Postpositivism.htm.

Dewey, J. (1916). *Democracy and education.* New York: MacMillan.

Dewey, J. (1929). *The sources of a science of education.* New York: Liveright.

Dewey, J. (1933). *How we think.* Boston: D.C. Heath and Co.

Dewey, J. (1938). *Logic: The theory of inquiry.* New York: Henry Holt and Company.

Gerke, R. (2007). *The proper assigning of an F grade: The lack of understanding best practice in grading.* Unpublished doctoral dissertation, Edgewood College, Madison, Wisconsin.

Imel, S., Kerka, S., & Wonacott, M. E. (2002). *Qualitative research in adult, career and career-technical education.* Columbus, OH: ERIC Clearinghouse on Adult, Career, and Vocational Education.

Kerlinger, F. N. (1964). *Foundations of behavioral research: Educational and psychological inquiry.* New York: Holt, Rinehart & Winston, Inc.

Lunsford, A. A. (2006). *Easy writer* (3rd ed.). Boston: Bedford/St. Martin's.

Mathison, S. (Ed.). (2005). *Encyclopedia of evaluation.* Thousand Oaks, CA: Sage Publications.

Mitzel, H. E. (Ed.). (1982). *Encyclopedia of educational research.* New York: Macmillian.

National Research Council. (2002). *Scientific research in education.* Committee on Scientific Principles for Education Research. R. J. Shavelson and L. Towne, Editors. Center for Education. Division of Behavioral and Social Sciences and Education. Washington, DC: National Academy Press.

Strunk, W. Jr. (1918). *The elements of style.* Ithaca, NY: W.P. Humphrey. Retrieved August 2, 2005, from: http://www.bartleby.com/141/

Strunk, W. Jr., & White, E. B. (2000). *The elements of style* (4th ed.). New York: Longman.

Trochim, W. M. K. (2002). *The philosophy of research*. Retrieved August 16, 2004 from: http://www.socialresearchmethods.net/kb/philosophy.htm. In Trochim, William M. *The research methods knowledge base, 2nd Edition*. Internet WWW page, at URL: http://www.socialresearchmethods.net.kb (version current as of October 20, 2006).

United States Department of Education. (2001). *No Child Left Behind Act*. Retrieved September 22, 2004 from http://www.NoChildLeftBehind.gov/index.html.

United States Department of Education. (2003, December). *Identifying and implementing educational practices supported by rigorous evidence: A user-friendly guide*. Washington, DC: U.S. Department of Education.

Wikipedia, the free online encyclopedia. http://en.wikipedia.org/wiki/Main_Page

Subject Index

A

Abstract 35, **45–48**, 50, 64, 127

Action research 6, **22–26**, 29, 41, 78–79, 84, 90, 165–166

ANOVA 52, **107–108**, 111, 140, 150–152

Antecedent variable 74, **95**

Applied research **41**, 49

B

Behavioral research 165

Blind review 12

C

Case-study research 78, **109–110**, 140, 142, 144, 165

Categorical data **15–16**, 95, 105

Causal-comparative 19, **25**, 78, 108

Central tendency 51, 52, **105–106**, 111, 149

Chi-square 51, 91, **107**, 111

Cluster sample 84

Coefficient alpha 56, **101**

Concept 3, 11, 12, 16, 22, 29, 34, 41, 54–56, 62, 69, 79–80, 98, 130, 136–138, 146, 160

Construct 34, **49**, 53, 55–56, 95–96, 100–102

Constructivism 37, **39**

Construct validity 55

Content validity 54

Correlation **50–52**, 55–56, 68, 100, **107–108**, 152, 156

Correlational study 19, 25, 75, **78**

Criterion validity 54–55

D

Data 33–35, 38, 40–42, **44–46**, 50–57

Deduction 5

Deductive **5**, 7, 9, 36, 44, 122, 141

Delphi technique **20**, 97

Dependent variable 7, **95**

Descriptive 22, **24–25**

Descriptive research 6, **22–24**

Design **5–11**, 18–20, 23, 25–28, 30, 41, 49, 73, 79, 98, 103

Developmental research 24

Dispersion 51–52, 74, **105–107**, 116, 149

Dissertation 4, 6, 15, **25–29**, 160

Dissertation research 6, **26–29**, 123, 165

E

Educational research **33**, 41, 142, 165

Empirical 4, 8, 11, 13, 17, 30, **36–38**, 40–41, 43, 48–49, 100, 135–136

Ethnography 6, 11, 17, **22**, 42

Experimentation 3, 18, 67, **95**

Ex post facto 9, 43, **77**

Extraneous variables 50

F

Face validity 54

Factor analysis 52

Field study 52, 77–78, **90–91**

Fundamental research 41

G

Grounded theory 22, 24, **109–110**, 147

H

Historical research 6, **22–23**, 78, 83, 102

Hypothesis **7–12**, 23, 48, 56, **68–69**, 76, 80, 115, 121–122, 139, 149, 151

Hypothesis testing 8, 56, **90–91**

I

Independent variable 7, 9, 43, 68, 74, 95, 108

Induction 5

Inductive 5, 9, 36, 40, 42, 111, 122, 141

Inquiry **3–5**, 12, 17, 23, 25–26, 35, 38, 40, 48, 61, 64, 69, 78, 81, 87, 92, 112, 118, 127, 129, 135

Interval data **16**, 21, 51–52, 55, 106–107

Interval sample 85

Intervention 6–7, 24, 74–75, 78, 89, 102, 111, 147–149

Interview research 165

Investigation 3–5, 35, 47, 49, 73, 153

IQ 55

J

Jury 12, 44, 100

L

Library research 34, 45, 64

Likert scale **20**, 98, 111, 149

Literature 4, 6, 18, 27–28, 30, 33–34, **43–48**, **61–64**, 67, 69–70, 79–81, 95, 100, 118, 123, 128–130, **136–139**, 161

M

Measurement **8–14**, 16, 19, 21, 40, 53–57, 74–77, 89–90, 96, 99–102, 105, 135, 140, 143, 150–151

Meta-analysis 11, 135

N

National Research Council **4–5**, 48–49, 52

Nominal data **15–16**, 21, 51

Nonparametric **13–14**, 16, 21, 51, 56

Normal population 107

Appendix

The Normal Probability Curve and Applied Statistics (from Wikipedia, http://en.wikipedia.org/wiki/Z_scores)

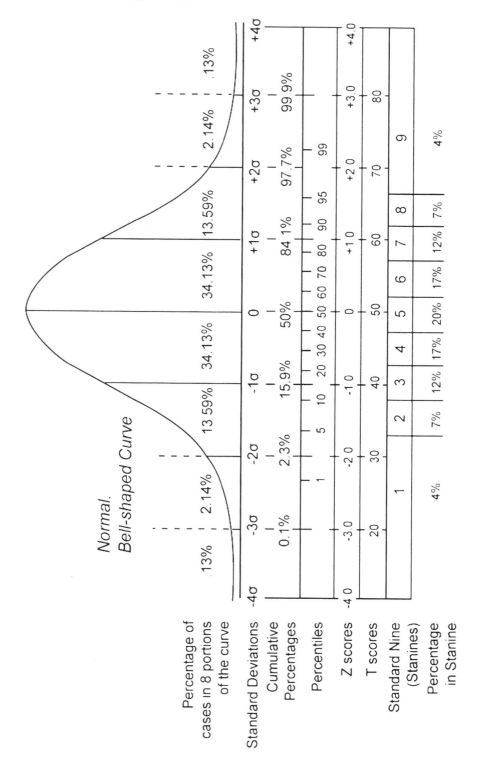

Notes

Notes

Notes

Notes

Notes

Notes

Notes